Managing and Marketing Tourist Destinations

Routledge Advances in Tourism

EDITED BY STEPHEN PAGE, *University of Stirling, Scotland*

Managing and Marketing Tourist Destinations

Strategies to Gain a Competitive Edge

Metin Kozak and Seyhmus Baloglu

Routledge
Taylor & Francis Group
New York   London

First published 2011
by Routledge
711 Third Avenue, New York, NY 10017

Simultaneously published in the UK
by Routledge
2 Park Square, Milton Park, Abingdon, Oxon OX14 4RN

Routledge is an imprint of the Taylor & Francis Group, an informa business

First issued in paperback 2012

Typeset in Sabon by IBT Global.

Library of Congress Cataloging-in-Publication Data
Kozak, M. (Metin), 1968–
    Managing and marketing tourist destinations : strategies to gain a competitive edge / by Metin Kozak and Seyhmus Baloglu.
        p. cm. — (Routledge advances in tourism)
    Includes bibliographical references and index.
    1. Tourism—Management. 2. Tourism—Marketing. I. Baloglu, Seyhmus. II. Title.
    G155.A1K684 2010
    910.68—dc22
    2010016343

ISBN13: 978-0-415-99171-1 (hbk)
ISBN13: 978-0-203-84230-0 (ebk)
ISBN13: 978-0-415-81148-4 (pbk)

Contents

Figures

Tables

Boxes and Exhibits

Boxes

Exhibits

Preface

The tourism industry had been ignored in the global research for development and wealth until the 1950s. Along with the end of World War II, tourism movements began to improve especially in Western societies, the developed countries of our present time. In relation to the recognition of its economic importance, tourism has become the fastest growing industry along with telecommunication and information technologies in the 21st century of global economy. In this context, tourism movements have lost the feature of exclusively addressing upper-level of income or aristocrats with free time and high income. Tourism has gained a massive characteristic that enables middle- and lower-income segments to get involved in both domestic and international tourism movements and thereby millions of people to move temporarily from their homelands to other regions or countries in order to meet their psychological, social and cultural needs (i.e. sightseeing, fun, resting, learning etc.). Such a movement makes one country a popular tourist destination while taking more or less proportion of international tourism figures.

Tourist destinations increasingly embrace branding techniques to develop unique positions, identities, and personalities in a highly competitive environment at national and international levels. Customer-based brand equity measures such as brand recognition, image, value, quality, loyalty and brand advocacy also provide valid metrics for destination benchmarking and competitive advantages. However, destination marketers (tourism offices or DMOs) have very little control over highly diverse and interrelated offerings of a destination or place. Community or resident support as well as groups of stakeholders and local politics create theoretical challenges for measuring brand equity (Gnoth, Baloglu, Ekinci and Sirakaya-Turk 2007). Therefore, some scholars debate that special models, principles and frameworks peculiar to place branding should be developed (Blichfeldt 2003; Morgan and Pritchard 2004; Hankinson 2004; Caldwell and Freire 2004; Pike 2005, Kneesel, Baloglu and Millar 2010).

Thus, marketing places and destinations are exciting as well as challenging (Fyall, Callod and Edwards 2003). Tourism systems and products are complex and influenced by economic, social, environmental and competitive forces locally and globally (Chi 2009). A sustainable destination will act for the interest of travelers and residents as well as for the protection of the resources (Kozak 2004a). A destination should operate in a way so that its economic interests, society or resident interests and environment interests intersect. Therefore, current marketing theories and practices need to balance the requirement for providing "memorable experiences" against the growing requirement of places and destinations to develop and protect their heritage, attractions, resources and human capital in the most sustainable way.

Strategic marketing planning takes place in a rapidly changing environment. Travelers today are more educated, demanding and experienced as well as more sensitive to environmental and social issues. They have more and quicker access to information and media and connectivity from home and office. They expect good value, quality and higher standards. They have multiple or changing lifestyles when they travel and demand more individualized experience based on idiosyncratic expectations.

Places or destinations have more interest than ever before in developing competitive advantages, more responsible tourism marketing strategies and tactics, tourism diversification such as medical tourism and disaster and crisis planning. The urgent need to become more competitive is augmented by the fact that place or destination marketing has some special characteristics. It is not only influenced by characteristics of services (such as intangibility, variability, inseparability and perishability), but also seasonality of tourist demand and the diversity and interdependence of tourism products. On top of all this, marketing decisions are to be made despite the different interests and goals of private and public stakeholders in a given destination.

This book discusses and synthesizes models, techniques and principles for strategic marketing and management of destinations. Global competition, coupled with more demanding travelers and highly diverse tourism "product", make place or destination marketing highly difficult and challenging around the globe. Competitive analysis of destinations is rapidly gaining in importance in the strategic marketing planning and positioning of destinations (Crouch and Ritchie 1999; Faulkner, Oppermann and Fredline 1999; Baloglu and McCleary 1999; Gursoy, Baloglu and Che 2009; Kozak, Baloglu, and Bahar 2010). The competitiveness may vary by type of competition, target market, and product mix. The destinations should create a competitive advantage by attracting tourists as well as developing and staging memorable experiences as good as or better than competitive destinations. The purpose of this book is also to discuss and present principles and guidelines to facilitate the marketing planning for tourist destinations. The principles and guidelines discussed equally apply to different product levels in travel and tourism such as museums, national parks, cities, regions and countries. Place or destination marketing today should go beyond traditional product or marketing orientation and adopt societal marketing or socially responsible marketing principles (perhaps a better term would be "sustainable marketing"), which balances the economic, social and environmental impacts of tourism.

The book is divided into three main parts. Part I expands the concept of destination competitiveness by discussing importance of destination competitiveness (Chapter 1), an overview of destination competitiveness (Chapter 2) and determinants of destination competitiveness (Chapter 3). Part II focuses on destinations' internal capabilities and management skills such as destination-based management strategies (Chapter 4), destination-based total quality management (Chapter 5), and destination benchmarking (Chapter 6). Part III extends the managerial approach of destination competitiveness into the perspective of destination marketing that also consists of the consideration of three main subjects. This part begins with the discussion of destination-based marketing strategies in general (Chapter 7), followed by the examination of other related subjects in detail such as destination branding (Chapter 8) and traditional versus "IT" marketing (Chapter 9).

Over the past few decades, tourist destinations have become a key component of the tourism system. Certainly, there are a number of reasons to indicate as to why the measurement and determination of destination competitiveness has become so important in travel and tourism (e.g. the existence of multiple destinations, the emergence of new destinations and so on). Each of these characteristics is explained in Chapter 1. These may also aid the readers to clearly understand the necessity of writing a textbook on the concept of 'destination competitiveness'. This chapter also discusses the distinctive characteristics of the tourism and travel industry along with tourist destinations and evaluating the main elements of destination attractiveness. Some trends on both the demand and supply sides were presented. This chapter also emphasizes that a strategic approach to marketing destinations is a necessity rather than an option in today's world. Along with discussing the reasons for using "place" competitiveness rather than "destination" competitiveness, Chapter 1 emphasizes the role of branding and experiential marketing in gaining a competitive edge.

The purpose of Chapter 2 is to review the concept of destination competitiveness and the multiple factors which influence it. The chapter first examines previous destination competitiveness research on the basis of their contents, strengths and limitations. The discussion dates back to the studies that came out in the mid-1970s. There was an increase in the number of studies published on the subject of destination competitiveness and its elements in the 1990s. An extensive review of the literature indicated that much has been written about competitiveness between different tourist destinations either at the regional/national or international level. Nevertheless, it is claimed that full competitive destination analysis has not received widespread recognition in the tourism literature.

As a result of weaknesses in earlier attempts to investigate and conceptualize the elements of destination competitiveness, Chapter 3 aims to provide a tentative framework in which each factor affecting competitiveness of tourist destinations in some respects is examined. Using Porter's (1985) terms, five major factors affecting the competitiveness level of international tourist destinations are then identified. These include the supply (or controllable) side, demand (or uncontrollable) side, tour operator operations, emergence of new destinations and emergence of substitute products and services. Each is explained in greater detail later in this chapter. Bordas (1994) suggests that competitive advantage can be created by following various steps in both management and marketing strategies: improving the quality of products and services, changing production processes, accepting new ways of distribution methods, adding new and attractive features and improving the infrastructure of technology. For these reasons, it is expected that a competitive environment at the micro level (business-organization level) and at the macro level (destination or country level) be established and people be encouraged to participate in this.

Chapter 4 aims to introduce an overview of major management strategies and their adaptation required to maintain the competitive advantage of tourist destinations (e.g. environmental management, human resources management, cooperation and collaboration). In order to be able to protect one from challenges of tourism and offer satisfactory products and services, there needs to establish a destination-based management program which requires a strong collaboration and co-operation among all the related bodies of a tourist destination. In order for the management of tourist destinations to give a distinctive appeal to such variables as leisure activities, sports, food, welcoming tourists and natural and cultural heritage, this chapter ends with the analysis of several measures that seem to play a key role in the success of managing the quality of tourist destinations.

As we know, the practice of total quality management (TQM) aims to satisfy both internal and external customers through continuous improvement in the level of service and product quality provided by an organisation. A successful implementation of a destination-based TQM practice can potentially assist to meet quality standards and enhance competitiveness. Ideally, this should also be the aim of a destination management organization in charge of managing sources, marketing products and setting policies. In the light of these statements, it is possible to suggest the practice of D-TQM as a significant contribution to the management of destinations in improving the quality of service provision. In addition, because the subsequent impact is expected to lead to an increase in the market share, this also would help to maintain the competitiveness of a destination in the international arena. Therefore, Chapter 5 aims to (1) emphasize the significance of quality management in successful improvement of the performance of tourist destinations and then (2) design a tentative model of

D-TQM, particularly suitable for the sustainable development of tourist destinations as well as application suggestions.

Chapter 6 briefly tries to outline how benchmarking may lead tourist destinations to enhance their competitive edge vis-à-vis their competitors. A short answer as to why benchmarking is relevant for tourist destinations includes the careful assessment of the trend of intense competition among destinations, not only as countries but also as regions. Tourists, from one day to another, have become more experienced and knowledgeable about the world and changes in their demand for consumption of products and services available in the international market. This results in a sensitive structure of tourists to even a very little negative experience during a vacation. Thus, the fake positioning of a small piece (e.g. let's say food poisoning or charging higher prices in this case) may distort the overall picture of the puzzle (e.g. quality of the whole vacation experience). Last but not the least, as a structure of human personality, customers compare not only themselves with others, but also make comparisons among their preferences and among various alternatives. A final decision is set as a consequence of the output derived from this decision-making process. Knowing about the performance of other destinations becomes important to take place in customers' final consideration sets.

The succeeding chapter attempts to cover all the relevant subjects that have now become very useful in today's contemporary business environment not only for the individual organizations but also managing the marketing of tourist destinations. In lights of various existing approaches, Chapter 7 provides an overview of existing marketing strategies and their implementation to destinations and then suggests several ways of marketing strategies in order to be able to maintain and even increase the competitive edge of tourist destinations worldwide. This chapter further suggests that monitoring competitors on a regular basis will enable one destination management to reinforce the analysis of the market and identify its own strengths and weaknesses and the potential marketing opportunity. This sort of analysis, in the end, may help to develop the correct positioning strategy. Some of the subjects included in this chapter are product diversification, market segmentation, innovation, market research, destination branding and destination positioning.

Most destinations today have excellent facilities and attractions, and every destination claims and promotes a unique culture and heritage, beautiful landscape, excellent facilities and very friendly locals. Therefore, creating a differentiated brand image is more critical (Morgan and Pritchard 1999). Chapter 8 is about branding tourist destinations. Success depends on essentially two dimensions: (1) the management of the tourism system as a system of networks and channels and (2) the management of brand attributes, their dissemination and consistency (Gnoth 2002). Destination branding should be managed strategically by destination marketing organizations to articulate and communicate a destination identity. This chapter provides concepts, tools and approaches of developing brands in travel and tourism to help destination marketers implement sound brand strategies and tactics. First, the concept of "destination" and "brand" definitions are presented. Then, branding challenges for destinations and larger context of brand-building processes were introduced. The components of brand image such as cognitive, affective and destination personality as well as destination tourism slogans are discussed. The chapter ends with a case study about destination slogans and branding destinations with unique selling propositions (USPs).

Consistent with the debate that the traditional travel distribution system is going through a very dramatic change, Chapter 9 aims to examine the present and potential impact of Information Technology (IT) on the tourism industry, tourism marketing and management and destination competitiveness. This chapter also examines the nature, structure and characteristics of distribution channels for tourism and travel service providers alongside the implications of IT as a new management and marketing instrument. This chapter further presents theoretical knowledge to examine developments in IT. It reports on how IT's current and potential use as a tourism marketing tool impacts the competitiveness of tourism and travel businesses in particular and tourist destinations in general.

This book discusses and synthesizes models, techniques and principles for strategic marketing and management of destinations. This book has an international focus. We wanted to discuss and present current theories, principles and practices to facilitate strategic marketing and management planning for tourist destinations. The principles and guidelines discussed apply equally to different product levels (small or large scale) in travel and tourism such as museums, national parks, cities, regions and countries. Several faculty members also contributed to this book by writing highly practical cases. We thank them for their support and contribution. We owe special thanks to the publisher, Routledge, for their patience and meticulous revisions. We finally thank our families colleagues for their support.

Part I

Destination Competitiveness

1 Why Destination Competitiveness?

Travellers today, domestic or international, are more educated, informed, demanding and experienced. As a result they expect good value, quality and higher standards. The changes happening at demand side, coupled with recent development in information and communication technology, influence all aspects of marketing strategy and travel behavior. From marketing theory perspective, the requirement of meeting or exceeding travellers' needs and wants should be balanced against the growing requirement of places and destinations to develop and protect destination attractions, assets and resources in the most sustainable way (Middleton and Clarke 2001). Certainly, there are a number of reasons to indicate as to why the measurement and determination of destination competitiveness has become so important in travel and tourism (e.g. the existence of multiple destinations, the emergence of new destinations and so on). Each of these characteristics is explained in this chapter. These may also aid the readers to clearly understand the necessity of writing a textbook on the term 'destination competitiveness'. This chapter also discusses the distinctive characteristics of the tourism industry along with destinations and evaluating main elements of destination attractiveness.

1.1. MAJOR CHARACTERISTICS OF THE TOURISM INDUSTRY

As a sub-sector of services, tourism has specific characteristics comparing with the manufacturing industry and other elements of the service industry. Such specific characteristics make the tourism industry differ in the management and marketing of tourist destinations, managing the host–guest relationship, and enhancing the competitive edge. These are listed below (for details, see Morrison 1989; Laws 1995; Kozak 2004a):

1. As the production and consumption coincide with time and location, tourists participate in the creation of the services they purchase. Tourists cannot sample the destination or its sub-elements before arriving for their vacations. But, they make their decisions either by looking

at brochures or obtaining feedback from their relatives and friends, which is so much different than making decisions to choose a physical product.

2. As a significant part of the service industry, tourist services are composed of intangible rather than tangible attributes. Service is consumed as long as this consumption activity continues. As a consequence of this, pricing of services is more difficult than pricing of products. The customer needs to use intangible products sought in travel and tourism operations in a shorter period because they are not re-consumable.

3. Tangible clues and evidence determine customers' assessment of the level of service quality (e.g. the type of furniture, the appearance of facility and staff uniforms and so on). This means that the quality of services is not a single criterion to be considered while evaluating tourists' overall judgment of tourism products provided during a vacation.

4. In tourism services, a much higher level of social interaction takes place among tourists, staff and local residents in buying tourist services than the one in buying tangible products. Thus, emotions and personal feelings, generated by service encounters, influence future purchase intentions. Those employees affiliated with a variety of tourist establishments and encounters contribute to forming an overall picture of tourist experiences with destinations, which might be unique to each user.

5. Distribution channels play an important role in the marketing of tourism products and services. A distribution channel is a set of independent organizations or individuals involved in the process of making a product or service available to the consumer or business user. Most distribution channels are more than simple collections of firms tied together by various flows. Because most channel members also get involved in promoting and selling the destination, an *integrated* communication and distribution strategy is also needed.

6. Customer experience is shaped by a set of products provided by various establishments and even by events to be participated during a vacation (e.g. advertisements by either governments or tourism establishments, recommendations by friends and travel agents, quality of food, shopping, social interaction with other customers and behaviour of local people). The risk refers to the failure on these elements that may lead to customer dissatisfaction and repeatedly negative word-of-mouth recommendation.

7. Obtaining objective prior information when purchasing services is more difficult than when purchasing products. Thus, word-of-mouth communication helps potential customers obtain information about the alternative services or tourist destinations they would like to purchase and, in turn, decide which one to be purchased.

8. Most tourism services are not easy to be copied. Rather, it may be impossible to be patented, either. Different hotel establishments may have rooms and restaurants with the same size and recreation activities with the same features. This is also the case for tourist destinations where several identical products exist (e.g. beaches, museums, nature, shopping and accommodation facilities).

9. The capacity of either a tourist establishment or a tourist destination is not suitable to be expanded quickly. For example, expanding the accommodation capacity of destinations takes months and sometimes years. Subsequently, such tourist services as beds and meals cannot be stored for sale in a following day when a growing demand appears.

What is served by the supplier and consumed by the consumer in tourism is called 'the tourism product'. It involves both tangible and intangible features. The tourism product is defined as "comprising attractions of a destination including images, sites, scenery, events and weather; facilities including accommodation, catering and entertainment; and accessibility with regard to the time and cost it takes to reach the destination" (Lewis and Owtram 1986, p. 204). As can be seen, attractions, events and accessibility play a pivotal role in the management and marketing of tourist destinations as they attract visitors; and, in turn, gaining the competitive advantage of tourist destinations. The primary marketing response to the above-mentioned travel and tourism characteristics has been managing and manipulating demand in the short term.

However, given the current trends such as sustainable tourism development and marketing as well as branding, a long-term planning and approach is a necessity, as well. In other words, the marketing responses should have both a strategic approach (long-term planning) and a tactical approach (short-term planning). And the tactics should be shaped and guided by the strategies. The term *sustainability* has emerged because of increasing consciousness of the countries about finding ways to develop their economies with minimal destruction of their environments and full consideration of the welfare of future generations (Carey, Gountas and Gilbert 1997; Rodríguez, Parra-López and Yanes-Estévez 2008; Prideaux 2009). A sustainable destination will act for the interest of travellers and residents, as well as for the protection of the resources. The triple bottom line suggests that a destination is operating in a way so that its economic interests, society or resident interests and environment interests intersect (Savitz 2006).

1.2. ATTRACTIVENESS OF TOURIST DESTINATIONS

Contributions to the work of classifying major elements of destinations include the following. In an earlier attempt to measure the tourist attractiveness of destinations, Var, Beck and Loftus (1977) note that it is a function of natural, social and historical factors, recreation and shopping opportunities, accessibility and accommodation performing above minimum touristic quality standards. Mill and Morrison (1992) state that a destination is composed of attractions, facilities, infrastructure, transport and hospitality. Similarly, Laws (1995) classifies elements which contribute to the attractiveness of a tourist destination under two main headings. Primary destination features include climate, ecology, culture and traditional architecture. Secondary destination features are those developments introduced particularly for tourist groups such as hotels, catering, transport and entertainment. Laws further claims that the primary purpose of tourists is to enjoy the primary features rather than the others, but the secondary features are necessary to reinforce the attractiveness of the destination. Goodall and Bergsma (1990) consider total cost as a fifth component in addition to attractions, facilities and services, accessibility and image. All these features together contribute to the attractiveness of a tourist destination.

Destination choice, image and satisfaction have all been the subject of considerable tourism research. Numerous attempts have been made to profile tourist motivations and link them to destination choice (e.g. Mayo and Jarvis 1981; Goodall 1988). Findings can be useful and helpful in directing future marketing efforts despite the fact that elements differ from one destination to another depending upon the type of destinations and tourist motivations (Kozak 2002a). In an empirical study, natural beauty, infrastructure, tourist facilities and climate were all found to be prime elements of the destination attractiveness (Gearing, Swart and Var 1974).

In other research, factors affecting tourist destination choices were listed as physical (infrastructure, superstructure, scenery, beaches, climate, historical sights), socio-psychological attractions (attitudes of the local people, cultural events, nightlife and entertainment, novelty of the destination, accessibility, food, quietness and so forth), political and social environment and cost and availability of time (Sirakaya, McLellan and Uysal 1996). In an attempt to investigate international travellers' destination choices and the factors influencing their choices, Kale and Weir (1986) found that the major factors in general were the availability of things to do and see, cost, climate and accommodation. It was also observed that major factors affecting respondents' choice of a specific destination were culture, scenery, history and food.

In a further analysis of tourist motivations, a category of *push* and *pull* factors is presented. Tourism literature emphasizes the importance of both push and pull factors in shaping tourist motivations and in choosing vacation destinations (Crompton 1979). Push factors are origin-related and refer to the intangible or intrinsic desires of the individual traveller (e.g. the desire for escape, rest and relaxation, adventure, health or prestige). Pull factors are mainly related to the attractiveness of a given destination and tangible characteristics such as beaches, accommodation and recreation facilities and cultural and historical resources (Uysal and Hagan 1993). As stated earlier, pull motivators indicate the extent to which each destination is attractive to its potential customers. Therefore, the destination choice process is related to the tourists' assessments of destination attributes and their perceived utility values (Kozak 2001a; Nicolau and Más 2006).

1.3. TRENDS OF THE TOURISM INDUSTRY

In figures of 2003, 691 million people who counted for approximately 10 percent of the world population were involved in tourism movements, and tourism revenues amounted to $523 billion (www.world-tourism. com). According to the World Trade Organization (WTO), these figures are expected to be 1.6 billion people and $2 trillion in 2020 and 2 billion people and $2.1 trillion in 2050, respectively (Cho 2003). Moreover, it is estimated that the total revenues of both domestic and foreign tourism will amount to $24.2 trillion in 2050 (Pizam 1999). World Travel and Tourism Council (WTTC) expected that tourism revenues would reach $7.1 trillion in 2006 with an increase of 50 percent, and this will count for 11.5 percent of the world Gross National Product (GNP) and 11.1 percent of the labour force in the next ten years (Crouch and Ritchie 1999). In such a fast-growing industry, the attempts of countries to increase their shares has accelerated competition in tourism and given way to new research perspectives. That is why a lot of tourism countries are in competition to take part in the international tourism market in order to especially acquire foreign exchange, create new fields of occupation and increase their annual GNP, which are surely required for the development of their economies.

1.4. WHY DESTINATION COMPETITIVENESS?

Whereas studies on competition focus generally on examining the exportation success of goods-producing or manufacturing firms, studies on the service industry including tourism are limited. Accordingly, we know very little about both the service industry and competition in tourism destinations. Nevertheless, the increasing weight of tourism in industrialized countries of today, counting for 60 to 70 percent of their GNP, has resulted in rising competition in this industry. It is known that the first studies on tourism competitiveness, in a particular reference to the subject of destination competitiveness that covers a significant proportion of the tourism literature, have been conducted by several researchers within the last few decades (Goodrich 1977; Haahti and Yavas 1983; Heath and Wall 1992; Kozak and Rimmington 1999; Kozak, Baloglu and Bahar 2010).

However, the most comprehensive study so far is that of Ritchie and Crouch (2003). They applied the competitiveness of the service industry

1. On the demand side, the most prevalent trends today are that travellers:

- Are better educated and more sensitive to environmental and social issues (generational markets).
- Have greater personal mobility and early retirement opportunities at younger ages.
- Are culturally diverse and have multiple or changing lifestyles when they travel.
- Demand more individualized experience and have idiosyncratic expectations.
- Have more frequent but short trips except for European market.
- Are more computer literate and technology-savvy.· Have more and quicker access to information and media and connectivity from home and office.

2. On the supply (destination) side, the market trends are as follows:

- More responsible tourism marketing and environmentally friendly travel (People, Planet, and Profit).
- More emphasis on disaster and crisis planning. Terrorism, pandemic diseases and natural disasters are forcing destinations and hospitality industry to better prepare and work together to respond to the disasters and crisis.
- Higher-speed transportation but increased fuel costs.
- More interest in tourism diversification such as medical tourism.

Box 1.1   Trends at Both the Demand and Supply Sides.

to the context of tourism destinations on the basis of countries, industries, products and companies. To these authors, the possibilities of a destination that provides a high standard of living for its citizens represent the competitiveness of that destination. Thus, the most competitive destination in the long term is that which most effectively creates well-being for its residents. Needless to say, Ritchie and Crouch state that it is also essential to set up the development of the destination on a sound basis in order to maintain a certain level of competitiveness.

The literature suggests that an area should have the following characteristics to be considered a tourist destination: a variety of natural, social and cultural resources and services, other economic activities, host community, a local council and an active private *or* public sector (Davidson and Maitland

1997). As stated earlier, a destination's performance is mainly related to the performance of these elements. When something is wrong with any of these elements, the outcome would be negative which will be reflected back to these elements. In such a case, tourists do not want to come back. The local community's quality of life would be negatively affected due to poor service standards. They would also earn less from the tourism industry. Employees would fear losing their jobs, resulting in a lower satisfaction with their jobs. Suppliers would earn less. Most important, all the cultural, economic and physical resources would be negatively affected if potential consumers withdrew because there would be less capital for reinvestment.

Due to its propensity to make a significant contribution to the national economy, the tourism industry has received particular attention from many governments and public authorities. As with every industry and business, many tourist destinations are in competition with each other (Kozak and Rimmington 1999; Kozak 2002b; Gomezelj and Mihalič 2008; Gursoy, Baloglu and Chi 2009; Kozak, Baloglu and Bahar 2010). As a result, the aim is to obtain much economic benefit from tourism activities by increasing the proportion of a country's tourism receipts out of international tourism. Given this, the following list includes various potential reasons to explain why we need to accept and discuss the term 'destination competitiveness' on the basis of both supply- and demand-based features.

1. Developments in international tourism and travel have intensified competition between international tourist destinations.

New destinations become established, some existing ones make further progress and others decline (Kozak 2000). Natural, cultural and historical resources, infrastructure, accessibility, attractions and facilities are accepted as elements of tourist destination competitiveness. Many tourists have experience with other destinations. It is, therefore, expected that visitors are likely to make comparisons between facilities, attractions and service standards (Laws 1995; Kozak 2001a, 2001b; Kozak, Baloglu and Bahar 2010). It is argued that a potential visitor selects a destination from alternatives and evaluates each alternative considering its potential to deliver the benefits sought (Mayo and Jarvis 1981; Decrop and Kozak 2009). Crompton (1993), for example, states that, in the evaluation of alternatives in the late consideration set, constraints (factors) associated with each of these alternative destinations become more effective.

2. Each destination offers a variety of products and services to attract visitors. However, each visitor also has the opportunity and freedom to choose from a set of national or international destinations.

As emphasized earlier, different factors might have an influence on destination choice (Nicolau and Mas 2006; Blichfeldt 2008; Decrop 2010).

For instance, each visitor might have different motivations and preferences for different destinations. Most studies of tourist destination selection and consumer choice behaviour have been related to the investigation of the relationship between attitude toward a vacation destination or the image of the destination and tourist preferences for the place as a tourist destination, as well as satisfaction or dissatisfaction with the destination. At this stage, Morrison (1989) presents two criteria: objective and subjective. These criteria help tourists decide which destination might have the potential to meet their own criteria best. Whereas objective criteria include prices, locations, physical characteristics of facilities or destination and services, the image of the destination is considered as subjective criteria. Both objective and subjective criteria are significant attributes in forming a destination image. For instance, the level of prices offered by any destination as an objective criterion has become an important attribute for tourists while choosing a destination from alternatives. These arguments also contribute to understanding of how and where one destination is competitive.

3. As a result of increases in the demand for package holidays for the last two decades, destinations have become more important than individual attractions and facilities.

Developments in the tourism and travel industry have created new destinations in addition to previous traditional destinations (e.g. seaside destinations and historical places). New developing destinations threaten mature destinations by offering affordable prices and unspoiled resources (e.g. Turkey, Tunisia and the Caribbean Islands as opposed to Spain). Destinations are the focus for attention because they motivate and stimulate visits and are the places where the majority of tourism product is produced and served simultaneously (Goodall 1990; Laws 1995). In other words, much of the tourism industry is located and much of the time is spent in destinations. Tourist satisfaction with a destination or its overall image rather than a facility may therefore lead to repeat visits. Previous research findings indicate that there is a significant relationship among tourist satisfaction, intention to return and word-of-mouth recommendation (Beeho and Prentice 1997; Kozak and Rimmington 2000; Um, Chon and Ro 2006).

4. The consumer psychology literature suggests that there is a strong association between attitudes toward an object and behavioral intention to repurchase or recommend it.

Thus, if attitude toward a country or a destination is positive, the intention to visit there is also expected to be positive or higher (Woodside and Sherrell 1977; Mayo and Jarvis 1981). As is explained in the following chapters of the book, there are numerous potential factors which can influence attitudes toward destinations. Of these, taking overdevelopment on board as an example, it has resulted in some significant environmental problems such as water pollution, noise and loss of landscape due to the lack of adequate planning controls at either the central or local government level. This may damage the image of the destination in the international market which in turn negatively impacts the benefits of tourism into the area in the long term. It is evident that authorities need to pay much attention to maintaining their resources if they would like to maintain their competitiveness levels and obtain benefits from tourism in a continuous manner.

5. From a tourist's perspective, there is a close relationship between all tourism-related facilities and businesses at the destination.

Tourist motivation has been shown to be multidimensional (Pyo, Mihalik and Uysal 1989). Tourists want to have more than one experience at a destination. When they visit, they stay at a hotel, often eat and drink somewhere outside the hotel, go shopping, communicate with local people and other tourists and visit natural, cultural or historic places. On the supply side, the trip is not a single product; rather it is made up of components supplied by a variety of organizations with different objectives. McIntyre (1993, p. 23) describes the destination as "the location of a cluster of attractions and related tourist facilities and services which a tourist or tour group selects to visit or which providers choose to promote". Coltman (1989, p. 4) presents a more comprehensive definition as being "an area with different natural attributes, features, or attractions that appeal to non-local visitors—that is, tourists or excursionists". All these elements make a contribution to tourists' experiences. As a consequence of the 'domino effect', lack of quality experience in even one of these areas may influence the overall satisfaction level detrimentally (Jafari 1983).

6. Due to the increasing role of information and transport technology and tour operator-based organized tours, tourists have gained an opportunity to increase their experiences with many destinations.

Tourists are becoming more sophisticated and looking for higher standards in quality, innovation and responsiveness as a consequence of developments in technology, increase in mobility and increase in the spread of word-of-mouth communication (Mill and Morrison 1992). Recent developments in technology and hearing about others' experiences give people access to all the information they need to learn about other places in the world. Increasing the mobility of potential tourists, technology has also provided easy access to the same or other destinations in either the short or long term. Each holiday taken may update a tourist's expectations for the next holiday and widen their experiences, resulting in a tourist group with higher expectations, needs and wants (Boulding, Kalra, Staeling and Zeithaml 1993). As a result, tourists know how to search for better offers and what to expect from their experiences with a national or international vacation. This highlights the importance of the quality of both services and facilities. Destination suppliers need to know what their customers look for while holidaying around the world and collect feedback regularly about the level of services they have received.

7. The method of distribution of tourism products is, to certain extent, different from that in some other industries.

The quotation by Ashworth and Voogd (1990, p. 18) underlines that "places [destinations] are obviously different from many other products on the market both in the composite nature of the product and the way it is used by the customer. The selling of the place is not the transfer of rights of ownership but only of limited and generally non-exclusive rights of use". A variety of supply- and demand-based reasons could influence visitors' decisions in the selection of a particular destination because they have to be physically present at a destination in order to have both psychological and physical holiday experiences (e.g. Gronross 1978; Um and Crompton 1990; Sirakaya, McLellan and Uysal 1996; Rust, Zahorik and Keiningham 1996). Of these, tourists have the opportunity to receive information about the destination through multiple information sources such as word-of-mouth communication, brochures, TV and other media and their own experience with the destination. In organizations, customers do not have direct access to the location where goods and services are produced or provided; they can purchase goods and services from retailers. In some cases, they may have experience with only a few attributes provided by businesses. For example, customers can conduct all the business relating to their bank account without speaking to any of the bank staff. They can just use the automatic bank teller machines to complete the process. The significant point here will be the overall image of the business among its customers and the efficiency of the machines. Such marketing differences bring the importance of distance, cultural differences between supply and demand, between destinations and between tourists as being factors influencing the investigation of destination performance and its competitive level.

8. Customer loyalty for destinations is lower than for organizations. Even in the situation where a customer may have visited the same destination on several occasions, visits will have been at the rate of once or twice per year.

This chapter supports the above statements, indicating that the majority of tourists visit a destination two or three times in their whole life. The same visitors may have been using products and services provided by individual organizations much more frequently in their routine life (e.g. supermarkets, department stores, restaurants and so on). Or they may have an experience with a tangible product until its life cycle ends (e.g. TV or car). Actual customer experiences in tourism expire once the vacation ends. The tourist has to take a new vacation for a new experience. This would be the consideration of a new destination for every vacation they take (McDougall and Munro 1994). Such a high level of customer turnover for tourist destinations brings the importance of the consideration of the needs, wants and demands of other potential customers who may arrange their first visits to a destination in the future, alongside the needs of those making repeat visits. This requires a continuous administration and a continuous measurement of the current performance of the destination.

It seems obvious that the term *tourist behavior* is different from the term *consumer behavior* in many respects (Gitelson and Crompton 1984). Expenditure is budgeted and time is planned much earlier because spending time on holidays is an expensive leisure activity. Because it is difficult for potential tourists to be familiar with destination services in advance, they need to physically exist there. Potential tourists also have a variety of alternatives due to the expansion in the number of domestic and international destinations. As a result, repeat business or regular loyalty may be less likely for destinations than it is for individual businesses, even where the destination fulfills tourist expectations, because tourists may look for similar but new experiences with different destinations (McDougall and Munro 1994) or they may have been dissatisfied with many aspects of their holidays. Tourists may even prefer a completely new destination for every holiday they take. For instance, it was empirically tested that package travellers tend to visit places once and then look for new destinations for future holidays (Hsieh, O'Leary and Morrison 1994).

1.5. A STRATEGIC APPROACH

This book discusses and synthesizes models, techniques and principles for strategic marketing and management of destinations. Global competition, coupled with more demanding travelers and highly diverse tourism "product", make place or destination marketing highly difficult and challenging around the globe. Competitive analysis of destinations is rapidly gaining in importance in the strategic marketing planning and positioning of destinations (Crouch and Ritchie 1999; Faulkner, Oppermann and Fredline 1999; Baloglu and McCleary 1999; Kozak 2004a). The competitiveness may vary by type of competition, target market and product mix. The critical issue is to create a competitive advantage by attracting and delighting tourists as well as creating a memorable experience as good as or better than competitive destinations. "The challenge of place marketing is to strengthen the capacity of communities and regions to adapt to the changing marketplace, size opportunities, and sustain their vitality" (Kotler, Haider and Rein 1993, p. 18). Therefore, strategic approach and marketing planning is a necessity rather than an option.

Tourism marketing's main role is to systematically link supply and demand. The starting point is often the supply side (product orientation) rather than the demand side (market orientation), except for man-made destinations. On the supply side, attractions, facilities, services, people (employees and residents), internal marketing and brand identity strategies and tactics all are marketing domains. On the demand side, understanding travellers' characteristics, perception and images, positioning, tourist experiences and behaviors as well as market trends are central to strategic place or destination marketing. The strategies and tactics are usually summarized under marketing mix variables, namely, product and service, pricing, promotion and distribution. Product development strategies need to be sustainable to foster triple bottom line from economic, social and environmental perspectives. Promotion strategy should integrate all efforts to build a strong brand equity and association and to stimulate visitation. Pricing strategy should be designed to provide a good value across target markets. The distribution strategy involves individuals and organizations to help place or destination get travellers to product (tour operators, travel agents, tourist offices, DMOs and so on). It also includes transportation (air, road, sea and rail). It should be noted that all these activities influence and contribute to the tourist-based brand equity of the place (awareness and recognition, value, quality, repeat visitation and positive word of mouth).

From "destination" competitiveness to "place" competitiveness. The destination competitiveness today is being redefined as the basis of competitive advantage shifts from tourism to a citywide integrated management. Therefore, the term "destination" is being replaced by "place" or "city" in tourism branding literature. Even promotion of tourist cities is changing shape to create an appeal that is aspiring to all stakeholders (tourists, businesses and residents). "Urban tourism now becomes a strategy for building quality services and products and sustainable management of the urban community, a means of attracting responsible tourists, and a way of developing competitive city destinations that combine a comparative supply able to meet the visitor's expectations with a positive contribution to the development of cities and the well-being of their residents" (Paskaleva-Shapira 2007, p. 108).

All stakeholders should be involved in strategic planning. The marketing issues and skills will be at the forefront for the upcoming decade to match between demand and supply. Place or destination marketing, however, will achieve a little without involving all stakeholders and combining their input and efforts into an integrated strategy. Therefore, "internal" marketing principles should be combined with tourism planning principles and policy formulation to coordinate the efforts of all stakeholders and residents, and engage them in the strategic marketing planning. The initial task in strategic place marketing is to organize an "internal" planning committee made up of residents, businesses and local government officials to ensure cooperation between private and public sectors. This is followed

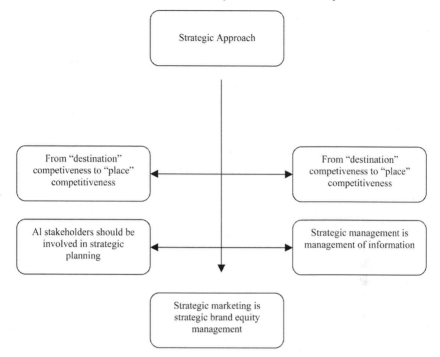

Figure 1.1 List of strategic approaches for marketing and management.

by improving four critical marketing factors: infrastructure, attractions, image and support from the community, which are to be utilized to attract and satisfy target markets (Kotler, Haider and Rein 1993). Destination management and marketing should act as tools and facilitators to achieve a complex range of strategic objectives, which will ultimately need to satisfy the needs and wants of stakeholders (Buhalis 2000). These objectives include both economic gains as well as social and environmental objectives to achieve sustainable growth, and not only ensure tourists' satisfaction but also stakeholders' and residents' satisfaction.

Strategic Marketing is Strategic Brand Equity Management.

Places need to develop brand equity to attract potential tourists and differentiate themselves from other destinations. Destination image is a critical component of customer-based brand equity models (Konecnik and Gartner 2007; Boo, Busser and Baloglu 2009) and plays a pivotal role in tourist demand management. A place may find its current image in the following situations (Kotler, Haider and Rein 1993): positive image, negative image, weak image, strong image and mixed or confused image. Destination marketing is not limited to physical attributes anymore. Affective and symbolic benefits (prestige and personality associations) provided by the destination have started to play a major role in strategic marketing. Developing and marketing favorable and differentiated images or brand associations has become the most powerful strategy in the marketplace.

Strategic Management is Management of Visitor Experience.

A tourism destination can be viewed as an amalgamation of places generating experiences. From a cultural perspective, places serve as storehouses of meanings that capture value in use and frame expectations for experiences (Snepenger, Snepenger, Dalbey and Wessol 2007). Tourist destinations should design and manage tourist experiences, which goes beyond entertainment. All destinations make some value propositions, and a memorable experience is every destination's proposition because all destinations are by nature in the experience business. An experience should take into account both rational and emotional expectations. Anything perceived and sensed (hear, smell, feel, see and taste) in the environment is an experience clue and must be managed (Schmitt 1999; Carbone 2004). Tourists or visitors will also sense what is missing in the environment based on their previous experience and background. Products, services, physical environment, local people and other visitors all emit clues which also carry messages. **The total destination experience** is a composite of all these and interactions (Carbone 2004). A typical experience will start at the airport (if not the destination) homepage and continue with the taxicab, hotel check-in, sightseeing, tour, dining and shopping experiences. Therefore, tourist destinations can create a positive total experience by arranging the hundreds of clues. If not managed, negative clues can ruin the whole experience by cancelling out the positive ones.

Strategic Management is Management of Information.

The destination marketing decisions should be fed by marketing research on a continual basis. Marketing intelligence should cover tourist, residents, and distribution channel perspectives. For example, Las Vegas has annual visitor, residents and travel agents surveys to assess characteristics, expectations, satisfaction and brand associations. Market research is needed for all stages of strategic marketing such as identifying trends and strengths and weaknesses, segmenting and target marketing, developing image and positioning, product development, pricing, promoting and distributing destination offerings.

1.6.   SUMMARY

The current trends requires an integration of tourism impact, cultural heritage tourism, city branding, visitor perception and experience

According to Kotler, Haider and Rein (1993), place marketing consists of four core activities: (1) designing the right mix of community tangible offerings and services, (2) developing appealing benefits for potential and current users/buyers, (3) delivering the place's experience in both efficient and effective ways, and (4) communicating the place's image to create awareness of the place's distinctive advantage. According to Pine and Gilmore (1999), there is a shift to an experience economy, which is the fourth phase of economic value after commodities, goods and services. In the experience economy, every business is a stage and work is a theatre. The new economy also demands new models and thinking. Pine and Gilmore (1999) argue that Las Vegas is the experience capital of America because almost everything about Las Vegas is a designed experience, from slot machines to themes resorts and from shopping malls to the shows. Schmitt (1999) discussed experiences under the concept of "experiential marketing". Experiential marketing focuses on customer experiences and replace sensory, emotional, behavioral and rational values with functional values. Schmitt (1999) discusses different types of experiences which he calls "Strategic Experiential Modules" (SEMs). SEMs include sensory experiences (SENSE), creative cognitive experiences (THINK), affective experiences (FEEL), physical experiences (ACT) and social identity experiences (RELATE). "Today, customers take functional features and benefits, product quality, and a positive brand image as a given. What they want is products, communications, and marketing campaigns that dazzle their senses, touch their hearts, and stimulate their minds" (Schmitt 1999, p. 22).

Box 1.2 Experiential Marketing of Tourist Destinations.

management and urban quality of life under the umbrella of sustainable tourism development and marketing. Moreover, because tourism is a labor-intensive industry, its development in economically less-developed places might offer advantages into the local and national economies. Tourists benefit from lower prices resulting from lower costs, and, as a result, additional jobs can be generated. Despite this, major elements of such places such as ecological and cultural values may be at risk to damage from tourism activities due to the lack of public and legislative control. This brings the trouble of declining and weakening the level of contribution to the economic prosperity of the place. In order to have a powerful economy, each destination has to compete with the others, attract technology-based investments and offer sustainable tourism products and services. The present chapter overviews the potential reasons as to study on the term 'destination competitiveness'. The succeeding chapter will focus on a critical overview of past research published on the competitiveness of tourist destinations.

* * *

CASE STUDY: MEDICAL TOURISM DESTINATIONS

Written by Dan Cormany, *University of Nevada Las Vegas, USA*

Hospitality has been linked to health issues for years, with travellers visiting foreign areas for spa therapies, alternative treatments, and using hotels as a home away from home as they have sought health diagnostic services, and cosmetic surgery (Nahrstedt 2004; Erfurt-Cooper and Cooper 2009). This had been a small specialty market but now there is a swelling tide of travellers, or "medical tourists", finding it either appealing or necessary to travel to other destinations for needed life-saving surgeries and orthopedic treatments. In the United States alone, the population of aging baby boomers is forming a "silver tsunami" (Maples 2007) about to crash on the shores of all available quality health care. Many of these baby boomers will elect to travel to benefit from the greatly reduced pricing of equally high medical services outside of the country (Demicco and Cetron 2006).

Hospitals from dozens of countries from Argentina to Vietnam have been raising their service levels, achieving international recognition, and furnishing themselves with cutting edge equipment along with physicians who can boast world-class training (Gahlinger 2008; Woodman 2008). For most needed or desired treatments, the potential medical traveller now has several world-class medical facilities in most corners of the globe from which to choose.

With these choices available, and more on the way, how does the potential medical tourist select a destination for treatment? What factors beyond top-flight medical care will give a destination an edge in this increasingly competitive field? For individuals looking to venture beyond national borders for care, what is the mix of facilities, policies and services that will be most important? As more and more areas are offering world-class medical services, what will distinguish one from another?

Marketing theory would partially answer these questions by suggesting that if treatment quality is equal, the traveller will make a selection based upon either choosing the lowest cost option or the destination that is best perceived to best serve the greatest number of that traveller's needs (Pike 2008; Kotler, Bowen and Makens 2010). These needs may vary from traveller to traveller, but it is in the meeting of these needs that hospitality needs to make a significant contribution to the growth of an area as a medical tourism destination.

A starting point is for a destination to consider the types of medical tourists it seeks to attract and what these tourists desire from their travel. Such travellers may be divided into six sometimes overlapping categories from general wellness enhancement to major surgery (as shown in the pie with each being one of the slices) (Cormany 2008).

These six categories may be further divided into specialty services. For instance, major surgery offered may concentrate on such expertise as heart care, cancer, joint-replacement, etc. Less major surgery may be focused on dental or bariatric treatments. For medi-spas, the focus may be on stress alleviation, learning healthier lifestyles, overcoming addictions, botox injections, etc. Alternative therapies may capitalize on regional expertise, offering acupuncture, Ayurveda, herbal therapy, reputable native treatments, etc. An area's specialty will result in particular types of hospitality support from the region's hotels, restaurants, and its destination marketing or convention & visitors bureau.

Often the first impression the potential traveller has of a destination is that he or she gains from the website of the official office charged with promoting the region. In the United States, this is handled on a city or state basis by local convention and visitors bureaus or state departments of tourism. In other countries, these efforts may be replaced or supplemented by national ministries or departments of tourism. In nearly all cases, these

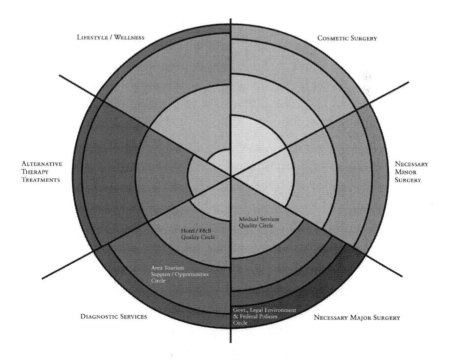

Figure 1.2 Major types of medical tourists.

are quasi-governmental operations, giving them a credibility that viewers might be less welling to extend to commercial websites (Pike 2008).

Such bureaus, departments or ministries not only provide a positive, comprehensive review of the area, but increasingly for business and leisure travellers, they have grown into roles of advocating for the development of appropriate services and facilities to extend the appeal of a destination or shore up a weakness that may be detracting from the area's appeal (Harrill 2005). Most have web pages dedicated to detailing items of interest to the leisure traveller and separate sections addressing services and facilities of need to the business traveller. However, only a handful has yet recognized that the medical traveller is a separate type of traveller, with needs different from either those of leisure or business travellers. With the exponential growth of medical travellers, even as other segments of travel have stagnated or shrunk in the current economy, the destination marketing executives who are not working with both the area hospitals or medical care cities, and the hotels, local transportation providers and area restaurants are missing a key element in helping build an area's reputation for medical tourism.

Leadership in these departments, ministries and bureaus are experts in marketing (Anholt 2009). So for them, it may be a lack of understanding of the needs of the medical traveller, or the potential business they represent for a city. If these destination marketing sites can promote "education tourism", "ecotourism", "GLBT tourism", "environmental tourism", "cultural tourism" and "volunteer tourism", as various sites currently do (links to many national and international destination marketing websites are available at the Destination Marketing Association International's website: www.destinationmarketing.org), it is incumbent upon those who would most benefit from an increase in medical tourism to communicate the potential value of medical tourists to these destination marketing executives while capitalizing on their expertise.

To do this, there may be a need to overcome what pragmatically may be called "bureaucratic inertia". As quasi-public institutions, many of these destination marketing efforts allocate next year's budget "in direct proportion to the amount of return [a segment offered last year] for a destination" to help justify this year's expenses, as notes Marshall Murdaugh, a leading marketing consultant for such organizations (Murdaugh 2005, p.31). Summaries of the numbers of visitors from outside the community served at area medical facilities, the average number of travelling partners with each, and the average out-of-hospital length of stay in the area, may all help to start the justification process for obtaining assistance from these destination marketing departments.

In turn, once the departments and ministries understand the potential of the medical tourism market, they may be valuable colleagues in communicating the market and profit potential to the rest of the local hospitality community. It is helpful to keep in mind that the main overlap of health and hospitality has been concentrated solely in operation of spas, which are usually operated as a separate profit center within the facility (Erfurt-Cooper and Cooper 2009). There needs to be education on the possible income a facility might enjoy as an aftercare facility, along with the special needs and expectations of such guests.

Departments of tourism, ministries or travel, or convention and visitors bureaus can also serve as a medical traveller advocate by encouraging disability-friendly facilities at regional airports, ground transportation capable of accommodating a wheelchair, and, with the direction of the medical experts, assisting restaurants to understand specific dietary requirements that may follow various medical procedures (Leibrock 2000). In cases where site-seeing may remain a pre or post-treatment option, aiding such tour operators to take into account guest limitations or to develop specially-designed experiences for medical guests are all roles for these destination marketing departments.

With regard to hotels, the type of services or facilities most beneficial may depend upon the nature of the medical treatments in which a region specializes. However when the traveller is seeking serious medical attention, the most common emerging model is that of a hotel as a facility serving the medical tourist briefly before medical treatment, and longer during the convalescence process prior to returning home (Cormany 2009). In essence, the hotel is an "aftercare" facility (MTA 2008), as the guest moves from medical facilities whereas his or her strength returns, healing occurs, and family members supplement the medical travel experience with tourism and relaxation. This recovery period may range from a few days for minor and cosmetic surgery to a couple weeks or more in the case of major surgery (Gahlinger 2008). Serving such patient/guests is relatively new ground for many properties, and it raises several new considerations.

These considerations include physical designs of guest rooms and access to facilities (Leibrock 2000), the ability of the hotel to meet dietary restrictions, and the offer of trained staff who understand their needs (Cormany 2009). Other factors include the availability of privacy, service levels, and proximity to medical help (Greenberg 2008). For instance, the availability of a nurse to help change bandages may be a valuable service provision.

A key point is that medical guests may be substantially different from leisure or business guests in their ability to participate, or "co-create" the necessary service (Zeithaml and Bitner 2000). After surgery, the guest is likely to be in a physically weakened condition, so routine processes such as waiting in a short front-desk queue, can be a daunting. Additionally, both the guest and his or her family members may be emotionally taxed, increasing the importance that the hotel staff has thought through their needs and coordinated such services so they don't need to (Stephano, personal communication, September 9, 2008).

In providing appropriate support properties a facility can distinguish itself as being "medical traveller friendly". Some service modifications that have proven helpful at some hotels include: scheduling specific housekeeping times to service the room offering personal shopping services, providing transportation (that perhaps can accommodate wheelchairs) to and from clinics, extending room service availability to 24 hours a day, and employing masseuses trained to complement recovery processes, cosmetologists skilled in "cosmetic camouflage" and medical-technology trained personal butlers able to respond to needs (Greenberg 2008). Some properties have also added nursing support to their staffs, whereas others have made such support available to their medical travellers through contracted third party providers (MTA 2008).

Concierge support, whether done by interacting only with the guest, in collaboration with personnel at the hospital, or as the local contact in conjunction with a medical facilitator in the traveller's home country, could also do much to aid the traveller and ease stress. At minimum, such a person serves to standardize communication between hotel departments and becomes a powerful marketing tool for the hotel. Such efforts also may provide an additional revenue stream for the property, much like a business center supports, and profits from, the business traveller. This contact person develops an expertise in the medical traveller needs, cultivates the unique contacts necessary to best serve the guest, and assures that services are coordinated for the benefit of both the guest and the various departments of the hotel.

Such services could be wrapped in and marketed with an all-inclusive hotel pricing for medical guests, making this a win-win for both the traveller and the facility. Almost by definition, medical travellers from the United States venturing outside of their country for surgery are doing so at least in part due to price sensitivity (Yim 2006). Additionally, a commonly voiced complaint of United States health care is the uncertainty of the final cost, as physicians, anesthesiologists, hospital facilities, medications, and other services each are billed separately, and may vary wildly from initial estimates (Gahlinger 2008). Many overseas hospitals have responded by providing a comprehensive price for their services, including that of their physicians. Hotels may want to avoid the perception of shifting the frustration of price uncertainty from the hospital to the hotel aftercare process.

By following the lead of international hospitals, hotels may not only find an all-inclusive price appealing to prospective medical guests, but also advantageous for the same reasons such pricing is often used in marketing resort destinations (Marsek and Sharpe 2008). From the property's perspective, this allows the hotel to capture revenue on three meals daily for the medical traveller and all of his or her family members. It also provides an income for a variety of support services the guest may or may not use. For example, these may include medical concierge support, a designated number of spa visits, ground transportation, possibly a specified number of nursing visits daily for the pre-determined duration of the stay, and even one or two light touring activities.

For the medical traveller, such price bundling removes apprehension over the final bill, and assures that if services are desired, they may be accessed.

There is another potential benefit of all-inclusive pricing. If medical insurance companies move toward covering travel expenses for such guests, it is conceivable that in the future hotels may be receiving direct payments from insurance providers. All-inclusive pricing contracts could clarify such coverage, assuring to both the hotel and the guest that prior approval has been issued for the total cost of the visit, and minimizing issues arising from questions of the guest's prerogative to utilize specific services. By limiting after-the-fact controversies of whether a nurse was essential, for example, or whether a medical traveller did or did not exceed an insurance-imposed meal allowance in ala carte ordering, the guest and the hotel are protected from extended post-trip haggling that so frequently drag out current insurance payments, and the insurance company is provided a pre-trip clarity of charges.

Eventually, all-inclusive price coverage, once clearly defined, may also afford those insurance companies a "value-added" measure of appeal if they wish to suggest medical travel as a cost-savings option to their clients (Marsek and Sharpe 2008).

Some lodging companies in key medical tourism destinations may also see an appeal to the medical traveller as a way to even out the seasonal ebb and flow of hotel occupancy, or as a sort of tourism that has more resistance to stagnation and decline than typical leisure destinations (Plog 2004). Others may be cautious about how well medical guests can be comingled with leisure and business travellers. Still others may pursue the strategy of Bodyline Resorts of Thailand, which accommodate exclusively medical tourists and their families.

For those facilities that wish to focus heavily on serving medical guests, some facility modification may eventually be required. Hotels may wish to extend their efforts into "medi-spas", transportation/lodging packages, or cooperative arrangements with area medical facilities. Separate, private check-in facilities, secluded restful areas, and reduction of hindrances to getting around the property are all simple, useful modifications. Guest rooms may be modified over time, by considering two basic factors—the recovering medical tourist is 1) more likely to spend a greater amount of time in the room than the average guest, so décor and utility details may be more critical to the comfort of their stay; and 2) more likely to have reduced amounts of energy and perhaps some mobility limitations, so convenience factors are especially important. With a little creativity and consideration of medical traveller needs, room modification may be done in a value-added way that enhances the appeal of the guest room to not only medical travellers, but all guests (Leibrock 2000).

Whereas hospitality firms may learn of the needs of specific conditions from the area medical personnel, they may also have some expertise to share with the hospitals. Many medical facilities are showing an interest in learning and imitating hospitality operations. Several medical centers are including concierge support, ground transportation arrangements, expedited hotel-like check-in processes, simplified billing, menus for food selection, and personal translators (MTA 2008).

Beyond medical and hotel facilities, destination appeal will also be directly affected by the area's ability to provide a pleasant, positive experience for the visitor. In fact, hotel hospitality and general area tourism offerings may be the distinguishing factor that allows an area to avoid relying solely on being the low price leader for a particular medical service. With increasing competition in medical tourism, a destination must avoid the perception that its medical services are simply a commodity, or it will be vulnerable to cheaper service offerings elsewhere. The potential medical visitor must also feel good about visiting the area. This brings us full circle back to the role of the destination marketing bureau, department or ministry.

In short, with increasing competition from more and more destinations entering the pursuit of medical tourists, areas are encouraged to take a holistic approach. Development of world-class medical service is an obvious first step, but a region's permanent status as a destination must factor in the blend of medicine and hospitality to serve specific types of medical tourists, and it must show a finesse by which tourism options are appropriately intertwined. Otherwise, its role as a medical destination may be short-lived, as newcomers compete to replace it as the cheapest provider of a particular treatment. Whereas cost will remain a driving motivation for many travellers, if cost is allowed to be the sole factor, there are likely to be only a few areas to emerge as winners, and development of full economic benefits for an area will remain restricted.

A model new to the world of tourism is beginning to emerge in many regions. In cities, states or countries, "healthcare clusters" or "medical cities" are being formed by leading medical providers to assist them in marketing efforts, enhance credibility, control reputation, and elevate standards of care (Stephano 2009). Frequently a part of these clusters are spas, resorts, and other tourism operators, united in coordinating a visitor's experience. These clusters then interface with national or state ministries of health, tourism, and economic development or export services, providing a coordinated voice and level of access to these governmental departments no one individual business could obtain.

Generally the formation of these clusters involves the establishment of standards by which those who are members will perform their services. This may include accreditation standards for medical facilities, minimum standards of experience for physicians, price ranges for treatments, etc. For the hospitality establishments, standards may include the provision of certain types or quality levels of facilities, and training staff on special needs of medical travellers. Adherence to the standards established by the cluster protects the area's medical tourism reputation, so membership as part of the cluster is a credentialing element for tourism operations serious about serving medical travellers. In some cases, this is further enhanced by the Ministry of Tourism certifying that tour operators have been trained in the specific visitor needs created by the type of medical services offered in a region.

The regional dominance of countries in medical tourism is highly unsettled in this newly emphasized service offering (Connell 2006). Thailand ushered in the current era of the medical traveller when an economic downturn in that country resulted in both hospitality and medical facilities underutilized. Bumrungrad Hospital in Bangkok, Thailand, became a leader in appealing to international visitors (Alsever 2006; Tatko-Peterson 2006); it is claimed that it hosted 50,000 Americans in the year 2007, demonstrating the size and scope of its operation (Woodman 2008). However, over 50 countries now wish to be known for offering medical tourism services, and this number is growing monthly. Table 1.1 lists the countries by region that currently have, or are developing, services in some form of medical tourism.

The ultimate scope of medical tourism and its impact on hospitality marketing and operations is yet to be determined. But by all indications, the hospitality element will remain, and grow, as an important component of a medical tourist destination's success.

Table 1.1   Destinations Developing in Medical Tourism

Africa	*Azores, Egypt, South Africa, Tunisia*
Australia & South Pacific	Australia, Brunei, Malaysia, New Zealand, Philippines,
Central Asia & Middle East	Cyprus, India, Iran, Israel, Jordan, Saudi Arabia, Syria, Turkey, United Arab Emirates
Central & South America	Argentina, Brazil, Colombia, Costa Rica, El Salvador, Guatemala, Panama, Venezuela
Eastern Asia	China, Hong Kong, Singapore, South Korea, Taiwan, Thailand, Vietnam
Europe	Belgium, Bulgaria, Croatia, Czech Republic, Finland, France, Germany, Great Britain, Greece, Hungary, Italy, Latvia, Malta, Poland, Spain
North America & Caribbean	Antigua, Aruba, Bahamas, Barbados, Cuba, Dominica, Dominican Republic, Grenada, Jamaica, México, United States

Source: Bookman and Bookman 2007; Gahlinger 2008; Woodman 2008.

It would seem like the perfect wedding when two of the world's largest industries find themselves together to support the globalization of health care and the comfortable provision of services to the medical tourist. But as the world of medicine and insurance has become introduced to the world of tourism and hospitality, the first impression is more of an arranged marriage between two strangers struggling to become acquainted after the wedding has occurred. Although each sector is rooted in being of service to its guests/patients, the approach to service and marketing tactics each have developed may seem strangely alien to the other. How familiar each becomes with the manner in which the other operates may well be a determining factor on whether medical tourism in a particular city or region succeeds or fails.

2 Destination Competitiveness
An Overview

There is intense competition in the tourism industry to obtain a greater role in international tourism by establishing various strategies, plans or objectives. The purpose of this chapter is therefore to review the concept of destination competitiveness and the multiple factors which influence it. This chapter first examines previous destination competitiveness research on the basis of its contents, strengths and limitations. The discussion dates back to the studies that came out in the mid-1970s and went through the early 2000s. There was an increase in the number of studies published on the subject of destination competitiveness and its elements in the 1990s. An extensive review of the literature indicated that much has been written about competitiveness between different tourist destinations either at the regional/national or international level.

2.1 DEFINITIONS

The review of the literature clearly indicates that there is not a certain definition of competition upon which is commonly agreed and which has a complete and perfect content (Chon and Mayer 1995). This is because it is almost impossible to integrate the characteristics of a number of countries and firms and distinguish some of them. Furthermore, the competition itself is a concept that includes perspectives in various disciplines, such as a price competition perspective, a strategy and management perspective, a historical and socio-cultural perspective, as well as a comparative advantages perspective (Man, Lau and Chan 2002). The major reason for attempting to develop a model of competitiveness that focuses specifically on the tourism industry is that there appears to be a fundamental difference between the nature of the tourism product and the more traditional goods and services. Unlike as for a certain manufacturing product, the competition among tourism destinations has a different structure. In terms of an integration of all the characteristics of the destination visited (Vanhove 2006), it contains the integration of 41 different sectors consisting of some small and some big branches of business which supply individual products and services (e.g. airline companies, sea lanes, trains, rent-a-car companies, travel agencies, intermediaries, restaurants and convention centers) (Lundberg, Stavenga and Krishnamoorthy 1995).

Competitiveness in the tourism industry has shifted from international and interfirm competitiveness to inter-destination competitiveness owing to the impacts of globalization. However, there are no special factors related to the determinants of destination competitiveness. Tourism competitiveness is a general concept that encompasses price differentials coupled with exchange rate movements, productivity levels of various components of the tourist industry and qualitative factors affecting the attractiveness or otherwise of a destination (Dwyer, Forsyth and Rao 2002). In addition, there are also available studies of other researchers (Ahmed and Krohn 1990; Woodside and Carr 1988). These studies investigate how to maintain competitiveness along with market shares among tourism regions. In this context, destination competitiveness can be defined as "the ability of a destination to proportionally provide the customers (tourists) tourism products with maximum satisfaction, more different, with higher quality, and better than other destinations, and to sustain this outcome."

As in every industry and business, many tourist destinations are in competition with one another to obtain a greater proportion of international tourism by attracting more foreign tourists (Goodall 1988; Heath and Wall 1992). Developments in international tourism and travel have intensified competitiveness among overseas tourist destinations. New destinations have emerged in the market, some existing ones make further progress and others decline as tourists and suppliers are now becoming more concerned about environmental and cultural values (e.g. the Caribbean and the eastern Mediterranean). Tour operators and the media are having an increasing impact on the market. Tourists are more experienced and knowledgeable due to their familiarity with other languages, using a variety of transportation, booking their holidays and having visited the same destination more than once. These pressures appear to be increasing the competition among tourist destinations. For this reason, it is important for destinations to be able to measure their competitiveness in order to identify their strengths and weaknesses and thereby develop their future strategies.

There has been an increase in the number of studies published on the subject of destination competitiveness and its elements in the 1990s. An extensive review of the literature indicated that much has been written about competitiveness among different tourist destinations at either the regional/national or international level. Some of these studies are summarized in Table 2.1. Nevertheless, it is claimed that full competitive destination analysis has not received widespread recognition in the tourism literature (Pearce 1997). One definition for destination competitiveness is given by Chon and Meyer (1995, p. 229), as a revision of the term competitiveness in economics, as below:

Destination competitiveness is the degree to which it can, under free and fair market conditions, produce services that meet the taste of international markets while simultaneously expanding the real income of its employees (citizens).

This statement shows that both quantitative and qualitative indicators are essential in defining the term destination competitiveness. A number of factors may influence a clear analysis of a destination competitiveness study, including the type of holidays taken either as part of inclusive tours or individually, the type of tour operators promoting destinations, differences between seasons or between climatic conditions and so on. Destination competitiveness analysis may be further inhibited by customer expectations, motivation, past experiences, the location and accessibility which could influence the competitiveness of destinations in each market.

A summary of other relevant definitions in the literature is illustrated in Table 2.2. As seen, Hassan (2000) defines competitiveness as "the destination's ability to create and integrate value-added products that sustain its resources while maintaining market position relative to competitors". He also points out that there are four determinants of market competition: comparative advantages, structure of demand, structure of industry and environmental responsibility. Competitiveness has been defined by d'Hauteserre (2000) as "the ability of a destination to maintain its market position and share and/or to improve upon them through time". Mihalic (2000) defines destination competitiveness from an environmental point of view, separating tourism components between natural and artificial as similar to the social and cultural environments. Pearce (1997) describes destination competitiveness as destination evolution techniques and methods that can systematically analyze and compare the diverse attributes of competing destinations within a planning context. Yoon (2002) evaluates this term as an ongoing innovation and change.

On the other hand, Go and Govers (2000) consider tourism competitiveness as an arising strategic value and destination competitiveness like the success in the integrated quality management. In their former study, Go and Govers (1999) measure a destination's competitive position relative to other destinations along seven attributes: facilities, accessibility, quality of service, overall affordability, location image, climate and environment and attractiveness. Peattie and Peattie (1996) think that price-oriented promotion activities play an important role in tourism competitiveness, and therefore they handle competitiveness in this context. Prideaux (2000) explains destination competitiveness with an analysis of bilateral tourist flows among countries and touches on the importance of transportation in tourism. Prideaux analyzes the factors that affect tourist flows under four categories: government responsibilities, private-sector factors, intangible factors and external political and economic factors. Prideaux emphasizes

Table 2.1 Overview of Previous Destination Comparison/Competitiveness Research

Author	Data	Side	Criteria
Goodrich (1977)	Primary	Demand	Tourist perceptions of similarities and differences among nine regions on water sports and sports, historical and cultural interests, scenic beauty, hospitality, rest and relaxation, shopping facilities, cuisine, entertainment and accommodation
Goodrich (1978)	Primary	Demand	Tourist perceptions of nine regions and their intention to choose them. Attributes were same as above.
Haahti and Yavas (1983); Haahti (1986)	Primary	Demand	Tourist perceptions of 12 European countries on value for money, accessibility, sports facilities and other activities, nightlife and entertainment, peace and quietness, hospitality, wilderness, tracking and camping, cultural experience, scenery and change from the usual destinations
Calantone, Benedetto, Halam and Bojanic (1989)	Primary	Demand	Tourist perceptions of several destination attributes (shopping facilities, hospitality, safety, food, culture, tourist attractions, tourist facilities, nightlife and entertainment, scenery, beaches and water sports)
Woodside and Lysonski (1989)	Primary	Demand	Developing a destination set where any destination is chosen among alternatives
Javalgi, Thomas and Rao (1992)	Primary	Demand	Traveller perceptions of European destinations (as 4 major regions) about 27 attributes
Edwards (1993)	Secondary Supply		Analysis of exchange rates and prices
Dieke (1993)	Secondary	Supply-Demand	Number of arrivals, purpose of visits, bed nights, accommodation supply, seasonality, tourism receipts, employment, tourism policies, market and tourist expenditures
Driscoll, Lawson and Niven (1994)	Primary	Demand	Tourist perceptions of 12 destinations on 18 attributes such as facilities, landscape, safety, climate, culture, modern society, different experience, value for money, accessibility, shopping facilities, organized activities, cleanliness, family-oriented, exotic place, outdoor activities, religious values, hospitality and nightlife and entertainment

continued

continued

Study	Type	Supply/Demand	Description
Briguglio and Vella (1995)	Secondary	Supply	Political factors, exchange rates, marketing, development of new products, human resources, hygiene and environmental factors and tourist services
Bray (1996)	Secondary	Supply-Demand	Analysis of prices, exchange rates, market and access
Pearce (1997)	Secondary	Supply-Demand	Market, access, attractions, accommodation supply, prices and development processes
Grabler (1997)	Primary	Demand	Accommodation, entertainment, ambience, cultural resources, level of prices, accessibility of amenities and destinations, location, originality, attitude, shopping facilities and food and beverage quality
Faulkner, Oppermann and Fredline (1999)	Primary	Demand	Analysis of travel agents' perceptions of core tourist attractions
Botho, Crompton and Kim (1999)	Primary	Demand	Tourist motivations and tourist perceptions of entertainment, infrastructure, physical environment and wildlife
Kozak and Rimmington (1999)	Primary	Demand	Tourist satisfaction with several attributes, tourist complaints, holiday-taking behavior with respect to destinations and years and seasons
Yoon (2002)	Primary	Supply	Stakeholders' perceptions of and attitudes toward tourism development and management was tested using a structural equation model of destination competitiveness and its relevant constructs
Enright and Newton (2004)	Primary	Supply-Demand	Performance measurement in lights of various business-based factors and attractors
Lopez, Navarro and Dominguez (2004)	Primary-Secondary	Supply-Demand	An analysis of supply-based performance indicators and presentation of the survey findings involving visitors' perceptions of 23 attributes

Table 2.1 continued   Overview of Previous Destination Comparison/Competitiveness Research

Author	Data	Side	Criteria
Bahar and Kozak (2007)	Primary	Supply-Demand	An analysis of the competitive position of Turkey vis-à-vis five similar countries in the Mediterranean area depending on both tourists' and practitioners' perceptions of 23 attributes
Kozak, Baloglu and Bahar (2010)	Primary	Demand	Through the feedback obtained from the nationally diverse market segments, the respondents compared Turkey on 23 attributes with the destination they selected to understand what attributes of their current trip in Turkey were perceived to be more or less competitive than the selected paired destination

Source: Own elaboration.

Table 2.2 Approaches to Definitions of Destination Competitiveness

Authors	Definitions
Chon and Mayer (1995)	The degree to which it can, under free and fair market conditions, produce services that meet the taste of international markets while expanding the real income of its employees (citizens).
Hassan (2000)	The destination's ability to create and integrate value-added products that sustain its resources while maintaining market position relative to competitors.
d'Hauteserre (2000)	The destination's ability to maintain its market position and share and/or improve upon them through time.
Pearce (1997)	Destination evolution techniques and methods that can systematically analyze and compare the diverse attributes of competing destinations within a planning context.

Source: Own elaboration.

that bilateral tourist flows between two countries should be analyzed under the light of these factors in order to understand tourism competitiveness.

Although it is known that the first studies on tourism competitiveness that cover a significant proportion of the tourism literature have been conducted by several researchers within the last few decades (Haahti and Yavas 1983; Heath and Wall 1992; Kozak and Rimmington 1999; Papatheodorou 2002; Enright and Newton 2004), the most comprehensive study so far is that of Ritchie and Crouch (2003). They applied the competitiveness of the service industry to the context of tourism destinations on the basis of countries, industries, products and companies. To this end, the possibilities of a destination providing a high standard of living for its citizens represent the competitiveness of that destination.

As seen, competitiveness has become the focus of consideration among empirical studies in tourism and hospitality, particularly in the last decade. An extensive review of the literature indicated that much has been written about competitiveness among different tourist destinations at either the regional/national or international level (e.g. Driscoll, Lawson and Niven 1994; Dwyer, Forsyth and Rao 2002; Papatheodorou 2002; Yoon 2002; Hsu, Wolfe and Kang 2004; Enright and Newton 2004). Some studies have attempted to estimate the competitive position of tourist destinations from the perspective of using quantitative measures (i.e. Papatheodorou 2002; Mangion, Durbarry and Sinclair 2005). This group of researchers usually referred to the assessment of secondary data such as prices, number of tourist arrivals and income. The second group of studies has taken the perspective of employing qualitative measures attempting to carry out a "one by one test" procedure for direct comparison (i.e. Driscoll, Lawson and Niven 1994; Yoon 2002; Enright and Newton 2004, 2005). It is also interesting to note the existence of some other studies making use of both quantitative and qualitative measures (Campos-Soria, Garcia and Garcia 2005).

Given brief information about the findings of such studies, for example, in a study by Mangion, Durbarry and Sinclair (2005), findings confirmed that price sensitivity of tourism demand varies from one destination to another; thereby, Malta and Cyprus are considered complementary rather than substitute target destinations for the international tourism market (Hoti, McAleer and Shareef 2007). Through the Duplication of Purchase Law and using primary data, Mansfeld and Romaniuk (2002) suggest that Scotland and Ireland compete more directly for the British market due to the position of their neighborhood locations. The same is also true for other substitute countries such as France and Italy, Hong Kong and Singapore and Mexico and Canada. Contrary to this argument, through the Market Share Analysis and using secondary data, Aguas, Rita and Costa (2004) identified that France, Greece and Spain come out as the winners, whereas Italy and Portugal are the losers in the competitive position of the European Union (EU) member countries in a period of six years between 1996 and 2001. In the context of evaluating business-to-business competitive performance, Campos-Soria, Garcia and Garcia (2005) note that service quality has not only a positive and direct effect on competitiveness but also an indirect effect on it via other variables such as occupancy rates and average direct costs.

2.2 A HOLISTIC OVERVIEW

The investigation of destination competitiveness research considers two mainstream approaches: conceptual and empirical. The former takes on board the proposed relevant factors affecting the competitive position of destinations. Of these, in an attempt to develop a tentative model, Crouch and Ritchie (1999) consider micro and macro (global) environment as the broad factors influencing destination competitiveness. The advantage of this model is its superiority in taking into account the role of destination management and entrepreneurs. However, it is based only on the elements of destination management, marketing and development, excluding external factors such as policies in tourist generating areas and the types of destination marketing channels used.

In general, the competitive performance of organizations is defined from the input and output side (see Figure 2.1). The input measure is based on physical and human capital endowment and research and development expenses. The output side covers profitability, market share, productivity, growth and so on (Jacobson and Andreosso-O'Callaghan 1996). Based on this grouping, the input side of destination competitiveness could be physical sources (tourist facilities, infrastructure and environment), human capital endowment (services) and marketing and promotion expenses. The output side is market share in both the number of arrivals and the amount of tourism receipts, productivity and so on.

As Pearce (1997) implies, a competitive analysis refers to comparative studies as the first step. Therefore, destination competitiveness can be evaluated both quantitatively and qualitatively (Figure 2.2). Quantitative performance of a destination can be measured by looking at figures such as annual numbers of tourist arrivals, amount of annual tourism receipts, level of expenditure per tourist and length of stay. However, there is also a need to take into account the qualitative patterns of destination competitiveness because these ultimately drive quantitative performance (e.g. socio-economic and socio-demographic profiles of tourists, level of tourist satisfaction, dissatisfaction or complaints, comments of tour operators or other intermediaries, quality of staff working in tourism, quality of facilities and services in tourism). Dimensions contributing to qualitative competitiveness include those attributes or items which tourists best liked during their vacation in the destination. The assumption here is that in arriving at a positive or negative view tourists will compare these attributes in terms of their experience in other destinations.

According to one approach (Bordas 1994), it is emphasized that the competitiveness is established between destinations and tourism organizations rather than countries because of the different aspects and features of the destinations in a country. This totally depends on how much a destination is more popular than its country (e.g. Edinburgh, Paris and Bali). Nevertheless, according to this approach, each geographical part of a country can be in competition individually with other similar foreign regions on the basis of facilities, cultural heritage assets and natural history. Given an example from Turkey, Istanbul, as a candidate for culture, business and congress tourism center may be in competition with its European counterparts; central Anatolia, as a center for culture tourism, with mainland Greece region and eastern European countries. In this sense, as a summer vacation

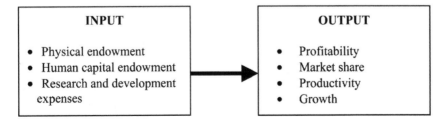

Figure 2.1 Input and output perspectives of organisation performance. Source: Own elaboration.

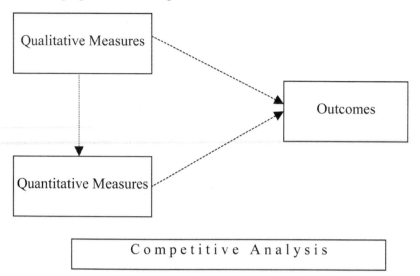

Figure 2.2   Role of qualitative and quantitative measures. Source: Own elaboration.

destination, the whole of Spain is not expected to be in direct competition with Turkey, but its Mediterranean coast may be in direct competition with the Aegean and Mediterranean coasts of Turkey.

2.3   OVERVIEW OF MODELS

The short- and long-term success of places is dependent on their competitiveness and effective positioning based on distinctive competencies. The conceptual frameworks and empirical research on competitiveness also indicate that place or destination competitiveness can be evaluated from two perspectives: (1) image and perception measures (subjective measures), and (2) economic, social and environmental indicators (objective measures). The former focuses on image development for specific destination attributes, branding efforts involving functional, affective and symbolic benefits and value propositions, customer-based brand equity measures and positioning strategies (Baloglu and McCleary 1999; Baloglu and Love 2005; Boo, Busser and Baloglu 2009). The objective measures are based on a number of indices and indicators related to economic and social development of a country or place, such as infrastructure, safety, purchasing power, human resources, environment quality and technology (Gursoy, Baloglu and Che 2009). For a more reliable and valid assessment, both subjective and objective approaches would be combined to assess the competitiveness of a place (Kozak, Baloglu and Bahar 2010).

As shown in Table 2.1, little has been done to perfectly examine the comparative performance of different international tourist destinations (Haahti and Yavas 1983; Haahti 1986; Pearce 1997). Both primary and secondary types of data-collection methods have been employed to carry out destination comparison/competitiveness research. Secondary data-collection methods primarily focus on the analysis of figures, whereas primary data-collection methods focus solely on investigating consumer attitudes toward or their perceptions of the attractiveness of several individual destinations. Of primary research, the researchers attempted to compare one destination's performance with other similar and competing destinations and to examine each destination's strengths and weaknesses on the basis of several generic variables (Goodrich 1977, 1978; Haahti and Yavas 1983; Haahti 1986; Pearce 1997). With limited exceptions (e.g. King 1994; Kozak and Rimmington 1999; Kozak, Baloglu and Bahar 2010), much of the research conducted using primary methods was undertaken without evidence that respondents had actually been to all sample destinations in person (indirect measure of destination performance), and research to date does not therefore provide a full account of destination performance and competitiveness.

Goodrich (1977, 1978)

This study was designed to compare tourists' perceptions of similarities and differences among nine tourist destinations on different generic dimensions, using multidimensional scaling, and the respondents' intention to choose among these destinations. The attributes included were water sports and sports, historical and cultural interests, scenic beauty, hospitality, rest and relaxation, shopping facilities, cuisine, entertainment and accommodation. Respondents were selected among those who had past visits to the sample destinations and requested to rate pairs of regions on a seven-point scale ranging from 'very similar' to 'somewhat different'. The study demonstrated that some destinations were perceived to be similar and some others different, and the same questionnaire could be used to assess perceptions of different destinations. This sort of assessment might be potentially relevant because destinations competing in the same market can understand their similarities and differences and design their marketing management strategies and policies. Despite this, the study concluded that the perception itself was not the only predictor of choosing a particular destination. From this result, it is evident that perception may not be the only predictor of measuring destination competitiveness, which means that its context needs to be extended.

Haahti (1986)

The objective of this study was to assess Finland's competitive position as a tourist destination compared with other countries by pointing out its strengths and weaknesses with respect to 10 major destination attributes. These are value for money, accessibility, sports facilities and other activities, nightlife and entertainment, peace and quietness, hospitality, wilderness, tracking and camping, cultural experience, scenery and change from the usual destinations. The study suggests areas where Finland was stronger and weaker. The research findings indicate that the strength of each attribute differs from one country to another. Sampling bias might have appeared because tourists had not completed their experiences with Finland (there were still on vacation) and that it is not clear whether they had any experience with or any information about the competing destinations.

Edwards (1993)

This research report was designed to examine the competitiveness of both short- and long-haul destinations on the basis of the comparison by the level of brochure prices for Inclusive Tours (IT), accommodation grades and the level of distance between the UK market and the holiday destination. Whereas some destinations are reasonable as a short stay with cheaper prices for the British market (e.g. Amsterdam, Bruges and Paris), others are expensive for holidays with shorter stays (e.g. Moscow, Budapest, Prague and Venice). The overall prices of long-haul holiday destinations are more than double that for short-haul destinations. With respect to the relationship between competitiveness and hotel grades, Caribbean and Mauritus are less competitive when grades rise. On the contrary, the South-east Asian destinations, together with Goa, Kenya and Sri Lanka, are more competitive as hotel grades increase. Despite the fact that the product, the length of trip and the place are the same, the level of tour prices differs from one tour operator to another, from mass tours to prestige tours and from one season to another. Some detailed information on the competitive position of countries worldwide is provided in Table 2.3.

Driscoll, Lawson and Niven (1994)

This is an example of measuring destination competitiveness from the perspective of the investigation of tourist perceptions. The respondents were requested to compare how better or worse they perceived the performance of 12 destinations on 18 attributes. These include facilities, landscape, safety, climate, culture, modern society, different experience, value for money, accessibility, shopping facilities, organized activities, cleanliness, family-oriented, exotic place, outdoor activities, religious values, hospitality and nightlife and entertainment. The weakness of this study is that it is not clear whether the respondents had personally been to the destinations under investigation.

Table 2.3 Price Competitiveness of International Tourist Destinations

COUNTRIES	CHARACTERISTICS
Inclusive Tours	
France	More expensive for independent beach holidays (especially for longer stays).
Greece	Cheaper for IT beach holidays and for independent travellers. The advantage rises as the holiday duration increases.
Italy	Expensive for IT beach holidays and very expensive for independent travellers.
Portugal	More expensive for IT beach holidays and less expensive than average for independent travellers.
Spain	Close destination to average prices for both IT and independent travellers.
Turkey	Cheaper for IT beach holidays and offers best value for longer stays.
City Breaks	
Austria	Rather expensive.
Belgium	Rather below average.
Czech Republic	Cheaper for IT particularly for longer stays.
Denmark	More expensive for both IT and independent holidays.
Egypt	Below average but can sustain its competitive position.
Germany	More expensive for IT with longer stays.
Greece	Cheaper for longer stays.
Hungary	Slightly below average.
Italy	Generally more expensive for both IT and independent travellers.
The Netherlands	Cheaper for both IT and independent travellers.
Portugal	Cheaper for both IT and independent travellers.
Russia	More expensive for IT.
Spain	Above average for independent travellers.
Turkey	Much cheaper for IT.
Long-haul Beach Destinations	
Antigua	More expensive.
Bahamas	Rather expensive.
Bali	More expensive for IT travellers.
Barbados	More expensive.
Florida	Fairly cheaper.
Goa, India	The cheapest for IT travellers.
Jamaica	More expensive.

continued

Table 2.3 continued

COUNTRIES	CHARACTERISTICS
Long-haul Beach Destinations *(continued)*	
Kenya	Much cheaper for IT travellers.
Mauritus	More expensive.
Thailand	Slightly below average.
Long-haul Touring Holidays (History and Culture)	
Australia	More expensive for independent travellers.
Canada	Average for independent travellers.
China	Quite expensive for IT travellers.
Egypt	Fairly cheaper for IT travellers.
India	Average for IT and cheaper for independent travellers.
Kenya	Cheaper for independent travellers.
Mexico	Fairly expensive for independent travellers.
South Africa	Below average for independent travellers.
Thailand	Slightly below average for both It and independent travellers.
U.S.	Close to average for independent travellers.

Source: Edwards (1993).

Chon and Meyer (1995)

Adapting Ritchie and Crouch's (1993) model of competitiveness, Chon and Meyer (1995), in their conceptual study, attempted to assess the competitive position of Las Vegas from the point of various dimensions such as appealing, management, organization, information and efficiency. However, as a limitation, the study lacks some other vital parameters of competitiveness, namely outputs, which are supposed to indicate the position of a destination on the table of leagues.

Pearce (1997)

This study was designed to compare a destination's attributes with eight other similar and competing destinations. He examined destination elements such as markets, air access, attractions, accommodation, prices and development processes and each destination's strengths and weaknesses. The findings demonstrated that Pearce's destination-based competitive analysis model could measure a destination's resources and policies and judge the potential performance of competitors.

Dwyer, Forsyth and Rao (2000)

In a more recent study, Dwyer et al. (2000), the authors carried out an econometric analysis to construct price competitiveness indices for key sectors of tourism for 13 countries of the origin and for 19 destination countries. Australia is taken as base, and its index is 100. The index score of less than 100 indicates that the destination under investigation is more price competitive than Australia. In a similar way, a figure of more than 100 shows that the destination is less price competitive than Australia. To this end, for instance, countries such as China, Thailand and Turkey are more price competitive than Australia for the Japanese tourist market, whereas other countries such as France, UK and Canada are less price competitive (more expensive) for the same market. In a further analysis, the authors calculated a price competitiveness index for each destination taking place in the competitor set using each of the selected major categories of goods and services. It is important to note that one destination country can be relatively cheaper than another country for a particular product because it is much more expensive for another category of tourism product/service. Given this, for example, Turkey is much cheaper (index=0.550) than Spain (index=0.950) for food because it is (index=0.780) much more expensive than Spain (index=0.370) for drinks. In addition, European countries, except for Spain and Turkey, seem to be the most expensive destinations in the competitor set. Asian countries are the most price-competitive destinations (cheaper than many destination countries) (e.g. Indonesia, China and Thailand).

Kim (2000)

This model of tourism competitiveness, too, was developed to explain competition and competitiveness in the tourism industry. In this model, Kim draws attention to four dimensions of competitiveness in tourism: primary, secondary, tertiary,and quaternary sources of competition. Kim states that the effect of every factor on competitiveness is different. In a study carried out in Korea, Kim points out that the effect of the quaternary sources on the competitiveness of the destination is far greater than that of the other factors.

Dwyer and Kim (2001)

The integrated model of destination competitiveness was developed by Dwyer and Kim (2001) in order to make comparisons between countries and between industries within the tourism industry. The model aims to determine what factors particularly affect competitiveness. The integrated model enlightens both the strong and weak points of various tourism destinations as well. Dwyer and Kim explain destination competitiveness by means of five factors: inherited and created resources, destination management, demand conditions, regional conditions and destination competitiveness. Handling the structure and indicators of destination competitiveness comprehensively, this model enables one to make comparisons between countries and between industries in the context of tourism development.

Ritchie and Crouch (2003)

As emphasized earlier, the most detailed work on tourism competitiveness so far is that of Ritchie and Crouch (2003), who attempted to explain destination competitiveness by developing a conceptual model. According to them, the most competitive destination is that which most effectively creates sustainable well-being for its residents. Policies implemented to achieve competitiveness should be founded on a sustainable basis. Competitiveness cannot set apart from the sustainability principle. If this principle is ignored, the fulfilled competitiveness will reflect an illusory situation. Crouch and Ritchie examine the factors affecting destination competitiveness under four categories: qualifying determinants, destination management, core resources and attractors and supporting factors and resources. Destinations using their resources in an effective and productive manner in the long term are those that are the most advantageous in obtaining competitiveness.

Bahar and Kozak (2007)

Taking the weaknesses of past research into consideration, the primary purpose of this study is to develop a practical method for measuring the direct competitive position of one country compared to other similar countries in the same set of competitiveness. The study presents the discussion of findings of a completed research project on the competitive position of Turkey vis-à-vis five similar countries in the Mediterranean area. The countries, self-selected by the foreign tourists visiting Turkey and the people engaged in the Turkish tourism industry such as hoteliers, travel agents or tour guides, and nominated as the direct competitor to Turkey, include Spain, Italy, Greece, France and Cyprus. Findings obtained from the two groups were then compared to each other. Results indicate that both foreign tourists and tourism practitioners agreed that Turkey is stronger on the friendliness of local people but is weaker on the physical distance to the target markets and the effective use of methods for promotion and advertising. The study suggests that the use of questionnaires eligible for direct comparison may have valuable implications for the competitive measurement of destination performance.

Kozak, Baloglu and Bahar (2010)

As in the study of Bahar and Kozak (2007), this study also develops a practical method for measuring the direct competitive position of one country compared to other similar countries in the same competitiveness set. In this respect, the competitive position of Turkey was studied relative to two other countries in the Mediterranean area. These countries were self-selected by respondents. This study has three parts: The first part aimed to identify 11 other Mediterranean destinations the respondents had visited at least once in their lives. The second part was designed to allow the respondents to choose from those destinations to compare with their current holiday. In the third part, the respondents compared Turkey on 23 attributes with the destination they selected to understand what attributes of their current trip in Turkey were perceived to be more or less competitive than the selected paired destination (positive or negative aspects of tourism). Through the feedback obtained from the nationally diverse market segments, findings of this study would be helpful for tourism authorities to evaluate their comparative performance with their major rivals.

2.4. Framework of Destination Competitiveness

Analyzing what factors affect competitiveness in the tourism industry requires the assessment of models postulated for competitiveness measurement. The models in question enable the determinants of competition and competitiveness to be examined differently from other industries. Therefore, it may be useful to give brief information about each model in order to better understand and evaluate the issue. Known as "dynamic diamond", Porter's model, which redefines the boundaries of strategic management (Melià n-González and Garaa-Falcon 2003), consists of an integration of four main internal variables and two external variables that enable the competitiveness of a firm to develop (Furman, Porter and Stern 2002). These are factor conditions, demand conditions, related and supporting industries, firm strategy, structure, rivalry and the roles of chance and government. According to Porter, dynamic diamond has a mutually reinforcing system. The effect of one determinant is contingent on the state of others. Therefore, it is impossible for a single determinant itself to sufficiently affect competitiveness (Porter 1990). There is a need for mutual interaction of all the factors together in order to improve competitiveness in the tourism industry. A drawback or problem in any factor is an obstacle to create a successful conclusion in competitiveness.

Following this brief explanation of the models of competitiveness in tourism, Table 2.4 summarizes the coverage, superiorities and drawbacks of the models. Putting all models together as a whole in a single table enables one to better understand the issue and enlighten the positive and negative aspects of the models. The similar point of the models of

Table 2.4   Models of Competitiveness in Tourism Industry

Authors	Coverage	Superiorities	Drawbacks
Porter(1990–1998)	1) Factor conditions 2) Demand conditions 3) Related and supporting industries 4) Firm strategy, structure and rivalry 5). Role of chance and government	1) Examines competitiveness in micro and macro perspectives, and handles the issue in terms of firm/industry and country 2) Provides a structure that is theoretically valid for all of the firms, industries and sectors in the economy, and examines the issue as a whole by integrating the economies and competitiveness strategies of other countries 3) As a dynamic model, it explains what factors affect the competitiveness among the national tourism industry	1) More applicable to the more advanced developed nations of the world, lacking applicability in smaller or developing economies. Therefore, it needs revising 2) Not taking into account some fundamental factors that affect competitiveness, such as exchange rates, labor cost, technology, foreign capital investments and globalization 3) Not much attention to human resources, which have a crucial role in tourism industry, in the process of developing competitiveness.
Ritchie and Crouch (2000) Crouch and Ritchie (1999)	1) Core resources and attractors 2) Supporting factors and resources 3) Destination management 4) Qualifying determinants	1) The most comprehensive model of destination competitiveness that has been developed so far. 2) Applies the competitiveness of services to tourism destinations on the basis of country, industry, firm and product.	1) Does not comprehensively examine many factors that affect competitiveness. Therefore, an integrated model of competitiveness has been developed to fill this gap. 2) Its empirical test is limited.

continued

Dwyer and Kim (2001)	1) Inherited and created resources 2) Destination management 3) Demand conditions 4) Regional conditions 5) Destination competitiveness	1) Allows one to make comparisons between countries and industries within tourism, and highlights the factors that affect competitiveness. 2) Provides alternative policies and strategies of competitiveness for the government and private authorities by determining the strong and weak sides of various tourism destinations.	1) The absence of an empirical test estimating the destination competitiveness. 2) Many factors that are included in the model have a qualitative feature.
Kim (2000)	1) Primary sources 2) Secondary sources 3) Tertiary sources 4) Quaternary sources	1) Destination competitiveness is determined by 17 factors included in the main four groups of determinants.	1) No scientific reason to divide the factors effecting competitiveness into primary, secondary, tertiary and quaternary sources. 2) Falls short of explaining the interaction among different factors and sources of destination competitiveness.

Source: Bahar and Kozak (2008).

Porter–Ritchie–Crouch and Dwyer–Kim is the absence of an empirical test in the determination of destination competitiveness. Kim's model differs from that of the others with its application into the practice.

2.4. SUMMARY

This chapter has examined past research on destination competitiveness and comparison on the basis of their contents, strengths and limitations. The discussion dates back to the studies that came out in the mid-1970s. There was an increase in the number of studies published on the subject of destination competitiveness and its elements in the 1990s. An extensive review of the literature indicated that much has been written about competitiveness among different tourist destinations at either the regional/national or international level. Nevertheless, it is claimed that a full competitive destination analysis has not received widespread recognition in the tourism literature. As a result, the succeeding chapter aims to provide a tentative framework, in which each factor affecting competitiveness of tourist destinations in some respects is examined.

* * *

CASE STUDY: TRAVEL AND TOURISM COMPETITIVENESS INDEX

Tourism competitiveness is multidimensional. A variety of interrelated factors such as health and hygiene, tourism-related infrastructure, political and economic stability, safety and security and prices determine a place competitiveness in the regional and global marketplace. The place competitiveness is critical given the fact that the World Economic Forum (2009) developed a Travel and Tourism Competitiveness Index (TTCI) and rated 133 countries. The TTCI aims to measure the factors and policies that make it attractive to develop the Travel & Tourism (T&T) sector in different countries. The TTCI spans the government, business environment and resources (cultural, natural, human, etc.). It is based on three broad categories of variables that facilitate or drive T&T competitiveness: (1) the T&T regulatory framework subindex, (2) the T&T business environment and infrastructure subindex, and (3) the T&T human, cultural and natural resources subindex. Each of the subindices consists of a number of individual measures of T&T competitiveness, with a total of 14 variables, as show in the following.

Subindex A: T&T Regulatory Framework

1. Policy rules and regulations (the extent to which the policy environment is conducive to developing the T&T sector in each country)

2. Environmental sustainability (the stringency of the government's environmental regulations in each country and the extent to which they are actually enforced, as well as other elements such as carbon dioxide emissions and the percentage of endangered species in the country)
3. Safety and security (the costliness of common crime and violence as well as terrorism, and the extent to which police services can be relied upon to provide protection from crime as well as the incidence of road traffic accidents in the country)
4. Health and hygiene (drinking water and sanitation as well as the availability of physicians and hospital beds)
5. Prioritization of T & T (the extent to which the government prioritizes the T&T sector, such as ensuring the country's attendance at international T&T fairs and commissioning high-quality "destination-marketing" campaigns)

Subindex B: T&T Business Environment and Infrastructure

6. Air transport infrastructure (both the quantity of air transport, as measured by the available seat kilometers, the number of departures, airport density and the number of operating airlines, as well as the quality of the air transport infrastructure for both domestic and international flights)
7. Ground transport infrastructure (the extensiveness and quality of the country's ground transport infrastructure, such as the quality of roads, railroads and ports, as well as the extent to which the national transport network as a whole offers efficient, accessible transportation to key business centers and tourist attractions within the country)
8. Tourism infrastructure (the accommodation infrastructure—the number of hotel rooms) and the presence of major car rental companies in the country, as well as a measure of the financial infrastructure for tourists in the country (the availability of ATMs).
9. ICT infrastructure (ICT penetration rates—Internet, telephone lines and broadband), which provides a sense of the society's online activity as well the Internet use by businesses in carrying out transactions in the economy
10. Price competitiveness in the T&T industry (the extent to which goods and services in the country are more or less expensive than elsewhere—purchasing power parity), airfare ticket taxes and airport charges (which can make flight tickets much more expensive), fuel price levels compared with those of other countries and taxation in the country (which can be passed through to travelers) as well as the relative cost of hotel accommodations

Subindex C: T&T Human, Cultural, and Natural Resources

11. Human resources (the education, training and availability of qualified labor)
12. Affinity for T & T (the extent to which the country and society are open to tourism and foreign visitors, i.e. the national population's attitude toward foreign travellers, the extent to which business leaders are willing to recommend leisure travel in their countries to important business contacts and tourism openness [tourism expenditures and receipts as a percentage of GDP])
13. Natural resources (the number of UNESCO natural World Heritage sites, the quality of the natural environment, the richness of the fauna in the country as measured by the total known species of animals and the percentage of nationally protected areas)
14. Cultural resources (the number of UNESCO cultural World Heritage sites, sports stadium seat capacity, the number of international fairs and exhibitions in the country and creative industries exports from the country)

The analyses can be conducted and presented on individual country and regional levels (i.e Europe, Asia and so on) or worldwide. These types of indexes are beneficial to places to assess strengths and weaknesses to determine their relative position and competitive advantage(s). Table 2.5 shows top-performing economies ranked based on their performances across index dimensions. Singapore, Hong Kong and Ireland are top ranked for policy rules and regulations, whereas Sweden, Switzerland and Denmark ranked as the top three in environmental sustainability. In contrast, Middle Eastern and Asian countries dominate the top of the price competitiveness pillar, with Egypt, Brunei and Indonesia ranked as the top three.

Table 2.5 Three Top-Performing Economies per Index Dimension

Country/Economy	Policy rules and regulations	Environmental sustainability	Safety and security	Health and hygiene	Prioritization of Travel & Tourism	Air transport Infrastructure	Ground transport infrastructure	Tourism infrastructure	ICT infrastructure	Price competitiveness	Human resources	Affinity for Travel & Tourism	Natural resources	Cultural resources
Australia	27	40	25	41	37	3	47	9	20	117	10	52	4	19
Austria	28	9	6	5	14	26	10	1	23	118	18	23	40	11
Barbados	24	29	26	40	19	33	12	42	26	83	32	2	121	59
Brazil	94	33	130	80	84	46	110	45	60	91	55	108	2	14
Brunei Darussalam	88	131	19	105	99	32	35	86	55	2	52	100	31	86
Canada	5	46	29	51	17	1	24	20	13	106	6	67	17	18
Denmark	4	3	4	28	91	12	6	23	4	131	2	72	77	26
Egypt	55	103	67	64	9	58	79	74	84	1	83	20	109	60
Finland	6	7	1	12	54	14	21	38	14	121	5	88	61	22
France	25	4	55	9	21	5	3	14	19	132	23	55	39	7
Greece	57	47	47	19	3	19	43	5	40	114	44	35	74	23
Hong Kong SAR	2	80	5	1	8	13	2	68	9	45	15	11	62	34

continued

Table 2.5 continued   Three Top-Performing Economies per Index Dimension

Country/Economy	Policy rules and regulations	Environmental sustainability	Safety and security	Health and hygiene	Prioritization of Travel & Tourism	Air transport Infrastructure	Ground transport infrastructure	Tourism infrastructure	ICT infrastructure	Price competitiveness	Human resources	Affinity for Travel & Tourism	Natural resources	Cultural resources
Iceland	21	13	2	4	20	18	34	13	2	128	3	17	73	50
Indonesia	123	130	119	110	10	60	89	88	102	3	42	78	28	37
Ireland	3	12	18	25	27	23	48	4	28	111	9	36	116	25
Italy	71	51	82	27	51	27	40	3	25	130	41	71	90	5
Lithuania	59	21	33	2	95	80	22	62	35	78	66	74	108	62
Malta	54	66	11	3	16	22	27	22	33	122	37	7	133	35
Mauritius	13	53	40	60	1	49	31	53	59	26	45	3	130	99
Montenegro	35	98	48	52	69	56	88	64	39	95	40	1	80	51
Norway	23	19	3	24	38	8	37	19	6	129	14	82	72	28

Singa-pore	1	42	10	53	2	15	4	37	17	27	1	10	94	29
Spain	74	31	66	35	4	10	20	1	31	96	31	48	30	1
Sweden	7	1	13	38	73	9	14	26	1	127	8	62	50	2
Switzer-land	18	2	8	13	7	17	1	7	3	123	4	34	15	6
Tanzania	89	32	98	127	33	113	116	118	120	43	122	33	3	108
United King-dom	14	10	78	46	31	6	17	12	7	133	12	99	26	3
United States	16	106	122	47	44	18	10	15	107	7	106	9	1	9

Source: World Economic Forum (2009).

3 Determinants of Destination Competitiveness

As a result of weaknesses in earlier attempts to investigate and conceptualize the elements of destination competitiveness, this chapter aims to provide a tentative framework in which each factor (adapted from Porter's [1985] competitiveness framework) affecting competitiveness of tourist destinations in some respect is examined. Using Porter's (1985) terms, five major factors affecting the competitiveness level of international tourist destinations are then identified. These include the supply (or controllable) side, demand (or uncontrollable) side, tour operator operations, emergence of new destinations and emergence of substitute products and services. Each is explained in greater detail later in this chapter.

3.1 FACTORS AFFECTING DESTINATION COMPETITIVENESS

Figure 3.1 shows major concepts of the term destination competitiveness. These include the supply side (or controllable), demand side (or uncontrollable), tour operator operations and external factors. The availability of supply-based factors distinguishes one destination from another and is regarded as important in maintaining competitive advantage. However, the demand side and tour operator operations, if the holiday is sold via tour operators, have been underestimated. The types of pull-and-push motivations driving tourists toward a particular destination will be of help to shape the type of attractiveness the destination has and its position on the set. In other words, a destination may have all the supply-based elements, but tourists may only want sunbathing, entertainment or a cheap holiday in the summer time or else. For some reason, the tour operator will not agree to sell the destination or the government may want to limit tourism development.

The tourism system includes accommodation facilities, tourist attraction sites, restaurants, entertainment, transportation and local inhabitants on the supply side and customers (visitors and travel agencies) on the demand

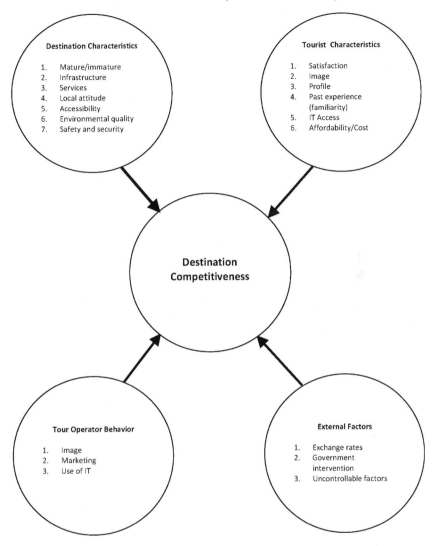

Figure 3.1 Concepts of destination competitiveness. Source: Own elaboration.

side. In a broader context of tourism economics, the tourism system is built up of its three elements: origin, destination and linkage (Laws 1991). Origin refers to the place where potential tourism demand exists. As the central element of the tourism system, the destination is the place where tourism demand is attracted to take a vacation. The linkage provides methods for bringing tourism to the destination and includes transport systems, distribution and communication channels.

All tourism demand is similarly constrained by money, political controls, time and fashion. Bull (1995) presents the factors affecting international tourism demand in three categories: (1) factors in the tourist generating area, (2) factors in the destination area and (3) link variables. Level of personal disposable income, holiday entitlements, value of currency, tax policy and controls on tourism spending are the main factors for the potential demand in tourist-generating countries. Next, general price level, degree of supply competition, quality of tourism products and economic regulation of travelers are listed as the internal factors in the destination countries. Finally, comparative prices between countries of origin and destinations, promotional effort by the destination countries in their tourist-generating counterparts, exchange rates and time and cost of travel are mentioned as the common link variables for both categories. The determinants of destination competitiveness evolve around these three elements between supply and demand.

In line with this background and using Porter's (1980, 1985) approach, in a broader context of destination competitiveness analysis, an equation model could be developed as below:

$$C = f (D + T + N + O + S)$$

Here:

C refers to the concept of destination competitiveness

D refers to the bargaining power of customers (the analysis of demand side)

T refers to the bargaining power of suppliers (the role of tour operators or travel agents)

N refers to the threat of the entrance of new destinations

O refers to the threat of substitute products and services

S refers to the competitiveness among existing destinations (the availability of supply-side abilities and impact of external factors)

Bargaining Power of Customers (Analysis of Demand Side)

Customers are becoming more sophisticated and looking for higher standards in quality, innovation and responsiveness as a consequence of developments in technology, increase in mobility and increase in the spread of word-of-mouth communication. Recent developments in technology and hearing about others' experiences give people access to all the information they need to learn about other places in the world and traveling. Increasing the mobility of potential tourists, technology has also provided easy access to the same or other destinations either in the short or in the long term. Each holiday taken may update a tourist's expectations for the next holiday

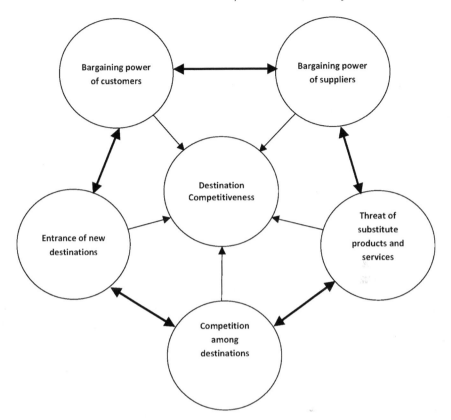

Figure 3.2 Elements of destination competitiveness. Source: Own elaboration.

and widen their experiences, resulting in a tourist group with higher expectations, needs and wants.

The socio-economic and socio-demographic profiles of tourism demand in potential markets are a determinant for affecting the choice of holiday and its direction toward particular destinations. The level of age, income, occupation, time, whom to travel with and personality play a significant role in determining the destination choice process (Um and Crompton 1990; Song, Wong and Chon 2003; Muñoz 2006). Potential tourists will be likely to choose destinations where any or all of these variables are well matched with what the destination offers. Taking income as a specific example, it was found to be a major factor on the amount of money spent on travel (Davies and Mangan 1992; Kozak, Gokovali and Bahar 2009), choices of destinations (Pyo, Uysal and McLellan 1991) and length of stay (Gokovali, Bahar and Kozak 2007).

Tourists are expected to mentally categorize destinations. One proposed categorization is grouped into 'consideration' (evoked), 'inert' and 'inept' sets (Woodside and Lysonski 1989). The 'consideration' set includes all destinations that a potential tourist is aware of and may be likely to visit. The 'inert' set represents all destinations that the potential tourist is aware of but has no intention of visiting in the short term. The 'inept' set refers to destination(s) that the potential tourist is aware of but has no intention to visit in a specific time period. The 'unawareness' set refers to destinations that the potential tourist is not aware of. According to Um and Crompton (1990), potential tourists are expected to select a destination from a set of alternatives in the 'consideration' set. Destinations effectively compete with each other for a place in the consideration set of their target customers. Research findings confirmed that familiarity, as one factor influencing the choice of destination in the consideration set, has a positive impact on the likelihood of revisiting a destination (Mazursky 1989; Milman and Pizam 1995; Court and Lupton 1997; Kozak 2001b).

Therefore, it is evident that familiarity could influence the bargaining power of both potential tourists and destinations. If tourists believe that the selected destination has matched their requirements, then they would come back or talk to others about their positive experiences (Kozak and Rimmington 2000; Kozak 2001b; Chi and Qu 2008). In contrast, leaving the destination with a feeling that it is not a good place for a holiday might increase the bargaining power of potential tourists due to the power of word-of-mouth recommendation while reducing the bargaining power of destinations for these tourist groups. As a result, in such a competitive environment, destination management authorities are expected to better know how both their positive and negative aspects affect tourist behavior (Alegre and Garau 2010).

The bargaining power of customers can be further examined from the point of their personality type as suggested by Plog (1974) to understand why destinations fall or rise in popularity. According to this approach, destinations move from 'allocentrics' to 'psychocentrics' because the latter attracts those who discover a new enjoyable place for a holiday. But as long as there is word-of-mouth communication and others are informed, the destination begins to attract fewer 'allocentrics' and moves toward 'psychocentric' travelers on the psychographic scale. The degree of movement largely depends upon the extent to which a destination becomes popular and how it is promoted and managed.

When it becomes increasingly popular by attracting any type of tourist groups and management has no control on over-development, it means that natural and cultural resources may deteriorate. Because the destination is likely to become an 'ordinary' place, 'allocentrics' will be replaced by 'psychocentrics'. This makes destinations lose their bargaining power because the psychocentric customers are likely to have increasing bargaining power. As a consequence, the destination faces several management and marketing problems because 'psychocentrics' are believed not to travel as often as 'allocentrics' do and stay for shorter time and spend less. Moreover, the destination might become more commercialized by losing the features which attract tourists and its competitiveness in the market.

Finally, as widely proposed and empirically tested, the level of tourist satisfaction is regarded as the most significant part of maintaining and sustaining competitive advantage because of the possibility that tourists become competitors of destinations. This means that any dissatisfaction with any vacation experience might distract tourists from a particular vacation destination. Or tourist arrivals might be slow when a considerable level of increase in place levels appears. Or tourists might seek free products or services in return for their commitment. All of these examples demonstrate why it is necessary to consider tourists as a source of destination competition due to the power of their negotiation.

Bargaining Power of Suppliers (Tour Operators)

It is clear that competitiveness between individual tourism organizations remains weak when mass tourism is the subject of discussion because the marketing and promotion of destinations are made by third parties such as tour operators, travel agencies and destination marketing organizations. In other words, the third parties sell destinations rather than individual accommodation establishments or food and beverage facilities. The following statement refers to the importance of overall marketing and promotion studies of destinations rather than individual establishments in maintaining competitiveness in international tourism (Murphy 1997, p. 3):

> Many tourism businesses believe they need to sell their destination before they can sell their individual offerings. This can be achieved by increasing the competitive advantage of the whole product mix, so that individual businesses benefit from the increased profile and trade.

This means that any individual accommodation establishment has to wait until its resort/destination is promoted by a travel agent abroad. As long as the number of tourists increases, it will also contribute to such individual establishments' profits by raising their occupancy rates and revenue margins due to the rules of multiplier effect in the theory of economics.

Where package tours are concerned, the extent to which a destination attracts the interest of tour operators and is included in their brochures might increase effectiveness in reaching the market. Tour operators feel themselves to be ahead of tourist destinations as they, as international suppliers and/or retailers, have to search for better products, applications or destinations for meeting customer requirements and following changes in their wants and needs. The image of the product (destination) is primarily influenced by tour operators' promotional activities in the tourist-generating country. Depending on the volume of income or the appearance of any problem, tour operators are likely to switch their customers to alternative destinations (Ashworth and Goodall 1988; Carey, Gountas and Gilbert 1997).

Tour operators consider themselves to be responsible for monitoring the situation in a destination; they offer holidays to alternative destinations if any threat is posed to their customers (Cavlek 2002). If a destination is considered unsuccessful, tour operators are likely to exclude such destinations from their portfolios for the following season (Goodall and Bergsa 1990; Grosspietsch 2006). In this regard, it can be claimed that any competition between tour operators plays a critical role in increasing the competition among international tourist destinations (Buck 1988). Financial supports or guidelines given by tour operators to increase the quality of tourism products in some destinations are also significant in influencing the balance of competition between destinations.

Given Butler's (1980) life cycle model, destinations in the 'consolidation' and 'stagnation' stages are more dependent on inclusive tours promoted by tour operators. As a result, the rate of increase of tourists slows, whereas total numbers are still increasing and the demand profile of the destination is dominated by repeat visits (Laws and Cooper 1998). The economic benefit gained from tourists using inclusive tour holidays is lower than that of others because the destinations dealing with inclusive tours are largely dependent on marketing channels via intermediaries, tour operators or travel agents who keep a high proportion of tour fees in their own accounts (Poon 1998). As a result, the destination would be at a disadvantage if intermediaries have more bargaining power than the destination itself. In short, marketing via tour operators presents benefits as well as threats for the competitive position of any destination in the international arena.

However, distribution channels in tourism and travel are undergoing a dramatic change as Information Technology (IT) is becoming increasingly vital for the efficient and effective management of operations and managing the distribution of products and services in the tourism and travel industry. Whereas large or international organizations have welcomed new developments in IT, seeing them as opportunities to be more competitive in the market, small and medium-sized organizations are forced to adapt themselves to the new business environment. Despite the benefits of IT, small tourism organizations may not be able to afford it. Thus, large organizations will be able to preserve their leadership by dominating IT marketing activities.

It is believed that the future competitiveness of tourist destinations will largely depend on the range of new telecommunication technologies being used and the extent to which destinations have access to the management, marketing and promotion opportunity via such technologies (Buhalis and Cooper 1998). Inequality in gaining access to IT may possibly create first- and second-class tourist destinations, organizations and customer groups (Rimmington and Kozak 1997). Such imbalance between developed and developing countries or tourist destinations could be the direct consequence of IT for international tourism and travel marketing. Tourist destinations and organizations with undeveloped telecommunication structures could be less suitable for IT marketing as being slower, weaker and more expensive. Such developments could strengthen the bargaining power of destinations which have access to IT, whereas the bargaining power of those which do not or which have limited access could be weakened.

Threat of Emergence of New Destinations

As Porter (1980) highlights, competitiveness becomes much fiercer when new competitors enter the market. A number of examples could be given from the tourism industry. Eastern Mediterranean or North African destinations now compete directly with western Mediterranean destinations in the European market. Despite the fact that there are thousands of destinations around the world, tourist destinations are subject to immense competition as potential tourists' ability to choose any of those from the set is limited (Woodside and Sherrell 1977). When tourists select a destination for their holiday at a given time, competing destinations will lose their opportunity because it is practically impossible for anyone to fulfill a desire to visit places all over the world. This refers to the importance of potential tourists' awareness and familiarity with the destination and the marketing potential of the destination management for taking a place in the consideration set.

Destinations in the 'inept' set therefore need action to bring them into the 'consideration' set. Although there is no evidence that all destinations in the consideration set will be selected by tourists choosing a vacation, it is important that those destinations in the consideration set are more likely than those in other sets to be considered by customers and take a higher place in the competitiveness set. If the destination is in the consideration set, it means that it is successful in conveying messages to reach potential customers. Otherwise, it fails to increase its attractiveness. For instance, Sandbach (1997) says that some newly emerging long-haul and exotic destinations compete with European destinations for European tourists. The reasons might be that Europe has become a mature tourist destination and has experienced difficulties adapting itself to meet changing customer needs and wants. Therefore, destination management always needs to be aware of what they and their competitors provide and how they perform due to the possibility of tour operators and customers exploring new destinations and changing their desires and expectations.

The empirical results suggest that there exist image differences across origin countries and differences in Turkey's image when compared to Greece and Spain regardless of respondents' nationalities. To better understand the nature of the significant differences found, an examination of the main effects showed that German and British tourists evaluated Turkey's competitive position more positively than Dutch/Holland tourists. In addition, British tourists rated Turkey better than German and Dutch/Holland tourists for "Quality of Services." Not surprisingly, Turkey was rated more competitive on "Cultural and Natural Attractiveness when compared to Spain than it was to Greece. In contrary, for "Quality of Infrastructure," Turkey was perceived less competitive against Spain when compared to Spain and Greece. The interaction effects showed that British and German tourists rated Turkey better than Dutch/Holland tourists for "Cultural and Natural Attractiveness," whereas British tourists evaluated Turkey's competitive position for providing "Quality of Services" better than both Dutch/Holland and German tourists. Therefore, strategic plans can focus on increasing the quality of service and perceived value as well as enhancing the destination experience by augmenting the tourism product and services in order to distinguish one destination from its major rivals.

Box 3.1 Perceptions of Multiple Destinations by Multiple Groups of Visitors. Source: Kozak, Baloglu and Bahar (2010).

Threat of Substitute Products and Services

The threat of substitute products and services could be examined under three broad headings: increase in demand for other non-tourism products and services, increase in demand for domestic tourism and increase in demand for using ITs or their variants such as virtual reality. It is claimed that destinations not only compete with each other but also with other products or services such as buying a new house, electronic equipment or paying fees for education, which are related to their existing or potential markets (Sirakaya, McLellan and Uysal 1996). Next, it appears that people sometimes prefer or are encouraged to take a vacation in their own country rather than going abroad due to the existence of personal or national economic problems. Finally, developments in IT could produce substitutes for tourism products. It is expected that people will not need to visit a particular destination because all variables in the virtual tourist destination such as sun and weather conditions can be modified to create the perfect virtual experience at lower prices (Cheong 1995; Williams and Hobson 1995; Williams and Hobson 1995). Although all these factors seem to be a substitute for tourism products and services in general, rather than specific destinations, the final outcome could influence destinations attracting tourists who have access or interest in such technologies.

Competition among Existing Destinations (Analysis of Supply Side)

When tourist destinations are considered as an element of the marketing mix (place), the importance of their performance levels seems clear. Zairi (1996) points out that competitiveness can be achieved when one is more innovative to develop new products and services and quicker to deliver them to their customers. Destination authorities therefore should be aware of what they and their competitors provide and how they perform due to the possibility of tour operators and customers exploring new destinations. They should also pay attention to developments in customer needs, wants and perceptions. For example, Greece monitors the changes over socio-economic, socio-demographic and holiday-taking patterns of its international customers (Kotler, Haider and Rein 1993).

There are notable contributions to classifying major elements of destinations. In an attempt to measure the tourist attractiveness of destinations, Var, Beck and Loftus (1977) note that it is a function of natural, social and historical factors, recreation and shopping opportunities, accessibility and accommodation performing above minimum touristic quality standards. Mill and Morrison (1992) state that a destination is composed of attractions, facilities, infrastructure, transportation and hospitality. Similarly, Laws (1995) classifies elements which contribute to the attractiveness of a tourist destination under two main headings: primary features (e.g. climate, ecology, culture and traditional architecture) and secondary features (e.g. hotels, catering, transport and entertainment). Laws further claims that the primary purpose of tourists is to enjoy the primary features rather than the others, but the secondary features are necessary to reinforce the attractiveness of the destination. Goodall and Bergsa (1990) introduce total cost and accessibility as new components. All the elements presented in Table 3.1 together contribute to the attractiveness of a tourist destination.

In marketing products, the place where a product is designed and produced is important to customers ('made in' label). They might assume that product X made in country Z has a higher quality than one made in country Y (Kotler, Haider and Rein 1993). In marketing tourism services, people might have a similar perception that one country has higher quality services than another. It has been shown that images of a tourist destination are a mixture of both positive and negative perceptions. If destinations seem otherwise to be equally attractive, the decisive factor will be where negative perceptions may be unlikely to occur (McLellan and Fousher 1983). Image could be affected by tourists' own familiarity with the place, recommendations from others and information provided by media and travel brochures (Fakeye and Crompton 1991; Milman and Pizam 1995; Grosspietsch 2006).

Table 3.1   Components of Destination Attractiveness

Group Heading	Criteria	Considerations
Natural Factors	Natural Beauty	General topography, flora and fauna, proximity to lakes, rivers and sea, islands, hot and mineral water springs, caverns, waterfalls
	Climate	Sunshine, temperature, winds, precipitation, discomfort index
Social Factors	Artistic and Architectural Features	Local architecture, monuments and art museums
	Festivals	Organised music and dance festivals, sports events and competitions
	Distinctive Local Features	Native and ethnic cuisine, handicrafts and products, dress, music and dances
Historical Factors	Attitudes towards tourists	Local congeniality and treatment of tourists
	Native Historical Settlements	The existence, condition and accessibility of native settlements
	Religious Significance	The religious importance in terms of past and present religious observances and practices
	Historical Significance	The extent to which a site may be well known due to important historical events and/or legends
Recreational and Shopping Facilities	Sports Facilities	Boating, canoeing, hunting, fishing, swimming, skiing, sailing, golfing, horseback riding
	Educational Facilities	Botanical gardens, aquarium, zoos, archaeological and ethnographic museums
	Facilities conductive to health, rest and tranquillity	Hiking trails, picnic and campgrounds, mineral and hot water spas
	Night-time recreation	Theatres, cinemas and other nightlife. Auto service facilities, groceries and necessities, souvenir and gift shops, handicraft shops
	Shopping Facilities	Highways and roads, water, electricity, gas, safety services, health services, communication networks, public transportation facilities and services
Infrastructure, Food and Shelter	Infrastructure above Minimal Touristic Quality	Hotels, restaurants, vacation villages, bungalows, motels,

continued

Table 3.1 (continued)

	Food and Lodging Facilities above Minimal Touristic Quality	Package tour prices, accommodation prices, food and beverage prices, shopping prices
Prices	Level of prices	Visa requirements, resistance to tourism development
Government policies	Entry barriers	Source: Adapted from Gearing, Swart and Var (1974); Var, Beck and Loftus (1977).

Source: Adapted from Gearing, Swart and Var (1974); Var, Beck and Loftus (1977).

The majority of customers may have experience of other destinations and so are likely to make comparisons among facilities, attractions and service standards of other destinations (Laws 1995). According to the theory of decision-making processes, it is argued that potential tourists select a destination among alternatives and evaluate each alternative considering its potential to offer the benefits they look for (Mayo and Jarvis 1981; Decrop and Kozak 2009). Thus, a competitive position can be achieved by both creating and transmitting a favorable image, which presents the destination as different from other similar destinations to potential tourists and by satisfying actual tourists (Goodall 1990). These are examples of how psychological repositioning (changing tourists' beliefs about facilities and services) and competitive repositioning (changing tourists' beliefs about their own and other destinations) might be introduced into the concept of destination competitiveness.

Tourist destinations are accepted as a key component of the tourism system. Due to developments in the tourism industry and changes in consumer behavior, more destinations, more choice of accommodation, a wide range of activities and special tours are now offered for tourists (Laws 1995). Each destination offers a variety of products and services to attract tourists. However, each tourist also has the opportunity and freedom to choose among a set of destinations (Laws 1991). Different factors may have an influence on destination choice. For instance, each tourist may have different motivations and preferences for different destinations. Research further suggests that attitude is a predictor of determining a destination to be selected among alternatives (Goodrich 1977, 1978; Mayo and Jarvis 1981; Um and Crompton 1990). Each destination therefore needs to know its performance levels through considering those strengths and weaknesses, which will affect both repeat visits and the nature of word-of-mouth communication to others considering a first visit (Selby and Morgan 1996).

Competition among destinations might contribute to the development of products and services. Providing better services not only gives an enhanced competitive edge but also raises standards in the industry, which in turn

Tourism Price Competitiveness Index (TPCI) shows the tourism price index across countries where the index value of '0' shows the least price competitive country and '100' represents the most price competitive country. It is computed using the Hotel Price Index and Purchasing Power Parity Index.

Human Tourism Index measures the achievement of human development in terms of tourism activity. It is a new index and is in line with various kinds of human development indices constructed by the United Nations Development Program (UNDP) to measure human achievement in various aspects of human development. The Human Tourism Index is calculated by taking the average of the Tourism Participation Index (TPI) and the Tourism Impact Index (TII).

Infrastructure Index shows the level of infrastructure development, combining the Road Index, the Sanitation Index and the Water Access Index. The Railway Index is not included because of the limited data available. An index value of '0' represents the country with the least infrastructure, whereas the value of '100' is for the country with the highest infrastructure.

Environment Index combines the Population Density Index, CO2 Emission Index and the Environmental Treaties Index. An index value of '0' shows the least environmentally friendly country, whereas the value of '100' is for the most environmentally friendly country.

Technology Index combines the Internet Index, Telephone Index, Mobile Index and HiTech Index.

Human Resources Index is proxied by using the Education Index obtained from the 2004 UNDP report. The education Index consists of the adult literacy rate and the combined primary, secondary and tertiary gross enrollment ratios.

Openness Index shows the level of a country's openness toward international trade and international visitors. The Openness Index is an aggregate index combining the Visa Index, Tourism Openness Index, Trade Openness Index and Taxes on International Trade Index.

Social Index is an aggregate social index, combining the Human Development Index (HDI), Newspaper Index, PC Index and TV Index. Total crime recorded is not included because of the limited coverage of the data.

Box 3.2   Indicators of Indices for Destination Competitiveness. Source: The World Bank (2004), World Development Indicators; The Human Development Report 2004. UNDP.

will be reflected to customers as a determinant of greater expectations. As a result, the customer's value chain would become an input of competitive advantage (Porter 1998). Understanding what a satisfied customer needs and wants is the basic ingredient of a recipe for arriving at successful marketing and improving competitive advantage (Czepiel, Rosenberg and Akerele 1974). Customers are an important source of identifying external ideas for many products and services; surveys enable them to reflect on their opinions about and experiences with the destination. When tourists are satisfied with the destination, the destination has the power to make its satisfied customers come back or recommend it to others. In contrast, when customers are dissatisfied, they will have the power to decide whether to come back or make favorable word-of-mouth recommendation and also to ask the destination authority to make the required changes to provide better service. As a consequence, customer-centered organizations or destinations will have a greater opportunity to win over the competition (Kotler 1994).

In order to talk about the competitive advantage of destinations, Crouch and Ritchie (1999) stress that value must be added to the existing economic resources, and the tourism industry must concentrate on the term *destination competitiveness* rather than *destination comparison* as the service industry is differentiated from the manufacturing industry by its more subjective features. They further suggest that economic and natural resources can be accepted as the determinants of comparative advantage because similar destinations may have these types of resource (e.g. warm weather, sea and beaches in Mediterranean countries). In other words, destinations with identical products will be alike. How to sell the experience of a vacation with the destination rather than the sale of the resource itself will be of great concern in maintaining competitive advantage. Therefore, value must be added to cultural, natural and economic resources by building accommodation near beaches or cultural heritage, organizing trips, removing the language barriers to communicate better with tourists, encouraging local people to be hospitable toward tourists or demonstrating local culture in its own surroundings. Such factors as feelings of safety and security, cleaner beaches and establishments, more hospitable and friendlier local people and better value for money could make one destination more competitive than or distinctive from others.

The development of tourism can make a considerable contribution to regional economic development. This has led the governments of some countries to take responsibility for investment, control, planning, co-ordination and financial issues within their nation's tourism industry. In this way, governments can control the flow of tourists to the country. Therefore, where tourism is considered to have a negative impact on social and natural structure, restrictions to entry or effective regulations can be established. Where tourism is considered to have a positive impact, governments strongly encourage the development of the tourism industry to attract more tourists and higher income. For example, in an attempt to increase the number of tourist arrivals, in the late 1990s, the Kenyan government decided to drop the visa charge for those from some European countries. The growth of public–private partnerships in tourism management and the promotion of countries such as Germany, Romania, Tunisia and India have also been observed. Such policies might result in changes in the destination's proportion of tourism incomes or tourist arrivals.

External (uncontrollable) Factors

Overall perceptions of tourists may depend on external factors which are difficult for destination management or local tourism businesses to influence. Factors disrupting flow to a destination may be economic, political or temporal features appearing in tourist-generating as well as tourist-attracting countries (tourist destinations) (i.e. age, income, occupation, personality, cost, time, motivation, distance, risk and existence of alternative destinations) (Mountinho 1987). There are also such uncontrollable factors as terrorism directed from outside a country (reference to the latest Fiji attack and other Alchida in Pakistan), spread of disease (MacLaurin 2004) and natural disasters (Huang and Min 2002; Huan, Beaman and Shelby 2004; Faulkner and Vikulov 2001) which may have a lasting effect when they happen. As the number of disasters and crises affecting the tourism and travel industry increases, it becomes evitable to understand the nature of these disasters and incidents, predict their potential impacts on the tourism industry and control their consequences.

Distance

How close a destination is to the tourist markets is another determination of destination competitiveness (Mill and Morrison 1992). Research findings revealed that there was a reverse relationship between perceived distance and intention to visit (Court and Lupton 1997) and revisit a destination (Mountinho and Trimble 1991). The competitiveness of short- and long-haul tourist destinations was examined by Edwards (1993) on the basis of comparison of prices levels, accommodation grading levels and distance levels between the British tourist market and the destination. Findings indicated that the level of prices were the strongest indicators of competitiveness between long- and short-haul destinations because the former destinations cost the customer about double that of the latter destinations. In a broader context, there is evidence to suggest that tourist motivations have a direct or inverse moderating effect on the influences of distance and prices (Nicolau and Mas 2006).

However, the distance may not always be important in affecting the flow of tourism demand to any destination. Some destinations such as the Caribbean and Mauritius could be less competitive when the grade rises, which means that accommodation costs are likely to increase. Surprisingly, some other destinations such as the South/Asian destinations, Goa (India), Kenya and Sri Lanka become more competitive when the accommodation grade rises. This means that there is doubt that the price may not always be an indicator of physical quality in the tourism industry, as opposed to arguments in the literature (Barksy 1992; Zeithaml and Bitner 1996). Therefore, it can be suggested that short- and long-haul destinations not be regarded as direct competitors against each other. Moreover, any destination in the short-haul destination can compete with the other. This means that most of the Mediterranean destinations, for example, could be in a direct competition on beach holidays (e.g. Turkey, Spain and Greece). This may be the same among long-haul destinations.

Because tourism and travel is a global activity, people may want to visit a place which is very close by or a long way away. In this case, cultural distance will appear as a main barrier (e.g. language, lifestyle, attitude, food and so on). Despite the fact that there is little or no difference between tourist receiving and generating countries' cultural values, how tourists perceive the style of local food, local lifestyle and local attitude toward tourists in a particular destination could influence their intention to either visit or not visit. As one of the factors in the analysis of supply and demand interaction, Burton (1995) examines the cultural links between origin and destination countries. Other things being equal, travel is more likely to occur between countries with some common cultural link such as common language and religion or shared political history (e.g. Malta, South Africa and the U.S. for British tourists and Turkey for German tourists). Cultural differences could sometimes be dependent on tourist motivations and encourage people to visit the place to learn more about the local culture if it is totally different (e.g. safari tours to Africa).

Risk

There has been increasing interest to discuss the potential impacts of such risk threats as terrorism, crime, natural disasters and spread of disease over the sustainable development of both domestic and international tourism and travel industries (Aziz 1995; Huan, Beaman and Shelby 2004; Fuchs and Reichel 2006; Kozak, Crotts and Law 2007). In this context, growing attention has been invested into organizing several academic conferences and industry meetings, a couple books have been published and a growing number of research papers have been authored. In a similar vein, there has been intensive media coverage of terrorism attacks (e.g. Afganistan, Philipinnes, Eygpt), health diseases (e.g. SARS, bird flu, H1N1) and natural disasters (e.g. earthquakes in Taiwan and Turkey, tsunami in Thailand, hurricanes in North America).

Generally speaking, the destination image in terms of risk and safety has a deterring impact on the likelihood of international visitors to travel to such places which are perceived to remain under threat. For example, one could note that those perceiving terrorism as a risk of travelling are likely to avoid the Middle East (Sönmez and Graefe 1998). Tourists have an image of Africa as a continent which is not safe in terms of health-related risks (e.g. HIV). Both Africa and Asia are perceived to be worse than Europe and Australia due to health risks stemming from the supply of poor food and water quality (Lepp and Gibson 2003). These findings are similar to those of later research conducted by Kozak, Crotts and Law (2007).

Among the main reasons for travel are pleasure and relaxation. Danger, disorder and threats to safety or health are compelling deterrents (Jefferson and Lickorish 1991). Long-term political stability of a country will make it a relatively more attractive destination for both investors in tourism and the tourists themselves. Internal social and political turmoil are the issues which need to be considered within the perceived risk of tourist destinations. The existence of unrest in some countries such as Romania, the former Yugoslavia, Tunisia and Egypt in recent years has affected their previous positive trends in the development of tourism activities at the international level.

As previously noted, the view that image is a critical factor in choosing destinations to vacation is widely supported (e.g. Goodall 1988; Court and Lupton 1997). Making tourists feel secure and safe before and during the vacation is essential to the international competitiveness of destinations. Additional destinations can be included in the consideration set of the destination choice model if a new destination is suggested and new information (e.g. recent violence or political or social unrest) is supplied either by friends or media (Sönmez and Graefe 1998). In his analysis of the Florida tourism industry, Brayshaw (1995) states that the negative image created by being unsafe may damage the tourism industry because the negative word-of-mouth communication which results from negative images cannot be avoided even if a destination has high-quality tourist attractions.

During a vacation, there is a possible risk of violence against tourists or petty crime in tourist destinations. Safety and security problems are higher in particular destinations which are experiencing rapid development in their tourism industry (Pizam, Tarlow and Bloom 1997). Survey results revealed that perceived risk and safety concerns were found to be strong predictors for not choosing regions (or some destinations) for vacation in the future (Sönmez and Graefe 1998). Tourists who perceived certain destinations as being 'at risk' are likely to avoid them in their future travel plans (e.g. the Middle East and Africa), whereas those who had previously travelled to the same destination (or region) were more confident and more likely to go back because their feelings of safety were increased. Similarly, older people were found to be more likely to return to the same destination (Gitelson and Crompton 1984; Ryan 1995; Juaneda 1996). The reason might be that this segment of tourists is more likely to attach greater importance to the increased perceptions of safety and security while travelling.

Another dimension of safety and risk concern is the fear of disease (Ritchie and Crouch 1993; Kozak, Crotts and Law 2007). Potential tourists are not recommended to visit and tour operators are unlikely to sell holidays to places known for high risk of diseases. Tourists also tend to complain about the lack of hygiene and sanitation for facilities, food and water and food poisoning. Because these are mostly third world destinations or countries experiencing disease problems, there may be imbalance in the tourism competition between developed and undeveloped countries as far as health and hygiene and sanitation issues are concerned.

3.2 SUMMARY

Using Porter's model, this chapter has presented five factors and addressed the question of how each factor could influence the competitiveness of tourist destinations: the bargaining power of both potential tourists and suppliers, the emergence of new destinations, the threat of substitute products and services and the competitiveness among existing destinations. Of these, the availability of supply-based factors distinguishes one destination from another and is regarded as a significant factor in maintaining a competitive advantage. Competitors could therefore be monitored on a regular basis

---

Based on the findings of an empirical study among those people visiting Hong Kong in 2003, it appears that North America and Asia were differentiated as the most risky destinations in terms of natural disaster. Infection disease was ranked as the highest factor, and terrorist attack was ranked as the second highest factor. This finding suggests that infection disease is a number one factor influencing travelers' choice of destinations regardless of the category of regions where they tend to travel. In terms of the probability of occurrence of such risks, regions such as South America, Africa, the Middle East and Asia are perceived to be riskier places for infectious diseases, North America is riskier for terrorist attacks, whereas Asia and North America are perceived to be riskier destinations with their higher scores of the occurrence of natural disaster. There is current evidence to support this finding: earthquake in South Asia, tsunami in Indian Ocean and hurricanes in North America. This is almost the same as how such places are perceived in terms of the magnitude of threat. It also appears that travelers are less likely to trust the efficacy of media in disseminating the information about the risks in South America, Africa, the Middle East and Asia.

Box 3.3   Risk Perceptions of Destinations. Source: Kozak, Crotts and Law (2007).

in line with the effective factors presented in this study, such as analysis of customers' characteristics, structure of marketing channels, destination image and tourist satisfaction, availability of tourist resources and their performance levels vis-à-vis other similar destinations and competitors' strategies. This might enable destinations to reinforce the analysis of their markets and identify their own as well as others' strengths and weaknesses. The findings of competitiveness analysis may help destinations develop the correct positioning strategy.

* * *

CASE STUDY: DESTINATION CHARACTERISTICS FOR MEDICAL TRAVEL COMPETITIVENESS

Written by Dan Cormany and Seyhmus Baloglu,
University of Nevada Las Vegas, USA

Competitiveness will vary by type of product and target markets. A starting point for a destination is to consider the types of medical tourists it seeks to attract and what these tourists desire from their travel. From this perspective, medical travelers may be divided into six categories ranging from general wellness enhancement to major surgery (please refer to the pie in Chapter 1 case).

Upon closer examination of the categories, it is possible for each category to reflect not only by the influence of a destination's medical services, but also by its hospitality support, tourism appeal and governmental policies (Bookman and Bookman 2007; Cormany 2008). For example, it would be expected that all medical tourists will make quality health care central to their destination choice (the innermost part for each slice of the pie). But for major surgery patients, the quality of aftercare facilities in hotels during their in-country recovery may be a crucial secondary factor and tourism opportunities of little importance. Those traveling for elective surgery or lifestyle reasons may give greater weight to resort accommodations and tourism opportunities which could supplement their visit. If the government has made the visa process easy or unnecessary, those needing immediate attention may favor one destination over another, whereas those seeking a specific alternative therapy available in only one area may be more patient in seeking a visa. In these ways, the four components affect various medical tourist categories in different ways, but the obvious point is that various aspects of hospitality and tourism will impact the traveler's destination decision in all cases, so it is important that an area wishing to remain competitive in the medical tourism market must supplement its top-level medical facilities with appropriate tourism support facilities and services. Elements of each of the four categories are identified in Table 3.2.

Table 3.2 Factors of Each Destination Component

Medical Facilities & Services Circle	Hotel & Food/Beverage Circle	Area Tourism Support Facilities & Services Circle	Governmental & National Factors Circle
1. Costs—medical	1. Costs—lodging	1. Costs—general labor	1. Political stability of country
2. Labor available—medical	2. Costs—food and beverage	2. Commonality of spoken & written English	2. Stability of labor force—union strike potential
3. Training available—medical (medical schools, nursing programs)	3. Number of 3/4/5 diamond—rooms available (Are int'l ratings available?)	3. Availability of educated translators	3. Currency fluctuations
4. Financial inducements for labor—medical	4. Hospitality labor availability	4. Airport a. Direct service from major American cities b. Airlines servicing area c. Accommodations for disabilitiesd. Airfare rates e. Frequency of flights	4. Access to money/credit
5. English commonly spoken among medical staff	5. Hospitality training available	5. Local transportation a. Avail. of taxis, limos b. Avail. of buses, other public transport in hospital/hotel areas c. Safety of available transportation options d. Accommodations for disabled available	5. Safety of country

continued

Table 3.2 *continued* Factors of Each Destination Component

Medical Facilities & Services Circle	Hotel & Food/Beverage Circle	Area Tourism Support Facilities & Services Circle	Governmental & National Factors Circle
6. Facilitiesa. Capacity b. Accreditation c. Licensure of staff d. Specializationse. Staff : patient ratio f. Ambulance service	6. Financial inducements for labor—hospitality	6. Reliability of infrastructure b. Public services c. Waste management	6. Respect for individual rights a. Culture of tolerance b. Gender equality c. Protection of disabled d. Freedom from unreasonable arrest
7. Equipment available for rental (oxygen, wheelchair, etc.)	7. English commonly spoken among hospitality staff	7. Safety from crime	7. Legal system a. Established laws b. Evenness of enforcement c. Ownership rights d. Legal recourse e. Protection of patients f. Malpractice recognized g. Accounting and financial disclosure h. Tax system i. Recognition of patents, intellectual property rights

continued

8. Private nurses available for hire	8. Availability of potable water in facilities	8. Local political stability	8. Ease of access a. Need for visa (by residents of target market) b. Visa access c. Visa processing time
9. Medications a. Availability b. Safety of medication quality c. Parallels to U.S. medication	9. Reliability of electricity in facilities	9. Distribution of b. Internet	9. Type of market (economic model) a. Capitalism b. Privatization c. Regulation/deregulation of areas impacting health care and tourism
10. Indigenous disease threats	10. Licensure & regulation for: a. Food & beverage operations b. Hotel accommodations c. Spa facilities	10. Ease of limited mobility maneuverability (wheel-chair, pedestrian friendly?)	10. Cultural strain a. Likeness of source and host country cultural b. Host country's citizen attitudes toward source country
11. Privately operated facilities	11. Dietary accommodations available (gluten free, low sodium, doctor prescribed)	11. Weather appeal for vacation and for recovery	
12. Operation of "aftercare" facilities?	12. Internet availability	12. Destination appeal a. City offerings b. Relaxation c. Education d. Culture e. Sight-seeing f. Traditional medicine as supplement/ alternative	

continued

Table 3.2 (continued) Factors of Each Destination Component

Medical Facilities & Services Circle	Hotel & Food/Beverage Circle	Area Tourism Support Facilities & Services Circle	Governmental & National Factors Circle
13. Ease of medical records transfer back to the home country	13. Hotel accommodations: a. Disability & special services accommodations b. Private baths c. Elevators d. Room service available (24 hours?) e. Proximity to hospitals f. Heat/airg. Value for services provided ratio 14. Presence of spa services a. Medical personnel associated with spa b. Spa treatments c. Traditional Treatments (acupuncture, herbal, Ayurveda, etc.) d. Instruction in relaxation, diet, wellness (tai chi, yoga, nutrition, etc.) e. Diagnostic services f. Exercise/workout facilities	13. Receptivity by locals to Americans 14. Current awareness/image of locale by Americans	

It would be safe to say that risk factors are more critical in medical tourism. Medical travelers are increasingly using medical tourism facilitators because of multiple competitive destinations and the importance of reliable information. Medical tourism facilitators (similar to travel agents or meeting planners) are more likely to have bargaining powers in such a system. The facilitators operate within the traveler's home country or the destination region and coordinate the whole trip.

Part II
Destination Management

4 Destination-Based Management Strategies

Tourism has many characteristics. First, tourism products are the most competitive products because there are many numbers of alternatives to the customers' offer. A customer might switch to another destination if they believe that there is the potential to meet their expectations. Second, offering a tourism product has an interest in many other practices and institutions which might impact upon tourists' cumulative experiences with a destination. As shown, in order to be able to protect one from challenges of tourism and offer satisfactory products and services, a destination-based management program needs to be established that requires a strong collaboration and co-operation among all the related bodies of a tourist destination. As a result, this chapter aims to introduce the major management strategies required to maintain competitive advantage of tourist destinations.

4.1. DESTINATION MANAGEMENT

Destination management, as a top management responsible for directing tourism demand and supply in the area, could have a similar position in destination benchmarking. Each destination management is supposed to be responsible for or representative of a particular place where any direct or indirect interaction among such elements as tourism supply (physical and human resources, products and services, tourism laws and legislation and tourism businesses), tourism demand (mass, individual, domestic or foreign tourist groups) and tourism suppliers (tour operators and travel agents) appears. All these elements and feedback to be received from this interaction may be helpful for destination management to make a comparison with its counterparts.

However, because success will depend on delivering the right mix of components to meet customer demand, a destination management program should involve consideration of all facilities and services which affect the tourist experience (Kozak 2004a, 2004b). In destination management, it is important to have co-ordination and co-operation between a set of organizations such as local and central government, private industry and the related international organizations (e.g. Kotler, Haider and Rein 1993; Hall 1994; Gunn 1997; Timothy 1998) because the public sector is responsible for releasing and approving plans and projects and the private sector is associated with running tourism or tourism-related businesses. Being aware of its advantages, several governments have recently begun to pay attention to the protection of natural resources and to upgrade and enhance the national heritage by developing an integrated approach involving collaboration between public and private sector representatives (e.g. France, Turkey and the Balearic Islands).

4.2. DESTINATION MANAGEMENT ORGANIZATIONS

Destination management organizations (DMOs) go under a variety of names such as convention and visitor bureaus (CVBs) or authorities, tourist bureaus, tourist organizations, tourist offices, councils and so on. They are funded by government or tax money and are mainly responsible for marketing destinations to current and potential visitors. However, their role also changes due to changes in the environment as DMOs need to satisfy the needs and wants of all stakeholders and achieve a complex range of strategic objectives. They start to play a critical role in managing economic, social and environmental resources of a destination. In other words, they are to articulate and implement sustainable development strategies of the destination. Such strategies focus not only on tourists and attractions but also on quality of life and residents.

DMOs should consider both leisure and business segments in strategic planning. Too often destinations only limit their target markets to leisure or pleasure travellers. Tourist destinations should also take business visitors into consideration as a heterogeneous market (conventions, meetings, trade shows, etc.) and develop facilities to attract them, as well. Places should also make themselves attractive for businesses and investors to come and invest in the community for both tourism and supporting industries. According to a study by the U.S. Travel Association in 2009 (Las Vegas Review Journal, 20 September 2009, p. E1), for every dollar invested in business travel, businesses experienced an average of US$12.50 in increased revenue and US$3.80 in new profits for the destination.

Place or destination marketing, however, will achieve a little without involving all stakeholders and combining their input and efforts into an integrated strategy. Therefore, DMOs need to coordinate the efforts of all stakeholders and residents and engage them in the strategic marketing planning. Their initial task in strategic place marketing is to organize an "internal" planning committee made up of residents, businesses and local government officials to ensure cooperation between private and public sectors. This is followed by improving four critical marketing factors: infrastructure, attractions, image and support from the community and answering three questions in a place audit (Kotler, Haider and Rein 1993):

1. What is the place's "livability" when it comes to attracting new residents?
2. What is the place's "visitability" when it comes to attracting tourists?
3. What is the place's "investibility" when it comes to attracting business and investment?

The Las Vegas Convention and Visitors Authority (LVCVA) is the official destination marketing organization of Las Vegas, a quasi-governmental agency established by a state law and funded by a county room tax. It has an autonomous Board of Directors involving both public- and private-sector members. The LVCVA's mission is "to attract visitors by promoting Las Vegas as the world's most desirable destination for leisure and business travel." The LVCVA's marketing function involves activities such as advertising, selling, digital marketing, research and strategic planning (http:// www.lvcva.com/about/about-marketing.jsp).

Creating a Powerful Team

The findings of empirical studies prove that multiple attributes affect the level of tourist overall satisfaction, word-of-mouth recommendation and repeat visit intention (Kozak 2001b). Thus, there is a close relationship between a destination's overall performance level and the performance of all the individual components which make up tourists' experience of a destination. All these elements of a destination bring about the importance of management in order to keep them and the development of the destination under control, create and stimulate demand for the destination and sustain a positive vision in the minds of customers, retailers and suppliers. In this sense, a destination manager could be considered as the authority in charge of directing resources, co-ordinating not only with local tourism establishments but also with leading national or international tourism and related organizations and directing TQM programs toward the implementation of the results to achieve goals and objectives. Basically, the potential role of destination managers may be providing local businesses and residents with services such as supervision and inspection.

Destination management should launch a powerful and expert team that will be familiar with the destination, the tourism industry and other destinations worldwide. The members of the committee might be selected from those who have a professional background and are capable of analyzing current developments within the industry. The implementation of TQM programs may provide a means of co-operative decision making, collaboration and communication. As Jafari (1983) suggests, tourism and other establishments need to be in harmony in the development and promotion of tourism activities in the destination. In this sense, destination management can be considered the authority which will direct TQM programs toward the implementation of the results. Therefore, it is essential to suggest the establishment of a destination marketing organization (DMAO) which will be in charge of directing tourism supply resources and co-ordinating with local tourism establishments and DMOs. Although DMOs are expected to have similar roles to DMAOs, the latter's activities are focused solely on marketing communications. The primary goals of DMOs can include:

- The development of a comprehensive tourism information system for the destination.
- The creation of a corporate image of the region or the country as a tourist destination.
- The creation of a greater awareness of the destination in the marketplace.

The development of a tourism information system is necessary to open a window to enhance communication between public authorities, between public and private organizations, between public authorities and the local community and between the responsible organizations and tourists visiting the area. It is also suggested that DMOs should collect the information about the destination internally and the environment (competitors) externally. Such information covers the following four sub-categories (Heath and Wall 1992).

These are necessary to achieve the strategies illustrated in Table 4.1 and could be taken into consideration from various perspectives. First, an internal information-collection system deals with the collection, storage and analysis of data such as hotel occupancy rates, number of tourist arrivals, tourist expenditure patterns, level of tourist satisfaction and complaints. Second, a marketing intelligence system includes collecting information from the external environment with regard to new laws and social, cultural and demographic trends on a regular basis. Such information is then distributed to tourism businesses. Next, an analytical marketing system provides a set of advanced techniques and models to understand, predict and control current or future tourism-related problems or threats that a destination does or will probably experience. Such a technique may be helpful for DMOs to review overall performance of the destination. Finally, a marketing research system is a way of carrying out a regular marketing research in order to understand what customers need and desire, and observe changes among them. Among the major information items related to tourists visiting the destination are the overall level of satisfaction, motivations and so on.

Table 4.1   A Revised Balanced Scorecard for Destination Competitiveness

Perspectives	Objectives
Customer Perspective	• Increase satisfaction
	• Decrease complaints
	• Increase compliments
	• Increase percentage of potential repeaters
Internal Businesses	• Identify and promote core competencies
	• Deliver a better quality service
	• Enable an effective relationship among organizations
Innovation and Learning	• Introduce new products
	• Revise destination positioning
	• Provide continuous improvement
Financial Perspective	• Deliver a competitive price
	• Deliver better value for money
	• Increase revenue per tourist
	• Increase average occupancy rates
	• Increase total tourism receipts

Source: Kozak (2004a).

Gaining Public- and Private-Sector Commitment

The tourism literature, to a large extent, suggests that co-ordination and co-operation between the public and private sectors is required (e.g. Inskeep 1991; Gunn 1997; Fyall, Fletcher and Spyriadis 2010) because the public sector is in charge of both releasing and approving plans and projects to design an urban or rural setting in a suitable manner, and the private sector has the responsibility of running tourism or tourism-related businesses. The benefits of such co-operation will be avoiding duplication and wasting financial resources and providing better communication channels to set plans, make decisions and put them into practice. Internal co-operation and co-ordination among government bodies (public sector) is required to use time and financial resources in a much more effective and productive manner as the private sector receives more profits and the public sector more tax revenue and a well-balanced economy (Poetschke 1995; Timothy 1998). Although there are several approaches in the literature to tourism development planning, at either a national or local level, it is beyond the primary purpose of this research to discuss either the advantages or disadvantages of each.

Forming a destination management consortium involving public sector, private sector, non-profit organizations and local residents is necessary to provide a sustainable form of tourism strategy because these take significant places in making decisions for tourism supply and generating tourism demand. In some countries such as Turkey, national tourism organizations take the responsibility of the development of the selected tourism areas, research, regularization of standards of facilities, overseas publicity, encouragement of tourism businesses and the establishment of overall tourism policy and promotion (Davidson and Maitland 1997). Moreover, the involvement of the public sector in developing countries appears to be acting as an investor and motivator for stimulating other businesses.

The members of the committee are to be selected from those who have a professional background and are capable of analyzing current developments within the industry. As discussed above, benchmarking requires effective collaboration, co-operation and co-ordination not only between members of the tourism industry but also between members and external organizations. As in organization benchmarking, the implementation of a TQM program may provide a means of co-operative decision making,

---

The earthquake in Indonesia in May 2006 destroyed several towns and many villages throughout the province of Yogyakarta. Extensive physical and infrastructural damage also occurred to vital infrastructure such as telecommunications, electricity supply, and transportation links. As well, parts of new buildings in Yogyakarta's Adisucipto International Airport collapsed and the runway was cracked, meaning no flights could arrive or depart. Tourism is a key economic sector for Yogyakarta, providing employment and income to thousands of people in the province, directly and indirectly. In response to the crisis to the tourism industry caused by the devastating earthquake, public and private tourism stakeholders in Yogyakarta and Central Java provinces have joined together under the patronage of the Coordinating Minister of Social Welfare and the Minister of Culture and Tourism to found the "Java Media and Tourism Crisis Center". Their mission is to assist in the rescue, relief, rehabilitation and recovery of the people, companies and organizations working in the tourism sector in both provinces and to keep the world informed as to the progress being made to return Yogyakarta to its normal status as an important cultural tourism destination, the heart of Javanese culture. Tourism is a multi-sectoral enterprise, and, as the Minister of Culture and Tourism noted, it will need the efforts and coordination of many government ministries working closely with the provincial authorities and private sector to carry out this mission.

Box 4.1   Yogyakarta Earthquake Affects Local Tourism Industry. Source: Noel B. Salazar posted for Trinet on 2 June 2006.

collaboration and communication. As Jafari (1983) suggested, tourism and other establishments need to be in harmony in the development and promotion of tourism activities in the destination. In this sense, destination management can be considered as the authority which will direct TQM programs toward the implementation of the results. Therefore, this study suggests the establishment of a DMAO which will be in charge of directing tourism supply resources and co-ordinating with local tourism establishments and DMOs. Although DMOs are expected to have similar roles to DMAOs, their activities are focused solely on marketing communications.

The growth of mass tourism has led to significant environmental problems in a number of critical areas (e.g. polluted sea and beaches and a noisy atmosphere). These areas could be a ground so as to underline why destination benchmarking approach is required to minimize the negative consequences of tourism. According to the policy of the Fifth Environmental Action Program established in 1992, the quality of planning, development and management of mass tourism particularly in coastal and mountainous areas needs to be improved. The program gives priority to sustainable forms of tourism and encourages tourists' awareness of environmental issues (Davidson 1998). In response, a number of initiatives have been introduced. National governments are asked to prepare inventories of their tourism resources and develop new policies. Co-operation between practitioners working in different regions who have similar problems and practices are encouraged to share both their positive and negative experiences. These co-operative relationships reflect the idea of destination benchmarking proposed in Chapter 6.

Human Resources Management

The subject of human resources is one of the top-priority investments in destinations to gain full competitive benefit. Porter (1985) views human resources as an important element of the organization's entire value chain driving through competitive advantage. As part of the service industry, tourism is significantly developing and is expected to continue to need many well-trained employees to offset labor shortages in the near future. It is widely known and accepted that tourism is an industry which requires intense face-to-face contact between hosts (local people and staff) and guests (tourists). Attitudes of local people toward tourists, approaches to tourism development and the development of programs to train both personnel and local people will indicate the position of a destination in the competitiveness set. Many destinations tend to employ students to deal with seasonal differences and high labor costs. It may take a long time to adopt them into the industry, and meanwhile there may be some dissatisfaction for both employees and tourists.

Local attitudes toward tourism and tourists may be positive in some countries and negative in others (Kozak and Tasci 2005). This applies to places which have a highly developed tourist industry as well as those which don't. The direction of attitudes on a positive and negative continuum can influence the direction of host and guest relationships in the same direction. Tourists cannot feel secure in places where local people's attitude is negative. When any negative image appears to exist in the attitude of local people, destination authorities need to encourage local people to be friendlier. Therefore, those having direct contact with tourists, particularly tour guides, taxi drivers, staff employed in hotels, restaurants and so on, and at airports, shopkeepers and others should be trained to behave politely because if these people give a bad impression, it can affect the whole of the local tourist industry. For instance, in Singapore, taxi drivers are trained to serve their customers better by improving foreign language skills and safety programs.

Effective Environmental Management

In an increasingly competitive business environment, the environmental quality of the tourist destinations represents a vital ingredient in the recipe for success. Poon (1993) stresses four key principles that destinations must follow if they are to be competitive. Of these, the environmental policy comes as the first, followed by other propositions such as making tourism a leading industry, strengthening the distribution channels in the marketplace and building a dynamic private industry. Therefore, to remain competitive in the future marketplace, both destinations and organizations must adopt environmentally friendly policies (Zahra 1999). Policies and programs which are designed to protect natural resources while making use of them have already been established by most tourist destinations and tourist organizations as customers are becoming more environmentally sensitive and aware. For instance, working with other governmental and academic institutions, the Caribbean Environment Programme is established to increase public awareness and environmental education through training and publishing materials and documents. Therefore, the reasons for considering effective environmental management as an element of destination competitiveness can be listed as below:

- Environmental consumption is a continuous process; therefore, its management must also be continuous in order to hand over to future generations an environment without damage.
- Environmental quality can influence tourists' first and subsequent visits to a particular place.
- Environmental quality can influence the image of tourist destinations and make them distinctive and enhance their competitive advantage.

Although environmental quality is considered to be a key element of the determination of competitiveness in tourism, the most distinctive part of the tourism industry (or tourism economics) is that it does not yet take into account the opportunity cost of environmental resources when producing a tourism product. Hence, it is believed that tourism services (or products) are cheaper because tourism suppliers think that such tourism resources do not need any cost to complete the whole product. Moreover, tourism suppliers are currently unwilling to accept their responsibility for the negative consequences of tourism development such as deregulation, overcrowding, traffic congestion, garbage and so on. There is an interdependent relationship between tourism development and the natural environment. This relationship is also complex. A clean and untouched natural environment may be required by tourism to increase financial benefits, but tourism may not be required by natural environment if tourism affects it negatively.

More recently, Tourist Ecological Footprint (TEF) frameworks were proposed to go beyond local environments and assess the broader ecological footprint of tourism activity at destination and product levels (Hunter 2002; Patterson, Niccolucci and Marchettini 2008). Such frameworks extend the environmental impact assessment to (1) origin destination (purchases made for the holiday package), (2) transit area (travel and consumption during travel) and (3) destination area (food and beverage, souvenirs, tours, water consumed, waste products and energy requirements) (Hunter 2002).

Environmental considerations are a significant element affecting a traveller's destination choice. Research findings revealed that about half of German tourists have considerable awareness of environmental quality issues when choosing a destination for a vacation (Ayala 1996). Moreover, because the quality of environmental resources has become an important part of destination development, tourist motivations and, as a result, of destination competitiveness (McIntyre 1993), any satisfaction or positive attitude or image which appeared following a vacation at one destination will likely stimulate subsequent visits and word-of-mouth recommendations. This will bring the first-time individuals from the unawareness set directly to the awareness set. Those who had favorable experiences will probably take the sample destination into a higher rank in their choice sets. Similarly, those who had a negative attitude or image toward a destination are likely to have less intention to visit and/or revisit but higher intention to make a negative word-of-mouth recommendation. As a result of widespread negative images of the environmental issues (degradation), Mediterranean destinations have begun losing their popularity in the European market. This brings a lower percentage of tourist flows and tourism receipts out of international tourism movements compared to the preceding years.

National tourist organizations have become increasingly conscious about the quality of the environment and its impact on successful destination management and marketing. The Scottish Tourist Board, for instance, is still in the process of launching new schemes for environmental management of tourist accommodations. One of those is to launch a unique 'environmental grading scheme' for accommodation establishments by

The three international leading tourism organizations (the World Tourism and Travel Council, the World Tourism Organization and the Earth Council) established a consortium in 1996 and released an action plan entitled 'Agenda 21 for the Tourism and Travel Industry: Towards Environmentally Sustainable Development'. The project aims to act toward sectoral sustainable development, identify areas in priority and provide further steps on how these objectives are to be achieved. The project requires a partnership among the government, the tourism industry and non-government organizations. The major priority areas include: (1) planning for sustainable tourism development, (2) training and enhancing public awareness, (3) providing exchange of information between developed and developing countries, (4) designing new products by considering their sustainability implications and (5) providing effective partnerships for sustainable development.

Box 4.2   Agenda 21 for the Tourism and Travel Industry. Source: http://www.wttc.org.

considering facilities according to their performance levels in such areas as energy efficiency, recycling and waste management. In addition to hotels, bed and breakfast accommodations and guesthouses, the scheme will also be extended to include tourist attractions (Stephens 1997). This eco-grading scheme is likely to be taken into account as the most important benchmark element which pays attention to the importance of the physical environment in the tourism industry. The name 'eco-benchmarking' can also be given to this element. As such, the Costa Rican Tourist Board gives a certificate to tourism businesses within the destination (called Certificate for Sustainable Tourism). This project categorizes and certifies each tourism business according to levels of its impact on or its contribution to sustainability.

Some local governments have recently begun to pay attention to the revitalization of destinations, such as towns, villages or cities, due to the problems appearing in their areas as a consequence of their increasing popularity in the market (e.g. traffic congestion, lack of pedestrian roads and cultural activities). Therefore, new projects are released in order to attract more visitors, meet their requirements and be more competitive in the market. Being aware of the significance of environmental resources in sustaining customer loyalty and improving destination competitiveness, the Tourism Council of the South Pacific introduced a list of guidelines to assist small accommodation facilities and resorts in safeguarding the environment. Font (2002), after reviewing the environmental quality certification initiatives made by numerous international public and private agencies, proposed a compliance assessment scheme

The European Blue Flag scheme has been established for recreational beaches as a part of the European Union's (EU's) environmental protection policy measures dealing with the quality of natural environment within the beach area. It is organized by the Foundation for Environmental Education in Europe (FEEE), a network organization whose aim is to promote environmental education and increase people's awareness of environmental issues such as efficient natural resources use. The scheme is based on 26 criteria for beaches and 16 criteria for marinas. The beach must be tested every two weeks during the bathing season and satisfy 19 criteria. The Blue Flag is awarded as an indicator of the quality of beach management encompassing three aspects: environmental education and information, beach management and safety and water quality. The blue flag has several stages beginning from forming collaboration between local government and organizations to the announcement of the award of the campaign. The two stages make the campaign outstanding. First, representatives of ministries responsible for the related subjects such as environment, health, tourism, sea, marine and so on come together as a national jury to discuss policies about the breakdown of responsibilities. Second, the award is made on the basis of a decision of an international jury made up of experts in the field.

Box 4.3 European Blue Flag Scheme. Source: Kozak (2004a).

for an international environmental quality accreditation or certification. Such an international eco-label program, however, needs to use general standards that would not be influenced by location-based features and regulations.

Co-operation Among Local Tourism Enterprises

A number of authors have emphasized the importance of collaborative strategies in order to achieve competitive advantages (e.g. Pikkemaat and Weiermair 2007; Parra-Lopez and Calero-Garcia 2010). In so doing, through developing collaborative networks, individual businesses via DMOs will be able to share information and communicate with others, commit resources to the network and encourage mutual trust. There are a wide variety of attractions and facilities which may be available to tourists visiting a certain place. Of these, for instance, shopping facilities play a key role in the attractiveness of a place as a tourist destination. Keller and Smeral (1997) suggest that destination-based factor endowments affect the competitiveness of a destination (e.g. natural and cultural resources, capital and infrastructure resources and human resources). The above-mentioned authors further state that quality in tourism encompasses three main components:

- Natural quality (environmental matters),
- Material quality (facilities such as accommodation, restaurants, shopping, sport and cultural events and so on),
- Non-material quality (services such as information guidance, housekeeping, speed of check-in and check-out procedures and so on).

The competitiveness of destinations is sensitive to these components. The implementation of factor-creating mechanisms such as education, research and development and investment programs are some of the most significant tools for creating a sustainable competitive advantage for international tourist destinations. Eliminating bureaucratic barriers could further improve tourist services and quality and reinforce the competitiveness of a destination (Keller and Smeral 1997). An efficient service is expected for check-in and check-out procedures at the destination airport, along with facilities for accommodation and food and beverages. Because time is limited, tourists do not want to waste time in queuing or complaining. As far as mass tourism and package tour holidays are concerned, tourists are becoming more sensitive about services, particularly at the destination airport and accommodation facilities.

Cooperation and Collaboration with Suppliers

Where package tours are concerned, the extent to which a destination can attract the interest of major tourism suppliers (e.g. tour operators, travel agents) and be included in their brochures will increase effectiveness in reaching the market. Suppliers feel themselves to be ahead of tourist destinations as they, as international suppliers and/or retailers, have to search for better products, applications or destinations for meeting customer requirements and following changes in their wants and needs. The image of the product (destinations) is primarily influenced by suppliers' promotional activities in the tourist-generating country. They have multiple and critical functions in destination marketing efforts such as promotion, distribution and image creation (Baloglu and Mangaloglu 2001).

Marketing via suppliers presents benefits as well as threats for the competitive position of any destination in the international arena. A good example can be given from Turkey. Most tourists visiting Turkey book via a tour operator. Turkey takes a higher place on the league table of international destinations when internal or external economic, social or political crises disappear and tour operators are promoting and selling Turkey. However, it has a lower ranking when any of these crises is in an upward trend and tour operators stop selling holidays to Turkey. The summer season of 1999 is a good example of this statement. For various reasons, the number of arrivals to the country via package tours sharply decreased.

For their significance in tourism sustainability (Gezici 2008), destinations cannot remain competitive in the long run without attractive beaches and sea, clean water and unspoiled landscape. Because the suppliers are the businesses that receive the greatest proportion of tourism revenues, they play a pivotal role in the competition among overseas tourism destinations and have to pay great attention to the environmental quality of destinations because it is the most important product they offer their customers (Wijk and Persoon 2006). It is unlikely to sell destinations characterized by dirty beaches and sea, noise and air pollution. Therefore, environmental guidelines or policies should be extended to include consideration of future generations.

As a result, it is believed that the future competitiveness of destinations will be based on the extent to which they are concerned with their sustainability (Rodríguez, Parra-López, Yanes-Estévez 2008). Therefore, existing tourist destinations are keen on developing new strategies and releasing policies on how to protect the natural environment and present themselves effectively to the market (e.g. eco-labelling, local agenda 21 and cleaner production etc.) (Lee 2001). The importance of environmental quality becomes clear when the degradation of beach quality at 'sea, sun and sand' holiday destinations leads to a negative impact on the number of tourist

---

As the first tour operator in the world to establish policies for environmental management, the TUI has developed its own environmental standards. Environmentally responsible tourism has become the main policy of TUI. It aims to be aware of the environment and sustain it in order to sustain the tourism industry. The TUI gathers information from more than 100 overseas destinations which is entered into an environmental database to be used for planning and designing catalogues. This information is used to keep customers informed about the environmental quality of the destination they are likely to go on holiday. The destination criteria used by TUI include beach quality, energy-saving measures, traffic control and so on. TUI also cooperates with accommodation facilities to monitor their environmental policies and practices. Along with the guidelines of TUI, the German Travel Agents Association, DRV, released a comprehensive program for environmental management. The DRV guidelines advise hotel management on how to be efficient and sensitive in water management, waste management, energy consumption, interior decoration, production and services of food, leisure facilities, staff training and communication skills with customers.

Box 4.4 TUI's Guidelines for Environmental Management. Source: Kozak (2004a).

arrivals, length of stays and number of repeat visits. As a consequence, a lower level of tourism income is likely to be generated (Dharmaratne and Brathwaite 1998).

4.3. SUMMARY

This chapter first introduces the requirement of establishing a broader organization that can be called DMOs and then emphasizes its role in developing major managerial strategies and their adaptation required to maintain the competitive advantage. The roles of destination management in national/international competitiveness might be to (1) search for which factors determine the competitiveness, (2) understand where the destination's competitive position is weakest and strongest and (3) observe trends in international tourism and how this may impact on the local tourism or what sort of lessons can be learned. Thus, this chapter also provides the analysis of several measures that play a direct or an indirect role in this respect.

* * *

CASE STUDY—MANAGING HUMAN CAPITAL IN TOURISM

By Peter Semone, *Assumption University, Thailand*

In 2009, some 2 million overseas visitors came to the Lao People's Democratic Republic (Lao PDR), generating export earnings of approximately US $300 million. In servicing these visitors, tourism in Lao PDR employs a core workforce of some 17,000 people with a further indirect employment effect of up to 167,000 people. Tourism is expected to continue to play an important role in Lao PDR's economic growth and prosperity, especially in terms of job creation. The Lao PDR tourism industry is estimated to account for 8% of GDP and 5% of the country's total workforce of 2,955,633. The growing demand for community-based tourism products is helping to create jobs in rural areas that complement employment in the agricultural sector.

The Lao National Tourism Administration (LNTA) estimates that there are some 2,460 hotels, guesthouses, resorts, restaurants and entertainment establishments in Lao PDR. Of the current profile of businesses, 73.2% are family-run businesses, 60% of companies have less than 10 employees and 30% among them have less than 5 employees.

The outlook for Lao PDR tourism is positive, and the industry is currently working toward meeting a number of challenging demand-side targets that will see overseas visitor numbers reach nearly 3 million in 2015

Table 4.2   Lao PDR Tourism Arrival and Revenue Statistics

Year	2005	2006	2007	2008	2010(*)	2015(*)	2020(*)
Tourist Arrivals(rounded/ millions)	1.1	1.2	1.6	1.7	2.2	3.3	4.0
Tourism Receipts (USD Millions)	147	173	233	276	313	392	500

International Tourism Arrivals/Receipts in USD with (*) LNTA forecast to 2020
Source: Lao National Tourism Administration 2010

and as many as 4 million by 2020. Reaching these ambitious growth targets set for the industry will require an expansion and an 'upskilling' of the tourism workforce at both operational and managerial levels. By 2020, it is estimated that direct employment in tourism will reach 40,000, with indirect and induced employment providing a further 250,000 jobs.

According to *Achieving Service Quality Through People—Tourism Human Resource Development Vision and Strategic Recommendations Lao PDR (2010–2020)*, a publication researched, written and produced by Luxembourg Development Cooperation on behalf of the LNTA, Lao PDR tourism faces a number of human resource-related challenges in its tourism sector which must be addressed if tourism is to achieve its central role in economic and social development.

These include:

- the quality and scope of existing training delivery does not meet industry requirements: the capacity of the tourism providers to deliver quality training does not yet meet minimum international norms;
- availability and access to more flexible training options for tourism businesses and its employees are very limited;
- developing the kind of workforce needed to service the needs of the Lao PDR tourism sector cannot be achieved through the provision of academic programs alone. There is an urgent need for practical skills training in traditional hospitality and tourism areas combined with generic skills such as problem solving, information and communication technology (ICT), cross cultural communication and life skills training;
- Lao PDR's international competitiveness is being jeopardized by poor service levels, and serious efforts must be made to improve the skills of personnel employed in the tourism sector. There is strong evidence to suggest the need to significantly invest in HRD as a means to strengthen and develop the tourism sector;
- research in support of the national HRD Strategy indicates that the tourism sector will require as many as 40,000 skilled workers directly

employed in the sector by 2020. As such, the existing 17,000 workers will require upgrading of skills through various short-term training interventions. At the same time, an additional 23,000 workers will need to be inducted into the industry workforce and be provided with foundation education and training.

Strategic Pillar 1: Provide stewardship and tactical directives for the strategic vision. This strategic pillar provides the technical and tactical support to achieve the vision. It is an intentionally flexible pillar in that it is comprised of a dynamic membership. This enables expert situational analysis over the course of time. Pillar 1 is the repository and aggregator of expert input, the monitor of effectiveness and efficiency in the overall strategy and the generator of implementation objectives for the diverse body of stakeholders described in Pillar 2.

Strategic Pillar 2: Develop frameworks for implementation of HRD in tourism and hospitality. This strategic pillar provides for implementation of the objectives derived by Pillar 1. This representative body of all stakeholders serves to develop work plans, identify synergies in partner resources and co-ordinate among all stakeholders with the overarching goal of continually developing the HRD in Lao tourism strategy. As the basis for a long-term coordination and partnership model involving all stakeholders in Lao tourism HRD and coordinated through the government and its agencies, this body's representation will be comprised from members of all five pre-identified stakeholder constituencies which include: private-sector entities, public sector, industry associations, education providers and the donor community.

Strategic Pillar 3: Develop international standard provision for management and vocational education in hospitality and tourism. This pillar focuses on providing tangible outcomes for the policy focus of the first two pillars. Outcomes will give priority to the development of a Lao National Institute of Tourism and Hospitality (LANITH) in Vientiane. The focus will first be on vocational education at the LANITH and then in various public technical/vocation education and training (TVET) schools throughout Lao PDR. A further step will be the development of a management institute for tourism in Lao PDR to provide for both initial and CPD needs. The network of the provision to meet the highest international standards will support the work of partner institutes in the private and public sectors while supporting the industry and upgrading the skills of its own personnel.

Box 4.5   List of Strategic Pillars for HRD.

The national HRD strategy also outlines what the HRD landscape in Lao tourism might look like in 2020, were the HRD strategic recommendations to be implemented and used as building blocks for a process of sustained further investment in, and development of, people as tourism's major asset. The landscape is painted by means of identifying 16 characteristics which will highlight best practices in HRD in the future.

These characteristics are not only important verifiable indicators of future success but also form the basis upon which three strategic pillars have been formulated. The three pillars can be summarized as follows.

Tourism has the potential to serve as a significant engine for local economic development given the sector's spatial distribution and the relatively low import content of the services it trades. Consequently, tourism is an important element in the further economic growth of the country. The Lao tourism sector is now at a turning point, and reaching the growth arrival and revenue targets set by the LNTA will require an enhanced performance across all sectors of the industry. This performance is likely only to be achieved in the context of parallel enhancements in product quality, service quality, an appropriately trained workforce and regional competitiveness. This in turn will critically require sustained investment in people.

5 Destination-Based Total Quality Management

In contrast to the emerging number of studies on quality measurement and total quality management (TQM) in tourism and hospitality settings, there is very little attention give to their application in a destination context. As we know, quality management (the practice of TQM) aims for sustaining an ongoing (continuous) improvement of the standard of facilities, products and services provided. Ideally, this should also be the aim of a destination management organization in charge of managing sources, marketing products and setting policies. In the light of these statements, it is possible to suggest the practice of destintation-based total quality management (D-TQM) as a significant contribution to the management of destinations in improving the quality of service provision. In addition, because the subsequent impact is expected to lead to an increase in the market share, this also would help to maintain the competitiveness of a destination in the international arena. Therefore, this chapter aims to emphasize the significance of quality management in successful improvement of the performance of tourist destinations and to design a tentative model of D-TQM, particularly suitable for the sustainable development of tourist destinations, as well as application suggestions.

5.1. PREMISES OF D-TQM

Tourism has diverse and complex characteristics. First, tourism products are highly competitive because there are many alternatives offered to visitors. Visitors might switch to other potential destinations if they believe that there is a better opportunity to meet their expectations (McDougall and Munro 1994; Hsieh, O'Leary and Morrison 1994). Next, a tourism product is an interest for many other practices and institutions which might impact upon visitors' cumulative experiences with a destination (Jafari 1983). Some attributes are not related to only one specific destination but could be a reflection of tourists' experiences with several destinations in the country (e.g. check-in and check-out services at the destination airport, local transport services and so on) (Kozak 2001b). For example, destinations are connected to each other by local transport services. A good network of public transport services would enable both tourists and local people to have access to other resorts and main tourist attractions.

When tourists visit a destination, they stay at a hotel, possibly eat and drink somewhere outside the hotel, go shopping, communicate with local people and other tourists and visit natural, cultural and historical places (Uysal and Hagan 1993). They evaluate their destination experiences not only on the basis of whether they like the quality of accommodation or food but also on whether the local people are friendly or natural and historical places are preserved. There is a common belief that the development of a tourist area depends on the quality of its natural resources (sea, land, forest etc.), economic conditions (the standard of life, infrastructure, superstructure etc), socio-demographic structure (e.g. local culture, religion, education, hospitality etc.) and their sustainability for tourism development. Specifically, the implementation of the TQM practice at the destination level includes various premises as indicated below.

First, from a tourist's perspective, there is a close relationship among all tourism-related facilities and businesses at a destination. Tourist motivation has been shown to be multidimensional (Pyo, Mihalik and Uysal 1989); tourists want to have more than one experience at a destination. When guests arrive at a destination, they may want clean rooms, streets and beaches, and they expect helpful and informative staff. If tourists have initial information about a destination's performance on these attributes or have previous experiences, then they may expect the destination to have facilities and services to meet their expectations and needs. For instance, if tourists observe one destination of a given "brand" with a clean environment and beaches and this attribute is advertised in relation to the brand, then they would expect other destinations to have similar features of attractions. The theory is that where expectations are formed and not met, there is an increased propensity for a negative experience and dissatisfaction. It is argued that a negative experience influences the likelihood of returning and of recommendation to others, thus impacting the overall performance of destinations (Kozak and Rimmington 2000).

Next, on the supply side, the trip is not a single product; rather it is made up of components supplied by a variety of facilities with different objectives (Kozak 2000, 2004a, 2004b). As a consequence of the 'domino effect', it is assumed that the lack of quality experience in even one of these areas may influence the overall satisfaction level detrimentally (Jafari 1983). There is a close relationship between a destination's overall performance level and the performance of all the individual components which make up tourists' experience of a destination. When something is wrong with any of these components, the outcome would be negative which would be reflected back to the destination either at the demand or supply side (e.g. leading to dissatisfaction or less income and so on).

Third, tourism is also dependent on the existence of natural and cultural heritage. Thus, the primary purpose should refer to assisting people to understand, preserve and provide access to nature and culture and to better make sense of the present. Sites, monumental objects and buildings are the major evidence to understand and analyse the past and the present. In order to do this, strategies need to be prepared for identifying, protecting, conserving and promoting natural and cultural heritage through partnerships among local authorities, landowners and businesses and through advice about protection approaches, alternative uses and appropriate designs. In such a model, both local and national authorities as well as members of the private industry and local people should recognize their primary protection role for natural and cultural heritage and use available protection measures accordingly.

Finally, tourists' needs and wants are changing as they are becoming more experienced and knowledgeable about their needs, wants and future holidays. Tourists make comparisons among facilities, attractions and service standards of alternative destinations because they may have experience with other destinations. It is argued that a customer selects a destination from alternatives and evaluates each alternative considering its potential to deliver the benefits sought (Mayo and Jarvis 1981). As a result, factors such as natural, cultural and historical resources, infrastructure, accessibility, attractions and facilities are accepted as elements of tourist destination competitiveness. In other words, although tourist satisfaction with a

---

Over the decades, it has become necessary to establish a public organization which would be in charge of promoting the national culture at both the national and international levels. In this case, many countries have launched the Ministry of Culture (e.g. Canada, Sweden, Spain etc.). The government of various countries has tended to establish a link between culture and its minor or major fields (e.g. the Ministry of Culture, Arts and Heritage in Malaysia, the Ministry of Culture and Education in Finland, the Ministry of Culture and Communication in France, the Ministry of Culture and Heritage in New Zealand etc.). More specifically, the link between culture and tourism is officially established. Heritage is also becoming an important part of the tourism industry and society as a whole, which is evident in some developing countries with the establishment of public organizations at the Ministry level (e.g. the Ministry of Culture and Tourism in Turkey, Malta, Moldova, Ukraine and Azerbaijan). Either as an ally or an enemy to each other, the interrelationship has led to such integration.

Box 5.1   Interrelationship Between Cultural Heritage and Tourism.
Source: Kozak (2007a).

destination may influence return, a destination area's overall image rather than a particular facility may be the key to making a first visit and thus be critical to making repeat visits, to creating loyal visitors.

5.2. EUROPEAN QUALITY AWARD: BASELINE FOR *D-TQM*

The European Quality Award (EQA) was launched by the European Foundation for Quality Management (EFQM) in conjunction with the European Commission in 1991. The EFQM is committed to promoting quality as a fundamental process for continuous improvement within organizations. The growing importance of quality in competitiveness within the European Union has brought about the idea to launch the award. The EQA model has two main parts with a total of nine criteria. The enablers consist of *leadership, people management, policy and strategy, resources,* and *processes.* The results include *people satisfaction, customer satisfaction, impact on society,* and *business results.* The level of customer satisfaction has the highest percentage (20%) within the whole model. The percentage weights are used to compare a company's scoring profile with the best in Europe. The award is given to the organization making a significant contribution with its approach to TQM by satisfying the expectations of consumers, employees and those of others who are interested in the organization.

In addition to criteria that are similar to those in the U.S.-based Baldrige Award, such as leadership, people management, policy and strategy, resources, processes and consumer satisfaction, three additional criteria, namely, people satisfaction, impact on society and business results, have been introduced in the EQA. The main difference between the Baldrige Award and the EQA is that the former follows a consumer-driven quality approach, whereas the latter takes the view that not only the consumer but also community and employees largely contribute to the definition of quality. In its present form, the EQA is suitable to be extended to include quality measurement of tourist destinations.

As in all other quality awards, organizations have a great opportunity to gain benefits of the EQA and its indicators launched in the public domain. This opportunity can be extended to include an organization's efforts to gain the award. Within the time period of preparing itself to apply for the award, the organization will have to review its overall performance, attempt to develop new techniques, look at others and, most notably, follow guidelines and consider what the organization requires itself to do for reaching the standards of the award. In addition, the criteria of the EQA model are used to benchmark organizations. For instance, Tang and Zairi (1998) used the enabler criteria of the model to benchmark education and financial sectors on the basis of leadership, policy and strategy, people management, resource management and process management.

In its present form, the EFQM is suitable to be extended to include quality measurement of tourist destinations and its improvement because a trip is not a single product and what a destination delivers is a mixture of various components (see Figure 5.1). Murphy (1997, p. 3) states that "many tourism businesses believe that they need to sell their destination before they can sell their individual offerings. This can be achieved by increasing the competitive advantage of the whole product mix, so that individual businesses may benefit from the increased profile and trade". In order for the management of tourist destinations to give a distinctive appeal to destination attributes of leisure activities, sports, food, welcoming tourists and natural and cultural heritage, this chapter is based on an overview of the following measures that seem to play a key role in the success of destination-based quality management practices (for details see Go and Govers 2000; Kozak 2004a, 2004b; Ozdemir and Kozak 2009): leadership, policy and strategy, people management, resources, processes, customer satisfaction, people satisfaction, impact on society and benefits for the destination performance (Table 5.1).

Leadership

Leadership, the first step, relates to the direction and behavior of destination management team to implement the programs to achieve the strategic objectives. It also oversees the implementation of a destination-based TQM program providing a strong collaboration and co-operation between local units, and units of other resorts and national institutions within a country. The TQM program would be the major responsibility of the destination management or the official DMO, which could be led by a 'destination manager' (Kozak 2000; Pikkemaat and Weiermair 2007). The management will be in charge of planning, organizing, leading or motivating staff, and controlling standards and information. The responsibility of management would include creating a vision for businesses, training its employees and educating local residents, planning promotion and advertising and conducting market research to gauge the level of customer satisfaction.

Policy and Strategy

As the second step, *policy and strategy* focuses on identifying the most appropriate venues as to how the destination management team formulates, reviews and implements their unique policies and strategies in tourism. All public and private businesses and organizations are responsible for maintaining a certain level of both physical and service quality within the tourist area. In order to achieve this broad objective, they are expected to consult with other stakeholders and be collaborative. As a direct outcome

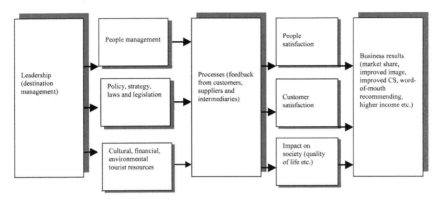

Figure 5.1   Application of EFQM model for destintations.
Source: Kozak, *Destination Benchmarking: Concepts, Practices and Operations,* Oxon: cabil, 2004. 0. 125. Reprinted by permission of CABI International.

of articulating a TQM-based destination management approach, and to make certain that the relevant aspects of a destination conform to both national and international standards in eco-label and service quality systems (Kozak and Nield 2004), It is also critical to make sure that developments in tourism do not bring any potential danger for other local or national institutions (e.g. agriculture, handcrafts, fishing and so on). This stage also consists of developing a sustainable tourism plan, respecting the cultural and natural environment and maintaining their sustainability.

People Management

This is the next step focusing on finding the most appropriate answers as to how the employees are managed to become productive and effective and how the local residents are involved. Given the characteristics of services, tourists have many interactions with employees and residents during their vacation. Thus, the level of satisfaction of employees and residents may directly influence the level of customer satisfaction with their services. Some of their contacts even take place in the host country, but particularly those in the destination country will be the major elements to shape their experience. This brings a number of relationships to exist between tourists and service providers, between tourists and the local people, among tourists, among service providers and so on.

Resources

This step focuses on finding the most appropriate answers as to how the destination management team is able to direct and supervise their existing

Table 5.1 An Expanded Version of EFQM-Based TQM

Criteria	Details
Enablers	
Leadership	The behavior of destination management team to accomplish its objectives.
Policy & strategy	The most appropriate answers as to how the destination management team formulates, reviews and implements their unique policies and strategies in tourism.
People management	The most appropriate answers as to how the employees and the local residents are managed to become productive and effective.
Resources	The most appropriate answers as to how the destination management team is able to manage their existing economic and human resources in an effective and efficient way.
Processes	The most appropriate answers as to how the destination management team identifies, manages and improves its processes.
Customer satisfaction	The most appropriate solutions as to what method is used to make customers satisfied with their present vacations and loyal to the destination in the future
Results	
People satisfaction	The most appropriate solutions as to what method is used to make both the employees and local residents satisfied with their visitors as well as with what they are doing and hospitable toward visitors.
Impact on society	The direct or indirect positive/negative impacts of what the destination management team tries to achieve in their tourism-based policies and strategies (impacts on society in terms of economic and social structure and natural environment).
Business results	What the local tourism industry has gained as a result of the practical application of policies and strategies through the use of benchmarking process (changes in the number of visitors, in the amount of tourism incomes, in the level of multiplier effect and in the proportion of income over GNP).

Source: Kozak (2004a, 2004b).

economic and human resources effectively and efficiently. These resources include the combination of both primary and secondary assets that are considered to be a potential for tourism development within the area. Leading to a success at the end of the way requires a strong co-operation and co-ordination among all elements of the destination, including all public- and private-sector bodies. The management of such resources assists all parties who are directly or indirectly related with the tourism industry to inventory their tourism assets, evaluate their potential use or benefits in tourism services and set goals and priorities for the development of tourism at the local level.

Due to the sensitive structure of cultural heritage, if it is gone, there is no way to return to its original setting. Just for protecting this cultural heritage, the political instruments have had to take several political and legal actions in many countries (e.g. the Ministry of Environment and Heritage in Australia, the Ministry of Culture and Tourism in Turkey etc.). In addition, some further actions have been taken at a broader scale. For example, various macro organizations have been established to take more active roles at the international arena by forcing local and national authorities to give utmost consideration to protecting their cultural heritage (e.g. the Council on Monuments and Sites [ICOMOS], UNESCO and so on). At the country level, similar types of agencies have been developed at the local or national level to control both the locals and the responsible authorities in terms of their ability to comply with the laws and regulations in this respect (e.g. the Council for Protection of Natural and Cultural Heritage in Turkey, the Directorate for Cultural Heritage in Norway). Such micro organizations are responsible for developing strategies and policies within the entire field of cultural heritage.

Box 5.2   Allocating Resources for Protecting Cultural Heritage.
Source: Kozak (2007a).

Processes

Being a bridge between inputs and outputs, *processes* focus on finding the most appropriate answers as to how the destination management team identifies, manages and improves its processes. Feedback to be gained through information collected from customers, employees, tourist organizations and local residents can be useful in reaching positive outcomes and delivering the right mix of components to meet the needs of the tourism and travel industry. For example, asking customers to list any problems they had or any improvement they could suggest might be a method of measuring customer satisfaction and could also provide valuable information about what needs to be changed or improved (Kotler 1994). In other words, it helps to have a list of *dos* and *don'ts* from the perspective of actual customers' comments or their observations while on a holiday in a destination.

Customer Satisfaction

As the last step of enablers, *customer satisfaction* focuses on discovering the most appropriate solutions as to what method is used to make customers satisfied with their destination experience and show loyalty to the destination in the future (Kozak and Rimmington 1999; Kozak 2004a, 2004b).

Thus, one should conduct regular surveys obtaining feedback from tourists about their perceptions of the destination quality and perceptions. A dissatisfied tourist is a threat to the destination's success in the future, whereas a satisfied tourist is a marketing officer promoting the destination at no cost. It should be noted that a destination usually targets multiple segments (e.g. relaxation, excitement, young people, elderly, low-income level etc.), and the destination should have the critical offerings and capacity to meet the needs and expectations of each group. As Peter Drucker points out, the quality in a product or service is not what the supplier puts in, it is what the customer gets out and is willing to pay for (Go 1998). This emphasizes the importance of how customers perceive the destination in terms of meeting their needs and expectations.

People Satisfaction

As the first step of results, *people satisfaction* focuses on discovering the most appropriate solutions as to how the employees and local residents are satisfied with the type of visitors and with what they are doing to be more friendly and hospitable toward visitors. One should organize training and education programs for both local people and employees. This is essential to ensure that both local residents (hosts welcoming tourists) and tourists (guests) are well aware of the cultural differences between each other (Reisinger and Turner 2002). The local people are expected to be hospitable and helpful, discouraging people from bothering tourists with hassle. Education programs can be conducted for local residents and those working in tourism to inform them about all aspects of tourism, how to preserve the local identity and heritage and how to behave toward foreign tourists (Kozak 2007b). An information packet can be prepared for tourists to inform them about local laws, regulations, traditions, ecology and natural and social environments. Representatives of the local community may also be invited to take part in destination management because they are affected by both positive and negative consequences of tourism development within the area.

Impact on Society

As an overall output, *impact on society* focuses on investigating the direct or indirect impacts of what the destination management team attempts to accomplish in their tourism-based policies and strategies (economic, social and environmental impacts on the society). Tourism development may affect the local people's quality of life by increasing problems such as air pollution, traffic congestion, over-commercialization and prostitution (Gunn 1997). As a result, the practice of D-TQM and its implementation in practice is important not only to tourists but also to the local community. The European Business Excellence Model, for example, considers 'the impact on society' (local community) as the eighth criterion for achieving quality and protection standards. In the tourism destination context, this criterion requires measuring and assessing the impact of tourism development on environmental and cultural resources. This includes such elements as natural resources, energy, safety and cultural heritage. As environmental consumption continually happens, the management must also be continuous so that future generations inherit an unspoilt natural environment and protected cultural heritage.

Benefits for Destination Performance (Business Results)

Also called "business results", *benefits for destination performance* refers to what the local tourism industry has gained after the implications of policies and strategies implementation through the use of a destination-based TQM process (changes in the number of visitors, in the amount of tourism incomes, in the level of multiplier effect and in the proportion of income over GNP). If customers are satisfied with a product, it is expected that they will be more likely to continue to purchase it and tell their friends and relatives of their favorable experiences with it. A seemingly obvious inference is that these ideas apply to tourism (Kozak and Rimmington 2000; Huan, Beaman and Kozak 2003). Baloglu, Pekcan, Chen and Santos (2004) investigate the relationship among attribute-based destination performance, overall satisfaction and behavioral intention (return intention and recommendation) for Canadian visitors to Las Vegas. The findings indicated that satisfaction is positively related to behavioral intent measures, such as recommendation (positive word of mouth) and return intention, and that the overall satisfaction is an intervening variable between attribute-based destination performance and behavioral intention for destinations.

Improvements in qualitative measures are sometimes expected to stimulate developments in quantitative measures as outcomes. As previously confirmed (Kozak 2004a), there may be a close relationship between various qualitative (e.g. tourist satisfaction) and quantitative measures (e.g. tourist spending). When tourists are satisfied, they tend to spend more, recommend their holidays or want to return. This probably increases the number of tourists in the following years and may also increase the total income from tourism.

5.3. PRACTICAL IMPLICATIONS FOR DESTINATION MANAGEMENT

As in every organization and industry, destination management authorities need to establish an effective mission statement which is feasible, motivating, distinctive and achievable and conforms to the general aims of management. Different destinations have different objectives and expectations from the tourism industry. Some destinations tend to offer a variety of tourist facilities and activities and be a year-round destination which attracts top-class customer groups, whereas some others only want to offer seasonal facilities and services for middle- or low-class customer groups. All such objectives will be related to destination management because they will influence the extent to which authorities are ambitious in the international market. There could be different marketing mix concepts for different market segments relating to tourist destinations because customers may have different personalities, needs and desires. Hence, for example, destinations can focus only on specific tourism products to approach the specific segments of the tourism market.

One should bear in mind that taking action is a significant stage in order to set goals for improvement and develop action plans. In this stage, the results can be reported to the people it affects or to whom it concerns (e.g. local authorities, airport management, tourism and travel businesses and associations and local residents). A new breed of tourists wants to spend vacations in unspoiled places and expects intermediaries to recommend the most appropriate destinations. As a result, intermediaries require tourism suppliers to pay attention to the preservation of the natural and cultural resources they supply and benefit from. If organizations or businesses within the destination fail to reach expected standards, customers may be advised to avoid this place to visit. As a final stage, tourism suppliers and destination authorities should provide several guidelines about how they expect customers (users) to behave and how to use resources without damaging the environment (e.g. keeping beaches and streets clean, keeping equipment at hotels safely and saving energy and water). Perhaps what is most important is that visitors should be strongly encouraged to be consistent with such guidelines.

As a result of the contribution of tourism services to the welfare of the local economy, local inhabitants should not be excluded from decision-making processes involving developments in their region. Hence, representatives of the local community could be another group to take part in a proposed destination-based TQM practice while taking action for improvement due to a high level of cross-cultural interaction and communication in tourism between hosts and guests (e.g. actual behavior toward tourists). They are the people whose quality of life is influenced by the consequences of tourism development within the area (e.g. air pollution, traffic congestion and over-commercialization) (Gunn 1997). As far as mass tourism is concerned, tour operators or their local representatives should also take part in such co-operative and collaborative work (Buhalis and Fletcher 1995). Some evidence can be seen in the tourism development of Mallorca where financial contribution and guidelines are provided by such foreign tour operators as TUI and Thomson.

5.4. LIMITATIONS OF D-TQM PRACTICES

Despite the fact that a destination-based TQM practice provides a number of benefits for both domestic and international tourism flows, some important issues need to be taken into consideration for a careful assessment of

Depending upon the Butler's model of destination life cycle, one can speculate that some resorts in Mallorca are now experiencing consolidation and stagnation stages at the same time. Such witnesses as the high number of visitors and the low level of tourism receipts, cultural and natural degradation indicate that Mallorca, as an island tourist destination, is in the mature stage of its life cycle and needs to refresh its appeal and re-establish its market position to avoid the possibility of decline. In response, as a part of long-term planning, the local authority has decided to revitalize the image of Mallorca, extend tourism to other seasons and attract 'niche market' customers including those travelling for conference and business reasons and sports such as walking, cycling, golf and yachting. In this respect, legislation has been introduced to tighten building controls and protect from further development. Investment in the product and tourist infrastructure is being made. The new Palma airport is an example of this. Old hotels and tourist facilities are destroyed, especially in Magaluf and Palma Nova, to create new places for gardens, landscaping and new resort facilities. Individual establishments are being provided grants to improve the quality of their signposting and presentation. More spaces are provided for cycle routes and pedestrianized areas. The local government empowerment and the collective action and partnership between local interest groups in Mallorca have been the major factor behind the success of the resort revitalization.

Box 5.3   Revitalization of Tourism in Mallorca Source: Kozak (2002c).

its application. For example, differences could be observed among different international destinations in respect of the organizational structure of their governments. As Keller and Smeral (1997) emphasize, keeping bureaucratic barriers to a minimum could improve tourist services and quality which would lead to enhancing competitiveness in the international arena. The former model may create bureaucratic problems and delays in making efficient decisions because the central government deals with everything in the country.

Political unrest may sometimes make it worse. In the latter model, local institutions are given the responsibility of regulating tourism businesses and activities, inspecting and supervising them and developing their own promotion campaigns, locally and abroad, in order to renovate and revitalize the attractiveness of the destination. Briefly, such differences are another piece of evidence indicating that cross-cultural differences in managerial practices could hinder the successful implementation of TQM-based research findings to be easily accomplished by a different political system. For example, there might exist several political factors that make the operationalization of destination-based TQM practice slow (e.g. passport, visa and custom control at the airport in a country).

Looking at the barrier in its practical application, the stage of taking action is possibly one of the most difficult parts of the decision-making process, as local authorities, tourism organizations and businesses may not intend to implement findings or make long-term decisions. This may be due to a lack of human or financial resources and the sensitivity of the tourism industry to economic, political and social changes. The establishment of action plans may also be influenced by cross-cultural differences in managerial practices, beliefs and values between peer destinations. It must also be stressed that achieving sustainable forms of tourism is not only the responsibility of stakeholders involved, governments at all levels, representatives of the private industry and local community in tourism destination countries, but it is also the responsibility of international organizations, environmental groups, tour operators, travel agents and potential tourists in the tourist-generating countries. However, it is the responsibility of the destination and of those who are involved in management to enhance competitiveness.

5.5. SUMMARY

As a result of this brief introduction on the significance of quality management in the success of improving the performance of tourist destinations, this chapter aims to design a model of TQM particularly applicable for tourist destinations and indicate the ways in which the model would work. This chapter is also based on the analysis of the several practical recommendations that seem to play a key role in the success of quality management in tourist destinations. The fact is that TQM is a commitment to the continuous improvement of customer satisfaction. Thus, an effective application of a destination-wide TQM practice requires a number of prerequisites to exist in practice.

*   *   *

CASE STUDY: 2005 UNIVERSIADE SUMMER GAMES AS AN EXAMPLE FOR D-TQM

Events often are seen as tools to promote economic activities and are regarded in a positive light (Dwyer, Forysth and Spurr 2006). Special events in fact have proved to be one way to achieve visibility and to build a reputation (Ritchie and Crouch 2003). Dickinson, Jones, and Leask (2007) explain the reason for adding events to attraction portfolio of destinations as to differentiate and compete in an increasingly competitive marketplace.

This case study introduces the 2005 Universiade Summer Games held in Izmir and assesses it from various perspectives in the context of destination marketing with a link to event and network management. The Universiade is an international multi-sport event, organized for university athletes by the International University Sports Federation (FISU). The assessment is based on the EFQM framework, from leadership to benefits and business results, and developed based on face to face interviews and a telephone conversation with people directly involved in organizing and promoting the event.

Leadership: Ministry of Foreign Affairs, Ministry of Youth and Sports and Izmir Municipality jointly declared the candidacy of Izmir in 2003, but it was accepted for the 23rd Summer University Games in 2005. The Summer Olympic Games was held with the co-operation of the Izmir Municipality, the Special Provincial Administration and the Ministry of Youth and Sports. About 9,000 people played some roles in the organization under the guidance of one general coordinator and three assistant coordinators, including a company from Istanbul that was designated as the sports consultant.

People Management: Three coordinators were responsibile for managing the voluntary and non-voluntary labor force people (a total estimate of 9,000) before, during and after the games. Commissions and subcommittees were formed for major areas such as safety and security, health and food and beverage. Coordination among the commissions was also necessary because of the overlap of responsibilities among the commissions. For example, the commission in charge of health was responsible for check-ups of both the sports people and workers, supplying food and beverage in hygienic standards and also drug controls of the sports people. The food commission is responsible for supplying food, beverage and lunch box for sports people accommodating in the village, workers, security officers and volunteers.

Resources: The resources were provided locally and statewide. Funding came from several sources such as the Municipality of Izmir, state institutions, civil initiatives and sports organizations. Many companies sponsored the event in different ways. Tansas Supermarket, as the main sponsor, supported the event in cash, whereas Adidas, for instance, provided the outfits of workers. THY (Turkish Airlines) organized direct flights to Izmir and provided free tickets as a sponsor company. The Foreign Affairs Department made it easier to obtain visas. Tickets were sold by Biletix (the largest seller of event tickets in Turkey), and the opening and closing gala of the games were watched by thousands of city people. At the end, all sports equipment and supplies were given to the sports federation for later use.

Processes: Several commissions were formed for a smooth operation and processes. They include accreditation, transportation, housekeeping, media and information technology (IT). The Village administration commission was responsible for the social activities and accommodation part of the facility with 10,000 beds for 15 days. The Games Village was considered to be a hotel to serve for 15 days only and was designed a year ahead.

Impact on Society: An event experience offers an opportunity for leisure, social or cultural experiences and builds destination brands. Given the size of the Summer Universiade in terms of the number of participating delegates and sports branches, the sports venues included not only Izmir but also other provinces such as Manisa and Aydın. Investments were made to improve infrastructure and superstructure. With the new facilities, Izmir hosts numerous sports activities and fairs and encourages the residents to participate in various sports activities.

Business Results & Feedback: The feedback from the sports teams and attendees were very positive. The Universiade helped to promote Izmir, and athletes and teams from 123 countries carried this back to their countries with positive word of mouth. The event was covered very positively in a significant number of broadcast and print media. About 255 journalists and writers mentioned the Universiade in their articles. The complete event, attended by 131 countries, was broadcasted live on TRT and partly on Eurosport, thereby promoting Izmir and Turkey in terms of successful organizations.

Hosting the Universiade as a mega-event has brought some economic and social benefits onto the businesses operating and people residing in Izmir as well as nearby provinces. The importance and impact of collaborative network management to involve relevant private and public sectors, and local, national or international organizations are highly visible while hosting globally prestigious events. A successful event is more likely if the EFQM is applied to the organization of the events.

Source: Ozdemir and Kozak (2009).

6 Destination Benchmarking

Although some literature is available concerning the relevance of several benchmarking models to the tourism and hospitality industry (see Kozak 2004a and references therein), it is limited with respect to their relevance to finding a proper answer to the question of how destinations' performance can be improved through the measurement of customer satisfaction. Moreover, one may see that past published academic works have paid little attention to building linkages between destination benchmarking and customer satisfaction and their relevance to tourism practitioners. Meanwhile, with their assumptions to make a comparison among multiple units or organizations, the majority fails to meet the basic conditions of a proper benchmarking investigation. Therefore, it is the intention of this chapter to focus upon expanding the field of this relationship while making the benchmarking concept more worth being considered in the future's conceptual and empirical studies and also keeping the attention of the related bodies (e.g. tourism authorities, practitioners etc.).

6.1. WHAT IS DESTINATION BENCHMARKING?

As in other forms of benchmarking studies (i.e. organization benchmarking, industry benchmarking), the term "destination benchmarking" also pays attention primarily to the continuous measurement and improvement of all services and facilities contributing to the visitors' cumulative experiences in a destination (Kozak 2004a). From the theoretical point of view, destination benchmarking has no distinction from other forms of benchmarking, whereas undertaking destination benchmarking studies is relatively more comprehensive and takes more time than organizational benchmarking studies. That is, to some extent, a plethora of internal (destination-based) and external factors impact the total performance of tourist destinations and, in some cases, also include operations of organization benchmarking studies (e.g. hotels, restaurants, leisure and recreation facilities and itinerary facilities). From the practical standpoint, it might be easier to control such factors influencing the satisfaction level of a user or visitor; but in a destination, those factors can hardly be related to a specific organization and not controlled by a single authority. Rather, this needs a general authority (e.g. DMOs) where various responsibilities are integrated to gain more power.

The value of destination benchmarking stems from the idea that the tourist experience is shaped through the provision of facilities and services on vacations, and the outcome of this ultimate experience forms the center of how destinations are likely to compete with each other (Kozak 2002a; Kozak and Rimmington 1998). Tourists, as temporary visitors, have no rights to vote the future of destinations or their citizens, but they are seemingly keener to vote by choosing better value destinations. In other words, the destination choice process heavily relies on the decision of tourists as either alternative-seekers or attribute-seekers (see Um and Crompton 1991; Moutinho 1987; Woodside and Lysonski 1989). This proposition refers to the two important points: (1) Destination choice process entails a number of alternatives in which tourists may switch from one to another in the same set, and (2) tourists know how to search for better offers and what to expect from their experiences with vacations. In such a case, what tourism practitioners, on the supply side, bear in mind is to search for better options to provide better values to meet their customers' expectations and keep this progress continuous by attracting new clients if not successful to keep the current ones.

In summary, a short answer as to why benchmarking is relevant for tourist destinations includes the careful assessment of the trend of intense competition among destinations, not only as countries but also as regions. Tourists, from one day to another, have become more experienced and knowledgeable about the world and changes in their demand for consumption of products and services available in the international market. This results in a sensitive structure of tourists to even a very little negative experience during a vacation. Thus, the fake positioning of a small piece (e.g. let's say food poisoning or charging higher prices in this case) may distort the overall picture of the puzzle (e.g. quality of the whole vacation experience). Last but not the least, as a structure of human personality, customers compare not only themselves with others, but also make comparisons among their preferences and among various alternatives. A final decision is set as a consequence of the output derived from this decision-making process (Payne, Bettman and Johnson 1997; Shafir, Simonson and Tversky 1997). Knowing about the performance of other destinations becomes important to take place in customers' final consideration sets.

6.2. RATIONALE FOR DESTINATION BENCHMARKING

As a performance management and improvement tool, it is generally accepted that benchmarking basically stems from Deming's quality management theory that aims to enhance quality and ensure its sustainability elsewhere it is applied (Kozak 2002b). Despite this, benchmarking has been defined in different ways by different organizations and authors within the period of last few decades although each aims to reach the goal of improved performance of a production and consumption unit, in this case a tourist facility or a destination (see Kozak 2002b and references therein). The Webster Dictionary defines a benchmark as 'a standard by which something can be measured or judged' (Camp 1989, p. 248). Regardless of how large this number is, it is possible to see so many examples of benchmarking definitions in the literature. What is especially significant in these definitions is that benchmarking studies are seen as a continuous process, not a one-time or temporary effort. As a result, those organization authorities who never believe the relevance of continuous measurement and improvement of performance are not advised to carefully consider getting involved in a benchmarking action and are advised to spend no time planning fake benchmarking studies.

The literature entails several forms of benchmarking carried out in the context of measuring customer satisfaction as an output of performance improvement. Of these, taking the hospital food service as a case study, Williams (1997) attempted to investigate how performance was improved through the analysis of patient satisfaction as a qualitative measure. This is a relevant example of both internal benchmarking (learning from itself) and external benchmarking (learning from others). Edgett and Snow (1996) performed an empirical study to assess the performance of the financial services industry. A number of qualitative and quantitative measures were utilized with regard to the assessment of customer satisfaction (e.g. increase in the number of customers, customer complaints and market share), product quality (e.g. increase in sales and income, reduction in costs) and product success (e.g. total sales, profitability). The recent study by Grigorous and Siskos (2004) is another piece of evidence in which benchmarking was applied for the purpose of maintaining continuous improvement through customer satisfaction. Contextually different, this study is designed to develop and install a national customer satisfaction barometer for the transportation-communication industry. The study ends with an emphasis on the fact that the estimated indices may provide a baseline against which future performance can be compared and it will be possible to track customer satisfaction over time.

Still, there have been far more conceptual papers on why benchmarking is important and how to operationalize it than empirical research focusing on methodological issues such as how to measure performance gaps. An overwhelming majority of researchers preferred establishing an empirical study based upon the supply side but avoiding the demand side (e.g. Warnken, Bradley and Guilding 2005). As a consequence of this, with minor exceptions (e.g. Kozak 2002b, 2004a; Fuchs and Weiermair 2004; Matzler and Pechlaner 2001; Vrtiprah 2001), little research has been undertaken on the empirical assessment of customer satisfaction as a qualitative measure of performance assessment and improvement in the tourism industry. The focus of these studies is how benchmarking can be used to improve service quality and customer satisfaction in a continuous and systematic way. Regardless of the type of industry or the nature of production or consumption, customers can expect organizations to have the responsibility of providing what they want and doing anything to better deal with their potential complaints relating to consumption experiences. This comes from the proposition that customers have psychologically future expectations and thus reflected to their lifetime ambitions to keep their lifecycle longer. This may also be the same in the case of organizations which need to keep their operations and lifecycles longer in their business.

Taking this as a departure point, it is possible to see that connections prevail between benchmarking and customer satisfaction. Although some literature is available concerning the relevance of several benchmarking models to the tourism and hospitality industry (see Kozak 2004a and references therein), it is limited with respect to their relevance to finding a proper answer to the question of how destinations' performance can be improved through the measurement of customer satisfaction. Moreover, one may see that past published academic works have paid little attention to building linkages between destination benchmarking and customer satisfaction and their relevance to tourism practitioners. Meanwhile, with their assumptions to make a comparison among multiple units or organizations, the majority fails to meet the basic conditions of a proper benchmarking investigation.

6.3. TYPES OF DESTINATION BENCHMARKING

Although the literature refers to the categorization of benchmarking under various titles, three main types can be listed: internal, external and generic. The literature suggests that organizations should first begin with internal benchmarking followed by external and generic benchmarking (McNair and Leibfried 1992; Zairi 1992; Kozak 2004a). Thus, they attempt to measure their own performance by collecting data on qualitative or quantitative measures. As Figure 6.1 demonstrates, there is a close relationship among all three types of benchmarking (Kozak 2004a). Internal benchmarking provides an introductory stage to undertaking external and generic benchmarking research. Self-generated data derived at this stage may be supplied to either the partner destination(s) or international organizations such as EFQM, WTO or WTTC to be used for exchange. The data produced may

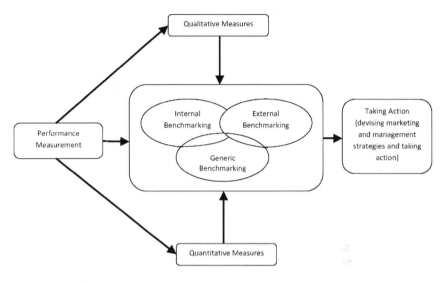

Figure 6.1 Elements of destination benchmarking.

then be redistributed or circulated to those who are interested. Because one objective of benchmarking is to search for the best practices and processes which come up with those results, generic benchmarking is supposed to give the destination an objective standard to aim at when internationally recognized best practice awards or classification systems are used as 'good practices' for improvement. This is obviously regarded as a part of external benchmarking.

Internal Benchmarking

This approach requires the benchmarking of each destination on an individual basis. In this approach, various methods can be used to evaluate the potential changes in a destination's current performance. First, the highest and the lowest scores for each qualitative measure are identified. Attributes with the lowest scores need improvement. These scores may not practically be applicable for comparison with those in past years due to a possible lack of data. Second, repeat tourists could be chosen as the sample in order to learn how the destination has changed compared with their previous visits and in what respects. Next, data on quantitative measures can be assessed to examine changes over the years. Annual reports may help to understand how the destination performs compared with its previous performance. The findings should indicate where the destination has problems and whether this can be eliminated using internal resources rather than external ones.

External Benchmarking

When external benchmarking is used, it is impossible to speculate on which attributes need to be taken into consideration for improvement until the comparison activity is completed and its results are fully presented. The reason is that the host and partner might both be performing well on attribute X. A negative gap on the part of the host will help to identify what to investigate further. In line with this, a model of external destination benchmarking with its main stages is suggested. It includes choosing a partner destination, collecting data, examining gaps and taking action (see Figure 6.2). Reflection on the literature review suggests that any kind of benchmarking begins by measuring one's own performance in order to specify areas which need to be benchmarked (Karlof and Ostblom 1993; Zairi 1992), with each destination needing to put into order their own priorities. It is proposed that both internal and external benchmarking help to identify these priorities.

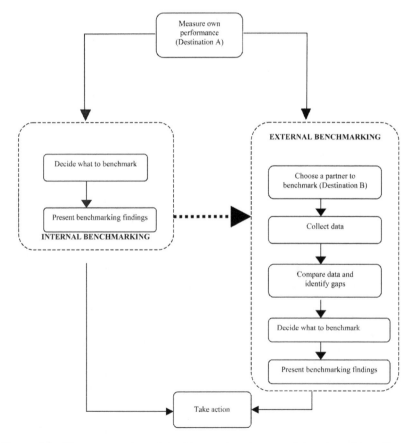

Figure 6.2 The proposed model of internal and external benchmarking. Source: Kozak (2004a).

Generic Benchmarking

Kozak (2004a) suggests that the common relationship between quality or eco-label systems and benchmarking is that the former is used as an example of the best practice benchmarking toward achieving continuous improvement of environmental quality. Therefore, this type of benchmarking introduces existing or proposed quality grading and eco-label systems as a form of generic benchmarking by trying to find an appropriate response as to how benchmarking, linked to external awards and grades, can offer advantages and bring about improvements in competitiveness for destinations. Although the typical benchmarking approach requires a partner to carry out the study, within the application of generic benchmarking, tourist destinations could look at either other destinations or international guidelines or standards in order to find effective solutions for their particular problems by having access to best practices recognized nationally or internationally. In so doing, destinations and their primary elements such as hotels, restaurants and beaches might identify ways of improving the environmental and service quality of their facilities.

Observations indicate that, in addition to academic-driven studies referenced above, there is also a growing amount of interest on destination

---

The Guildford Tourism Strategy Action plan can be given as an example of these recent developments in destination benchmarking. This plan proposed that a destination benchmarking survey be carried out every three years. Accordingly, the first was undertaken in 2000 and the second in 2003. More than 400 visitors coming to the town were approached for interview to investigate their reasons for visiting, origins and perceptions of the town as a destination. Findings are compared to those collected three years ago, which can be accepted as a kind of internal benchmarking. In terms of the quality of visitor experience, overall perceptions are generally positive and a high level of satisfaction appears to be present on various indicators. The town is also benchmarked against other historic towns where the same survey is carried out. From this comparison, it is seen that the average expenditure of visitors to Guildford is higher than that for the other destinations under investigation as partners. As one may expect to see in a purely visible benchmarking research report, the tourist board has made its decision to use these findings to carry further on their perceived strengths while developing ways to address perceived weaknesses. This can be considered as a good example of external benchmarking.

Box 6.1   An Example of External Destination Benchmarking.

benchmarking particularly from the regional tourist boards in the last few years, particularly commencing from the early 2000s (see Box 6.1). We also see that the industry organizations or the local tourist authorities try to do their best to comply with the standards or guidelines of a perfect benchmarking study. Of these, Lennon, Smith, Cockerell and Trew (2006) published a book by taking into consideration the concept of destination benchmarking from the perspective of NTOs. This study is a good example of destination-oriented organization benchmarking research as it provides the key lessons learned through benchmarking. NTOs provide crucial evidence for establishing the basic structure of how NTOs approach e-media, partnerships, office rationalisation and emerging markets, team management and communication, branding, and MICE tourism. On the other hand, it neglects nominating partners and taking actions and the evaluation of best practices as the fundamental feature of a benchmarking study.

Second, in a similar but much broader subject of destination benchmarking, tourist authorities in the South-west part of England have recently begun developing their own benchmarking scheme by gaining more interests from other partners. The need to measure and compare the performance of destinations, in order to encourage continuous improvement to best practice standards, has been the motivating force behind the South West Tourism's destination benchmarking program. In 2004, the seventh year of the national scheme was celebrated, in which 105 destinations participated, providing a broad basis for comparison across all destinations. The benchmarking service, which measures and compares visitors' opinions gathered through face-to-face interviews, is available for historic towns, seaside resorts, large towns, cities and market towns. Having a database of more than 100 destinations can be regarded as a very productive way of improving one's own performance by looking at others and making multiple comparisons with any destination they may choose as a potential partner. This example is also worthy of discussion to figure out how a basic benchmarking investigation should be carried out.

6.4. MEASURES OF DESTINATION BENCHMARKING

The issue of benchmarking has gained considerable momentum to become a focal point of tourism research in the last decade. One may observe that previous research was essentially oriented toward emphasizing the importance of benchmarking and its practical application for both tourism organizations and destinations (e.g. Min and Min 1997; Leslie 2001; Matzler and Pechlaner 2001; Vrtiprah 2001; Wober 2002). Despite the growing amount of published research, both academic and practice driven, in this field, practical studies designed to particularly develop tourism-based measures are yet to be well established, which should be the first stage of any benchmarking study. Developing and using measures helps to identify the current performance and monitor the direction of changes over a period. Measures identified during the planning stage of benchmarking may also help to determine the magnitude of the performance gaps and select what is to be benchmarked (Vaziri 1992; Karlof and Ostblom 1993). It is also possible to shape up future strategies depending upon the measures and their findings obtained in a benchmarking project.

Thus, it is crucial to introduce several performance measures and discuss their rationale in destination benchmarking (Kozak 2004a). An overview of the related literature clearly demonstrates that both researchers and practitioners tended to use both qualitative (textual) and quantitative (metric) measures usually by collecting data via questionnaire surveys, secondary sources and observations (Kozak and Nield 2001). Qualitative measures of performance are superior in revealing insights about destination performance in developing long-term value. However, as already illustrated in Figure 6.3, alone, qualitative measures are not enough; rather, they are expected to contribute to expanding zones of output measures (e.g. gaining higher income). As such, quantitative measures seem to be more objective and more process-oriented, but relatively easier than qualitative measures to be used in any kind of performance measurement studies. Success in such measures is expected to gain success in qualitative measures.

Qualitative measures are considered as the degree of perceptual values assigned to each numerical value (e.g. number '1' means "not satisfied," whereas number '7' refers to the term "very satisfied") (Moser and Kalton 1971; Hair, Anderson, Tatham and Black 1995). The level of a customer's satisfaction is regarded as a part of qualitative measures (non-metric or non-quantitative) because it indicates only relative positions and perceptions in an ordered series (Kozak 2004a). Customer-oriented examples of

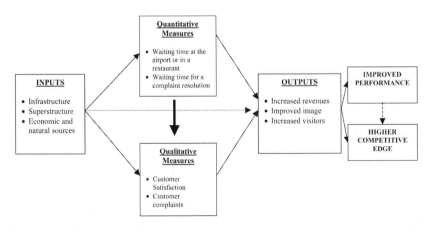

Figure 6.3 Roles of qualitative and quantitative measures in destination benchmarking. Source: Own elaboration.

qualitative measures involve "an increase in satisfaction among surveyed customers from 50 percent to 75 percent" or "a decrease in consumer complaints from 4.8 to 3.8". As a result, qualitative measures seem to be relatively subjective and more output-oriented, but important for drawing visible conclusions to develop both management and marketing strategies.

In quantitative measures, differences between two or more points are mathematically equal (or at the same distance) and refer to an absolute value (Hair et al., 1995). For instance, let us assume that a visitor pays US$40 for a single room, whereas another pays US$60 for a similar type of room in a different resort or country. In such a case, the difference is certainly US$20 under all circumstances around the globe. Both interval and ratio scales are examples of quantitative measures (Balm 1992). Quantitative measures can be extended to include some other measures relating to the level of tourist satisfaction (customer perspective) (e.g. the length of check-in and check-out at the destination airport and at accommodation facilities, time spent waiting for transport, the time waiting for food to be served in a restaurant or the time spent in waiting for a response about a complaint) (Kozak 2004a). An example of customer-oriented quantitative measure includes "a decrease in the waiting time for a passenger from 6 minutes to 5 minutes".

6.5. DESTINATION BENCHMARKING AND CUSTOMER SATISFACTION

A substantial body of research has emphasized the importance of identifying needs and wants of the potential demand as the first stage of consumer behavior, which may influence, to a great extent, the customer's decision-making behavior in subsequent stages—namely, information search, evaluation of alternatives, choice and post-consumption process (Howard and Sheth 1969; Engel and Blackwell 1982). Specifically, Camp (1989) notes that understanding and benchmarking outputs against the best in the industry reveals the elaboration of true consumer requirements. The best practice examples may not exist if not preferred by end users or consumers. In the tourism context, if the objective is to investigate strengths and weaknesses of one particular destination or differences between the two sample destinations, then it would become necessary to observe these attributes of destinations with lower or higher satisfaction levels to test if such differences really exist and identify root causes of outcomes.

The intangibility of tourist industry renders the assessment of product and service quality through customer feedback to be a vital component of effective management of tourism organizations and tourist destinations alike. During the last few years, measuring customer satisfaction has taken on a noticeable importance in academic marketing publications (e.g. Oliver 1980; Churchill and Surprenant 1982; Fornell 1992). But this interest is not exclusively academic-driven, as many companies have begun to appreciate customer satisfaction as a key variable for gaining a competitive edge. Monitoring tourist satisfaction can provide invaluable feedback for detecting problems that cause dissatisfaction with vacations and have a negative impact on future visitation (Cronin and Taylor 1992; Bloemer and Ruyter 1998; Baker and Crompton 2000; Kozak 2001b).

Like in individual organizations, there are also several ways of enhancing competitive advantage of tourist destinations. As the most significant tool, measuring the level of customer satisfaction either overall or with each specific attribute will show us how we are progressing and what we are doing in order for visitors to leave with positive experiences or memories at the end of their vacations. This proposition is sufficient to claim that how we are good enough could be a considerable criterion to become a target destination through the eyes of our potential visitors and also competing with our competitors working with similar patterns of tourism products and targeting similar types of market segments.

In a context of destination management and marketing, many elements have the potential to be an ingredient of benchmarking measures. Why a tourist visiting X is less satisfied with almost everything provided, whereas the other going to Y has more complaints about the bad quality of food, a dirty coast, insufficient beach facilities and so on. As indicated in Figure 6.3, all these observations may influence their intention to spend a certain amount of money during their vacations within the destination or their total satisfaction, and a great experience may contribute to maintaining a positive image of the destination elsewhere in the world or encouraging tourists to spend more because they think that they experience a nice vacation wherever they are visiting. Regardless of whether these are, to some extent, correct or false speculations, it does not matter. What does matter is a tourist experience interrelated with many attributes of a destination producing various elements can be disseminated as a valuable information as outputs (i.e. satisfaction, dissatisfaction, positive/negative image, coming or not coming back in the future, recommending this vacation to their neighbourhood or not, spending less or more).

Taking into consideration this increasing attention from the practitioners, like the previously developed national customer satisfaction barometers (Grigorous and Siskos 2004), a similar approach can be followed that refers to a group of destinations both internally and externally. Whereas the existing barometers were designed to measure the overall satisfaction level of citizens with different products, the proposed barometer might consider the inclusion of various destination attributes (e.g. level of prices, attitudes, services, transport, facilities, accommodation etc.). An average index can be calculated for the destination itself by processing the information available in the form of either metric or textual data. Such an approach constitutes the measurement of customer satisfaction on a regular basis to make comparisons against the baseline index which can be accepted as a standard value of a potential benchmarking investigation. This will provide useful information about consumer behavior (e.g. how they are satisfied, dissatisfied, how likely to visit, how much to spend) and carefully assess if there are any changes in such indicators both internally and externally (e.g. attributes where the level of satisfaction increases or decreases, to what extent tourist spending changes). This helps to identify priorities for improvement on each occasion and also to develop a uniform barometer which will be useful for those interested in performance measurement and improvement.

6.6. MOVING FROM BENCHMARKING THROUGH BENCH LEARNING

Because some commentators take the term "benchmarking" from an experience-based learning perspective, there is no doubt that this approach is right as long as problems appear with the apple-to-apple comparison studies (Karlof and Ostblom 1993). In other words, one may not find a prospective partner to work on in order to make reliable comparison by using any qualitative or quantitative measures of destination benchmarking. In such a case, rather than trying to make a "one-by-one" or "step-by-step" comparison, sharing experiences or making observations may also be the effective ways of reaching the conclusion by finding solutions or answers to those questions taking place in someone else's mind. In some cases, this proposition refers to a "bench-learning procedure". Some other commentators also suggest that benchmarking should be perceived as a process of adaptation, but not adoption (Watson 1993). From this perspective, it is not just a question of copying what exactly others are doing; the power in benchmarking comes from exchanging ideas, which is a learning process from others' both positive and negative experiences.

Through such a learning experience, organizations can benchmark their potential inputs such as human sources, economic and natural values and their abilities to come up with a better output. As long as these inputs are brought to the desired level to make customers satisfied at an acceptable level, which may then impact upon developing the margins of quantitative measures, these measures will then directly contribute to the overall performance of the destination, as outputs, by gaining increased revenues, visitor numbers and improved image. Even the local people will perceive the positive impacts of tourism development within the area; they may also want to help take both measures and procedures that need to be taken to move forward, in contrary to keeping their resistance forward. A benchmarking study being conducted via the process of developing qualitative measures indirectly contributes to the improved performance and gaining a higher competitive edge.

In the case of a relationship between benchmarking and customer satisfaction, the answer as to "why?" is expected to refer to the statement: "because a higher customer satisfaction is maintained by elaborating our own performance on the basis of either self experience-based learning or learning through looking at others". The response to "how?" may include: "how we can achieve a higher customer satisfaction or how others might have been successful in doing so?" or "what tools we need to consider about?" In the context of destination benchmarking, it is not worthy at all how many visitors one attracts to the destination per day or per year, if their contribution to the local economy is not at the desired level and even they hardly get what was promised to come up with a satisfactory experience at the end of their vacations. What happens in such a case is a good example of how an input-output analysis model does not work as it should do. There is no problem in terms of gaining more inputs, but the expected outputs for both the demand and supply sides is a big deal (e.g. gaining lower satisfaction for visitors or obtaining a smaller amount of money per visitor for a destination).

6.7. IMPLICATIONS FOR DESTINATION COMPETITIVENESS

This study has introduced various propositions for use in practice and has also emphasized the importance of customer satisfaction for performance measurement and improvement of destinations and the role

---

The LVCVA's international brand strategy program consists of sales, marketing, public relations and other promotional activities. The LVCVA has established three distinct market segments, providing more focus and flexibility to achieve the objectives. Major markets include Canada, Mexico and the UK, which collectively account for 70 percent of overall international visitation to Las Vegas. The branding strategy of Las Vegas is dominated by two major elements: movies and special events. Cities highly depend on events to build a strong brand as they would be more effective than advertising campaigns. Movies and events are memorable experiences and natural vehicles to create emotions or emotional attachment to the destinations. Other similar destinations that are likely to promote themselves in the case of event tourism may take the branding strategies of Las Vegas as a model to be applied into their own destinations. There would be some potential for these destinations to record improvement in their overall performance through learning about pros and cons of Las Vegas.

Box 6.2 Event Tourism and Branding: The Case of Las Vegas.

of benchmarking on it. Identifying the level of destination performance based on the feedback about the outcome is vital in order to provide a useful indication of its current position of tourism, demonstrate the extent to which it takes place in the international competitiveness set and determine how much improvement is required. As noted, benchmarking means neither making an "apple-to-apple comparison" or competitive analysis nor how exactly copying others. The main two questions in benchmarking are related to finding proper answers to such questions as "why are differences in performance observed?" and "how can a higher performance be obtained?" Rather than copying what others are doing, benchmarking could be considered "a learning process for drawing lessons from one organisation and translating them into the unique culture and mission orientation of a different organisation", as Watson (1993, p. 6) suggests. It is also called a "fast learning" process from external sources (Fuchs and Weiermair 2004). In addition, it is worth noting that benchmarking should be perceived as a tool not only for performance management and improvement but also for revising management and marketing strategies, if required.

Because benchmarking was first applied in the manufacturing industry in the late 1970s, it was often perceived to become a manufacturing-driven quality improvement tool. However, one may observe a growing interest in the service industry in the last decade. Therefore, what has been used so far is the assessment of production units or capacity per day or per year as quantitative measures. As already discussed above, these are metric values so that it is easy for anyone to compare themselves with other rivals in order to evaluate their current performance and estimate how they may be performing in the future. As a result, from the demand side, little attention has been paid to how the customer segments see the overall performance of organizations or the quality of each of their products or services. The practical implication here refers to the significance of customer feedback in conducting performance evaluation studies regardless of how much or how many one organization or destination produces or how better it performs than its rivals from this perspective.

In this respect, one should also pay careful consideration not to overlook the fact that the philosophy of benchmarking resembles that of the TQM approach. Both approaches have identical objectives (e.g. commitment to the continuous improvement and customer satisfaction) (Codling 1992; Zairi 1992, 1996). Both methods need close cooperation to support one another to achieve a world-class performance, thus reaching national or international standards. The literature entails growing empirical evidence to suggest that applying one of these approaches helps to come up with a successful outcome with the application of the other approach (Balm 1992; Nadkarni 1995; Zairi 1996). Thus, organizations adopting a TQM program are expected to be successful in conducting effective benchmarking projects. In a similar vein, those initially adopting benchmarking programs also obtain a positive outcome from their TQM projects (Taylor and Wright 2006). From this perspective, Kozak (2004b) suggests that, because TQM is a commitment to the continuous improvement of service performance and enhancing customer satisfaction, its effective application requires a number of prerequisites to exist in practice, which can also help identify the context of destination benchmarking.

First, both public and individual organizations are expected to encourage a personal commitment to learning (e.g. training and being keen on new practices) (continuous learning). They need to seek new practices by looking at others' successes and mistakes (e.g. keeping eyes on others) (learning organization culture). In line with this, they should establish a partnership with others and with research institutions in order to regularly update their skills and knowledge and create an open-minded atmosphere (e.g. sharing information with those engaged in tourism) (learning partnerships). As a breathtaking point of benchmarking, one needs to provide a two-way communication (e.g. listening to each other and visitors) (team-working). Listening to each other means establishing collaboration between the private and public sector and among those working in the local tourism industry. It is also the fact that continuous improvement needs to be maintained in offering product and service quality (e.g. looking for best practices) (quality management). These criteria are where the success relies on gaining a better positioning in terms of destination performance and customer satisfaction in the tourism and hospitality industry.

6.8. SUMMARY

In lights of our observations over the past few years, we may conclude that tourism is a dynamic industry making a positive contribution to the development of towns and cities and other tourism destinations and the well-being of their residents. As a practical tool to achieve such a conclusion, destination benchmarking may be vital in providing better quality facilities and services and increasing inputs through tourism activities on the supply side. The concept of destination benchmarking aims to provide international tourist destinations with an opportunity to increase their economic prosperity, protect environmental resources, preserve cultural value s and increase the residents' quality of life on the supply side. On the demand side, benchmarking aims to maintain a high level of tourist satisfaction and loyalty by offering a high standard of facilities and services to meet customers' needs and expectations. This is also expected to lead to an increased intention of word-of-mouth recommendation through an improved image in the future. As a result, we may better visualize the relationship between destination benchmarking and maintaining the competitive edge of tourist destinations.

*   *   *

CASE STUDY: T-MONA AS AN EXAMPLE FOR APPLIED DESTINATION BENCHMARKING

Written by Peter Kratochvil and Andreas Neumann *(MANOVA GmbH, Austria)*

T-MONA (Tourism Monitor Austria) is an example of a successfully implemented benchmarking system developed in cooperation with the Austrian Tourism Board (Österreich Werbung) and MANOVA. Since 2004, more than 50,000 interviews have been conducted throughout the country using a consistent survey methodology, where results are processed into a specifically designed online solution with a user-friendly interface. The methodology enables participating destinations to not only have insight into their own data, but it also offers a comparison to the results of other participating destinations. Through this methodology, an understanding of the destination's strengths and weaknesses can be achieved. A sophisticated weighting system based on the national overnight statistics guarantees comparability even with disproportionately scaled samples. Integrated filter and segmentation options allow in-depth analyses by organizing the data into important business segments.

T-MONA was designed as a Web-based management information system to enable tourism managers flexible 24/7 access to score evaluation and analyses, no matter how diverse and complicated the project requirements are. The functionality of the system is displayed in the following real case of an Austrian region focusing on "wellness".

The task of the destination manager (Tom) is to examine the most important guest segments for his region. The first results based on vacation types show that two thirds of the vacation guests in the region call their stay a "wellness-vacation". Tom can now set a filter to analyze wellness guests only. With one mouse-click, T-MONA provides the information: "Wellness-guest" averages 47 years, comes mainly from Austria (92 percent) and has a regular guest ratio of 25 percent. Using a consistent survey and interview method enables monitoring and display of developments over the years (internal benchmarking). Tom sees that the structure based on countries of origin shows barely any changes, but that the age average dropped from 50 to 47 years and that the regular guest ratio collapsed considerably from 62 percent to the mentioned 25 percent. In fact, what seemed to be a reasonable score turns out to be a problem.

As mentioned, T-MONA does not only offer insight to your own scores, but also features benchmarking with other destinations (external

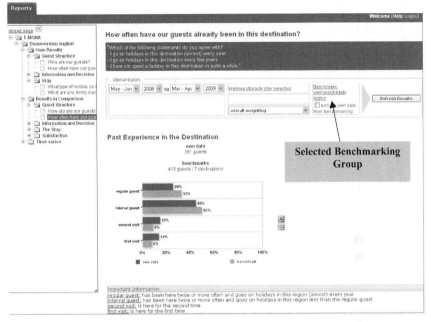

Exhibit 6.1   Travel experience of the guests 2008–2009.

benchmarking). Comparisons in T-MONA are available as aggregated national results, state results, regional results and, after mutual agreement, even one-to-one comparisons with individual destinations. Tom is concerned about the development in the regular guest segment and would like to find out if there is a trend in the industry, specifically the wellness industry. After choosing the benchmarking group "wellness regions" in T-MONA, he discovers that the regular guest ratio has decreased in the entire wellness tourism industry from 45 percent to 30 percent.

In the next step, Tom looks at the motives of wellness guests to travel to his region. A top-10 list shows the most important decision criteria compared to last year's data. "Wellness offer" is the most chosen criterion. What is new is that many other aspects have gained importance for choosing his destination. On the one hand, elevated "price-performance ratio" and "proximity/reachability" criteria tell him that a price-sensitive audience was attracted, especially from "nearby" markets. In comparison with other wellness regions, he can see that these two criteria were mentioned more often in his own destination. On the other hand, "variety of offers" and "quality of service" scored worse than the benchmarking group.

In its survey, T-MONA includes both quantitative and qualitative variables. An example for a quantitative variable is "guest expenses". The cumulated expenses of wellness guests in Tom's region are 128 Euros per person

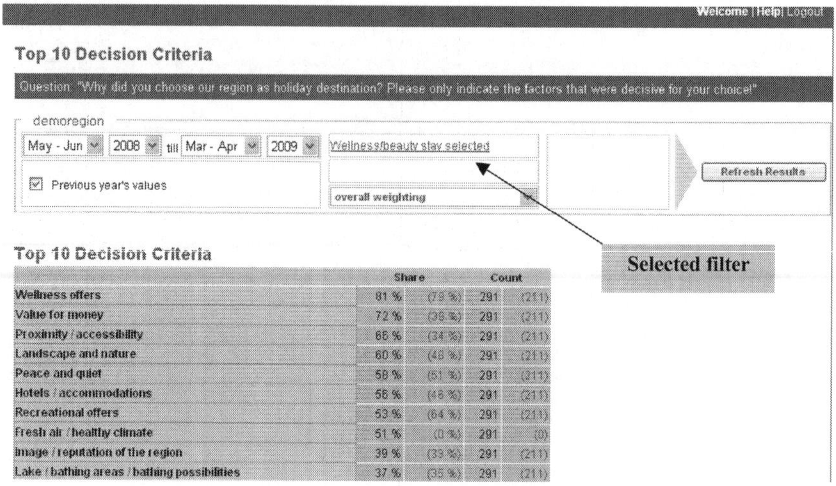

	Share		Count	
Wellness offers	81 %	(79 %)	291	(211)
Value for money	72 %	(39 %)	291	(211)
Proximity / accessibility	66 %	(34 %)	291	(211)
Landscape and nature	60 %	(48 %)	291	(211)
Peace and quiet	58 %	(61 %)	291	(211)
Hotels / accommodations	56 %	(46 %)	291	(211)
Recreational offers	53 %	(64 %)	291	(211)
Fresh air / healthy climate	51 %	(0 %)	291	(0)
Image / reputation of the region	39 %	(33 %)	291	(211)
Lake / bathing areas / bathing possibilities	37 %	(35 %)	291	(211)

Exhibit 6.2 Top-10 decision criteria for selected guest group.

and day. The good news: It is 21 Euros higher than two years ago. The bad news: It is 12 Euros less than travelers spend in other wellness regions!

Besides quantitative variables, qualitative variables play an important role in assessing the performance of a region. T-MONA captures numerous satisfaction ratings to guest activities and offer components of a region. The satisfactions are gathered on a six-stage scale, with 1 being extremely satisfied and 6 being rather unsatisfied. The scale was purposely chosen to be positively distorted because of the low variance of data. Especially for qualitative variables, benchmarking serves as a vital grading instrument to properly scale assessments. The comparison of satisfaction rates over periods of time defines trends and allows destination managers like Tom to react and initiate counter campaigns. Satisfaction developments also reflect the success of newer investments. With its time-series charts, T-MONA offers an advantageous tool. Equally important is the comparison with the competition (external benchmarking), which delivers the necessary orientation for SWOT analysis.

In order to gain an impression of his region's performance regarding "wellness guests," Tom examines their satisfaction rates in detail. Tom's region scores (in comparison to other wellness regions) are worse in most satisfaction characteristics, excluding the wellness and beauty offers. This fact needs to be pointed out because this item is the most mentioned decision criteria of wellness guests when choosing their destination. Regarding accommodations, which are also a top-10 criterion for choosing a vacation spot, the assessment is on average not a bad rating, but not as positive as it shows on competitors' sides. The deficits in "sports offers" should be a motivation to kick off new plans for improvement.

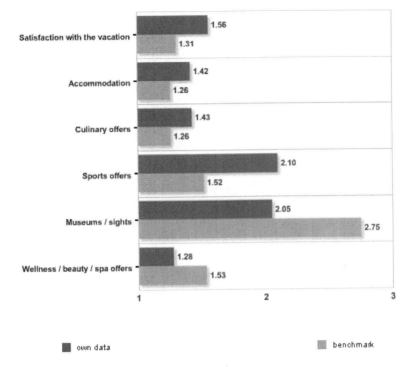

Exhibit 6.3 Satisfaction rates (the lower the better).

T-MONA can directly derivate strengths and weaknesses based on satisfaction comparisons with the chosen benchmarking group and display them in a SWOT analysis.

Currently, the German Tourism Board (DZT) is also using this benchmarking tool under the name "Qualitätsmonitor Deutschland Tourismus" for strategic marketing, positioning and branding. The German and Austrian national tourism board use this system to successfully derive their marketing campaigns, as well as more than 70 regions, provinces and states to reach phenomenal results in destination development.

Part III
Destination Marketing

7 Destination-Based Marketing Strategies

In light of various existing approaches, this chapter provides an overview of existing marketing strategies and their implementation to destinations, and then suggests several ways of marketing strategies in order to be able to maintain and even increase the competitive edge of tourist destinations worldwide. This chapter further suggests that monitoring competitors on a regular basis will enable one destination management to reinforce the analysis of the market and identify its own strengths and weaknesses and the potential marketing opportunity. This sort of analysis, in the end, may help to develop the correct positioning strategy. Some of the subjects included in this chapter are cost leadership, product diversification, positioning, satisfaction and image measurement, market segmentation and product development. The implementation of these strategies could be adapted to the field of destination competitiveness as follows.

7.1. COST (PRICE) LEADERSHIP

The price elasticity of tourism demand is assumed to be high (e.g. Crouch 1995; Song, Wong and Chon 2003; Muñoz 2006, 2007). Thus, any percentage change in prices is expected directly to encourage or discourage travel to a certain place. For instance, those who went to Greece were found to be so sensitive toward the level of price changes in the destination that higher prices lessened tourism demand (Syriopoulos and Sinclair 1993). In a recent empirical study, Muñoz (2006, 2007) confirmed that tourism demand is very sensitive to prices while traveling to Spain. Cost leadership is one of the two primary objectives for gaining competitiveness (Porter 1985). The relative prices of a destination in comparison to some other places are the main destination attribute for motivation to travel. Smeral (1997) contends that some mature destinations are forced to compete with others at price levels but are less competitive in prices or costs. For instance, destinations such as Turkey, Cyprus and Greece with their cheaper labor and production costs have an advantage over Spain, Italy and France.

Given the results of a brochure-based price competitive analysis, some researchers have attempted to measure the competitiveness of destinations. For instance, Turkey was found to be cheaper than Malta for the German market and than Mallorca for the British and German markets (Briguglio and Vella 1995). Nevertheless, value for money is a key variable, other than price itself, influencing choice behavior because it combines the price and qulity evaluations and is a comparison between what customers get compared to what they give (Porter 1985; Murphy and Pritchard 1997). The relationship between quality and price is not well developed. One may increase, whereas another may decrease (Bowman and Faulkner 1994; Bojanic 1996).

To maintain cost advantage, organizations need to maintain above-average industry quality standards while simultaneously offering lower prices. This is believed to bring higher returns in the market. However, this view may not be applicable to the tourism industry due to the features which distinguish it from some other industries. It seems unlikely to benefit from cost advantage on the basis of destination competitiveness because tourism is a combination of a variety of tangible and intangible inputs. A destination market price includes accommodation and transport costs but may not reflect the cost of other main production factors such as the physical and cultural environment. The impact of marketing through third parties also makes it difficult for local authorities or tourism organizations to control market prices. This is explained in detail in the following sections of this chapter.

In international tourism competitiveness, there is a close relationship between changes in exchange rates and changes in the level of prices. In other words, positive or negative changes in exchange rate of a particular country against those of tourist-generating countries may lead to an increase or a decrease in the level of tourist product and service prices (Icoz, Var and Kozak 1998). For instance, Switzerland and Japan have become more expensive countries, whereas Israel and Greece are relatively cheaper in the eyes of potential tourists as a result of fluctuations in exchange rates. A similar case is apparent for Turkey, perceived as a cheaper destination among European citizens. Moreover, Middleton (1994) notes that, for international tourism, price is complicated not only by the combined effects on holiday prices of exchange rates between tourist-generating countries and tourist-receiving destinations but also by the comparative level of inflation in the destination area compared with the area in which potential demand is to be found. The next variable to these price complications is the cost of oil which is especially important in all forms of air transport, but it is difficult for destinations to control this factor.

In the theory of tourism marketing, a tourist is expected to prefer traveling to a destination where the value of his own currency is higher than others. Findings of empirical research with respect to major economic variables influencing foreign tourism demand through Turkey indicated that the foreign currency exchange rates had a significant impact over tourism demand (Bahar and Kozak 2006). Turkey was seen as a cheaper country by European tourists because the value of the Turkish Lira (TL) against Euro has decreased considerably in recent years. As a result, the cost of rooms has remained at a low level, stimulating the interest of foreign tourism demand and tour operators. A very recent crisis in the Turkish economy (early 2001) forced the government to devaluate the TL against other foreign currencies by 20 percent to 25 percent. This makes the country much cheaper and increases its attractiveness as a favorite tourism destination in the international market. The results show that EU membership and thereby the use of Euro does not directly affect the destination preferences of the selected EU citizens. Other findings are that Turkey, being out of the EU and not using Euro, has a positive effect on traveling preferences through the country, and also it does not matter whether the target destination is a member of the EU.

7.2. PRODUCT DIFFERENTIATION

This strategy includes the process of making products more different than what competitors are still supplying, and priority must be given to investigate the potential products to be used in the market (Kotler, Armstrong,

---

Kotler and Fox underline four types of pricing strategies: cost-oriented, competition-oriented, demand-oriented and a combination of the three approaches. Cost-oriented approach refers to marginal costs or total costs. Because the level of cost does not rely on the number of visitors, changes in tourism demand do not influence the level of prices. Competition-oriented approach refers to the level of prices provided by competitors and needs a careful analysis of their pricing strategies. This strategy may be a driving force of competition among destinations offering similar type of products and serving for similar group of visitors. Demand-oriented approach, unlike cost-oriented approach, refers to the relationship between tourism demand and the level of prices. Thus, once any change in tourism demand or in tourist perceptions of price levels appears, then the level of prices is likely to move around. The combination approach includes a mixture of all three pricing approaches where and when needed. Our competitors might be offering a tourism product/service at a higher level of price, but there would be nothing much for us to follow if tourism demand through our destination is not at a satisfactory level.

Box 7.1 Types of Pricing Strategies. Source: Kotler and Fox (1985).

Saunders and Wong 1999). As such, from the destination marketing point of view, the product differentiation strategy may depend upon the variety of resources a destination offers. If it has limited resources of tourism activities to attract various market segments due to various reasons such as climatics, structural or institutional factors, then the establishment of this strategy will fail to enhance success in practice. Destinations with diverse products and services and the ability to present them as a package of tourism products can have more opportunities to be successful in competition.

As a consequence of efforts to diversify tourism products recently observed worldwide, tourist destinations have become distinctive in terms of crerating different names such as rural tourism, agro-tourism, medical tourism, thermal tourism, heritage tourism, wine tourism and so on. Those in the Mediterranean region provide visitors with the opportunity not only to experience culture, history and nature but also to have the experience of sunbathing, water sports, food and nightlife (e.g. Spain, Greece, Turkey, Egypt and Cyprus). These are the most competitive products because there are many alternatives (substitutes) to the customers' offer. A customer might switch to other destinations if s/he feels unhappy with a particular one. Given this, what destination authorities need is to carry out extensive research to identify their existing and potential tourism resources and how each can be used.

International tourist destinations differ depending upon the types of tourism activities and tourism demand they have. A Mediterranean destination may be dominated by mass holiday tourism, whereas for an eastern European destination it may be by heritage tourism. It is also important to note that two destinations in the same country in terms of tourism supply and tourism demand may be very different (e.g. Blackpool and Edinburgh in the UK). Destination competitiveness research should therefore consider the main characteristics of every destination. To some extent, competitiveness research can be carried out between very different destinations (business tourism and winter tourism) when only limited types or service levels of accommodation or food and beverage facilities are the subject of the research.

Because customers are the main elements of the subject, there may be very little difference in terms of diversity and levels of service offered. Similarly, provision of infrastructure and superstructure as basic needs for tourism and travel might be the same for all destinations and customers. Nevertheless, it may be impossible to compare the overall performance of a destination dedicated to business tourism to that of another dedicated to mass holiday tourism due to the varying nature of tourism demand and tourism supply.

7.3. DESTINATION POSITIONING

The concept of destination positioning can be defined in different ways. One definition is "the art of developing and communicating meaningful differences between a region's tourism offerings and those of competitors serving the same target market" (Heath and Wall 1992, pp. 114–115). Following a similar way of understanding, another definition is "the process of establishing and maintaining a distinctive place for a destination in the minds of potential travellers within target markets" (Crompton, Fakeye and Lue 1992, p. 20). Both definitions have in common that destination positioning is a marketing term to emphasize that a destination is different from its competitors in various ways. Thus, several authors contend that instead of developing a marketing plan based upon what tourism authorities believe the destination is expected to offer, the starting point is to identify what exists in the minds of visitors and reinforce these key elements (Botha, Crompton and Kim 1999; Mykletun, Crotts and Mykletun 2001).

One destination might have the potential to serve a variety of products and services, but it might need to focus on improving a specific one(s) which could probably make itself distinctive from other counterparts. An effective positioning strategy may provide competitive advantage to a destination trying to attract more tourists (Goodall 1990; Crompton, Fakeye and Lue 1992; Grabler 1997) or longer- stay tourists (Sainaghi 2010). In Porter's terms, true positioning may differentiate one destination from its competitors on attributes that are meaningful to tourists. It is also important to bear in mind that positioning is a vehicle to make a destination more attractive and competitive to certain markets. Attributes making one destination distinctive or more competitive than its rivals are described as "determinant" attributes in the marketing literature (Swan and Combs 1976). Like organizations, destinations also need to offer something different from their counterparts. This could be better value for money, a higher quality of services, a new product, easier access to technology and so on. Sometimes there would be more than one attribute that is important to visitors, and that makes the destination distinctive.

Positioning strategies can be based on identifying strengths, weaknesses, opportunities and threats for tourist destinations. Strengths are items the destination is good at or something that makes a significant contribution to delivering tourist satisfaction and repeat business; weaknesses are items the destination lacks or something that causes tourist dissatisfaction and may prevent repeat business; opportunities are potential dimensions and elements at the destination that could lead to tourist satisfaction and repeat business in the future, if developed effectively; threats are potential disruptions, such as physical environmental problems, lack of quality and interest, lack of facilities and activities, that will possibly decrease tourist satisfaction and demand in the future. It is extremely important in maintaining competitive advantage in international tourism to know how to sell the experience of a holiday in a particular place (Crouch and Ritchie 1999). Such factors as cleaner beaches and establishments, more hospitable and friendlier local people and cheaper prices could make one destination more competitive than others.

As far as marketing strategies are concerned, it might be possible to keep the attention of repeat tourists or attain new tourists, promote holidays with self-catering and bed and breakfast, attract those traveling alone or with less companions and those taking shorter holidays. Focusing Porter's (1996) variety-based positioning strategy, specific products and services differentiating one destination from others could be focused. The level of prices can be reduced to attract tourists in the off-season period. In line with Porter's (1996) 'needs-based positioning strategy', a particular segment of customers might be targeted (e.g. family groups in Alcudia and young independent tourists in Arenal in Mallorca or the use of homogeneous market segmentation strategy) (Fornell 1992). Or new products can be developed, as Mallorca currently does (e.g. improvement of sports and recreation activities).

7.4. MARKET SEGMENTATION

As the right place differs from one segment of customers to another and the right customer differs from one group of destinations to another, the positioning process implies a segmentation process where a destination targets the right kind of visitor (Mykletun, Crotts and Mykletun

---

Variety-based Positioning Strategy: This type of strategy is based on the choice of product or service varieties rather than customer segments. This makes economic sense when one destination can promote particular products or services using distinctive sets of its activities. For example, specific products and services differentiating one destination from others could be focused.

Needs-based Positioning Strategy: This type of strategy shall be applied while targeting a particular segment of customers (e.g. family groups or young independent tourists). It appears when customer segments are different in their needs from each other and methods are developed to satisfy these needs. Activities should also be different while meeting each segment's needs.

Access-based Positioning Strategy: One segment's needs may seem similar, but the ways to access them are different. The size of the place where potential customers live and the size of the group to which they belong are the factors influencing the successful implementation of access-based strategy.

Box 7.2   Porter's Positioning Strategies. Source: Porter (1996).

2001). The strategy of market segmentation seeks to achieve competitive advantage by focusing on a specific type of customer segment and designing the existing products and services according to their values or socio-economic and socio-demographic characteristics (Kotler, Bowen and Makens 2009). Those who expect the same benefits or are in the same category of consumption patterns are classified as one segment of the market.

Thus, Heath and Wall (1992, p. 91) states that "market segmentation is based on the assumption that different market segments have different needs [and different sets of personality, expectations and wants], different levels of present and potential consumption, different levels of awareness of the product and are exposed to different communication channels". Thus, different marketing mix concepts should be devised for different market segments through the destination. As every destination has a different product to attract customers from different markets, it is unlikely that all destinations are able to compete for all market segments. In this sense, the most important and competitive products should be developed in each segment (Hoti, McAleer and Shareef 2007).

Having reviewed earlier studies in the literature (Calantone, diBenedetto, Halam and Bojanic 1989; Goodall 1990; Heath and Wall 1992; Song, Wong and Chon 2003; Díaz-Pérez, Bethencourt-Cejas and Álvarez-González 2005), it is possible to suggest several categories of market segmentation strategies relating to the marketing of destinations (e.g. by socio-economic and demographic characteristics such as nationality, age, income and occupation, by product-related characteristics such as types of activity, number of repeat visits and length of stay, by psychographic characteristics such as attitudes, interests and motivation and by geographical characteristics such as day trippers, domestic and foreign tourists). The first two strategies discussed above are also considered within the market segmentation strategy. A destination might offer cheaper services to those with lower income levels in the off-season or attract only explorers for adventure tourism.

For example, Spain is a strong player on beach tourism, whereas Switzerland thrives on winter tourism. If a destination relies heavily on summer vacations and offers cheaper holidays with longer duration, it can attract tourists with low levels of income who intend to take vacations in the summer. To be competitive, a specific type of market segment can be attracted in a specific period of time (e.g. youth, elderly people, explorers, fun-seekers, family groups etc.). This would reduce costs and increase benefits sought in favor of the customers (value for money). This is the result of both tour operators and destination facilities. Tour operators can promote a specific destination for a particular country, and tourist facilities can offer different levels of prices for those at higher or lower income groups depending upon the quality of facilities and services provided.

7.5. TOURIST SATISFACTION

The customer's value chain is another input of competitive advantage (Porter 1985). Understanding what a satisfied customer needs and wants is the basic ingredient of a recipe in arriving at successful marketing and improving competitive advantage (Czepiel, Rosenberg and Akerele 1974). Attention is drawn to the importance of tourist perceptions in successful destination marketing because they influence the choice of a destination (Song, Wong and Chon 2003), the consumption of goods and services while on holiday and the decision to return (Kozak 2001b). The reason for this is that the majority of tourists have experience of other destinations with which they make comparisons, for example among facilities, attractions and service standards (Laws 1995). Customers are an important source of identifying external ideas for many products and services; surveys enable them to reflect on their opinions about and experiences with the destination and can be used to benchmark many aspects of performance against competitors.

The measurement of customer satisfaction provides benefits for both customers and organizations. The feedback from customers can be used to increase the level of service quality and employee motivations which in turn lead to more satisfied customers and employees. Therefore, the importance of the examination of destination competitiveness arises from the fact that motivations (psychographic attributes) are important factors for choosing a destination. When customers are not satisfied, they will not return, and on their return home they will discourage their friends and relatives from visiting. Similarly, positive experiences are expected to lead to customer satisfaction and positive word-of-mouth recommendation (e.g. Beeho and Prentice 1997; Kozak and Beaman 2006; Um, Chon and Ro 2006). As a consequence, customer-centered organizations or destinations will have greater opportunity to win over the competition (Kotler 1994).

The main feature of a destination management may be to assist all those concerned with the destination performance to think out of the box when they want to be aware of what customers think and benefit from knowledge of activities elsewhere and their impact upon customer satisfaction and tourism receipts. Destination managers therefore should be aware of what they and their competitors provide and how they perform, due to the possibility of tour operators and customers exploring new destinations. They should also pay attention to developments in consumer needs, wants and perceptions. For example, several destinations regularly monitor the changes in the socioeconomic, socio-demographic and holiday-taking patterns of their international customers (e.g. Greece) (Kotler, Haider and Rein 1993).

7.6. DESTINATION IMAGE

Past studies indicate that the image of a destination influences tourist behavior (see Pike 2002 for a list of publications). For the potential success of a destination, tourists are expected to have first an awareness and next a positive image (Milman and Pizam 1995). Um and Crompton (1990) claim that because potential tourists usually have limited information about the attributes of one destination where they have not previously visited, from the visitors' points of view, the image and attitude dimensions are likely to be critical elements in the destination choice process. A distinctive image perception will perhaps make one destination different from its competitors in the minds of visitors (Baloglu and McCleary 1999; Prebensen 2007).

For example, one may perceive a tourist destination as being relatively cheaper, offering a variety of entertainment options and being extremely popular among one particular segment. Thus, in marketing of products, the place where a product is designed and produced can be important to customers ('made in' label). They could assume that product X made in country X has a higher quality than one made in country Y (Kotler, Haider and Rein 1993). Similarly, in marketing tourism services, people can perceive that one country has higher quality services than those in another and image perception varies from one person to another.

Research demonstrates that images of a tourist destination are a mixture of both positive and negative perceptions. If destinations seem otherwise to be equally attractive, the decisive factor will be where negative perceptions may be unlikely to occur (McLellan and Fousher 1983). It is also argued that comprehensive destination image studies are an effective tool for assessing the strengths and weaknesses of tourism destinations particularly regarding the perceptions of actual and potential tourists (Selby and Morgan 1996). Because tourists want to have more than one experience, there is a close relationship between all tourism and related facilities at the destination (Pyo, Mihalik and Uysal 1989). All these elements, some of which have already been explained in this chapter, make a contribution to the image studies of destinations as well as the satisfaction levels of tourists.

As repeatedly emphasized in this book, destinations are in competition to attract more tourists. Due to developments in the tourism industry and changes in customer behavior, more destinations, more choice of accommodation, a wide range of activities and special tours are now offered for tourists (Laws 1995). The majority of tourists may have experience with other destinations and make comparisons between service standards of various destinations. Thus, a competitive position can be achieved by both creating and transmitting a favorable image, which presents the destination as different from other similar destinations to potential tourists, and making actual tourists satisfied with the destination (Goodall 1990). These are examples of how psychological repositioning (changing tourists' beliefs about facilities and services) and competitive repositioning (changing tourists' beliefs about their own and other destinations) can be introduced into the concept of destination competitiveness.

The image of one destination are formed by various sources of information, including promotional literature (travel brocuhures, posters etc.); the opinions of other people (friends or travel agents) who haf either been to the destination or obtained initial information by reading, watching or listening to others; the general media such as movies, newspapers and TV and radio programs; and finally tourists' own experience (Fakeye and Crompton 1991; Echtner and Ritchie 1993; Beerli and Martín 2004). Bojanic (1991) concludes that advertising is an effective tool to improve positive image. Word-of-mouth communication, the other element constructing the destination image, could be either negative or positive; each of these will have varying impacts on tourists' desires in different ways. The majority of people said that they had received travel information from their friends and relatives taking holidays around the globe (Gitelson and Crompton 1983). In sum, in order to attract more tourists, the suppliers of tourism products/ services should improve their service quality and upgrade their brand image (Song, Wong and Chon 2003; Muñoz 2006).

7.7. DESTINATION LIFECYCLE AND NEW PRODUCT DEVELOPMENT

Like products, destinations are also believed to have a lifecycle through their existence in either the domestic or international market or in both markets together. Tourist destinations go through a cycle of evolution similar to that of normal products. Number of visitors and their socio-economic and socio-demographic characteristics are the main indicator of movements in lifecycle of tourist destinations, whereas this is the number of products sold and their objective and subjective features. A model of destination lifecycle was developed by Butler (1980) to examine the impacts of tourism development in an area and show how it moves from one stage

---

Research undertaken among the U.S. citizens on their image perceptions of various Mediterranean destinations demonstrated that Turkey was perceived to be superior to Greece and Italy on good value for money and unpolluted environment. On the other hand, Turkey was perceived to be inferior to the same competitor destinations on good nightlife and entertainment, standard of hygiene and cleanliness, and quality of infrastructure. These are the areas where one destination is better (more competitive) or worse (not competitive) than others. Depending upon the research findings, it was pointed out that those attributes with the highest ratings may not be those that differentiate competitive destinations from each other because some attributes are likely to be viewed as being the same.

Box 7.3   Image Perceptions of Mediterranean Destinations. Source: Baloglu and McCleary (1999).

to another. Commencing from the early stage when the place is explored as a tourist location to the last one when the place is about to fall, this model refers to the subsequent six stages as indicated below.

Exploration: the area is not so popular yet it attracts a few *allocentric* type of tourists.

Involvement: The number of visits begins to increase and local people offer services primarily for tourists.

Development: The area is on its way to becoming a well-known destination while putting itself at risk of losing its originality because it attracts more investment and is widely advertised.

Consolidation: The major part of the local economy is generated by tourism income. Tourist arrivals continue to increase but at declining rates.

Stagnation: Carrying capacity is reached and various economic, social and environmental problems begin to appear. The area is no longer popular.

Rejuvenation: There are two options in the last stage: (1) either ambition on earning from tourism will decline or (2) dramatic changes need to be established to reshape the existing image.

This makes clear that, in the 'consolidation' and 'stagnation' stages, destinations are more dependent on inclusive tours. As a result, the rate of increase of tourists slows, whereas total numbers are still increasing and the demand profile of the destination is dominated by repeat visits (Laws and Cooper 1998). The yield gained from tourists using inclusive tour holidays is lower than that of others because the destinations dealing with inclusive tours are largely dependent on marketing channels via intermediaries, tour operators or travel agents. The destination will be at a disadvantage if intermediaries have more bargaining power than the expected level.

By classifying the psychology of customers in tourism under two headings such as 'allocentric' (those who have active personality) and 'psychocentric' (those who have passive personality), Plog (1974) suggests that such typology could be effective in understanding why destinations fall or rise in popularity. According to his approach, destinations move from 'allocentrics' to 'psychocentrics' because the latter attracts those who discover a new place to vacation and enjoy. But as long as there is word-of-mouth communication and others are informed, the destination begins to have fewer 'allocentrics' and move toward 'psychocentric' travellers on the psychographic scale. The degree of movement largely depends upon the extent to which a destination becomes popular and how it is promoted and managed. When it increasingly becomes popular by attracting any type of tourist groups and management has no control on over-development, it means that natural and cultural resources may deteriorate. Because the destination is likely to become an 'ordinary' place, 'allocentrics' will be replaced by 'psychocentrics'.

As a consequence, the destination faces several management and marketing problems because 'psychocentrics' are believed not to travel as often as 'allocentrics' do and stay for a shorter time and spend less. Moreover, it becomes more commercialized by losing its features which attract tourists and its competitiveness in the market. In such a situation, Plog (1974) suggests that destinations attracting more 'mid-centric' to 'psychocentric' tourists need to evolve new strategies in order to reach those who travel more often and spend more.

As a vital instrument particularly for those destinations working with the rejuvenation of mature markets, innovation and improvement of new products may be of help to gain the competitive advantage (Pikkemaat and Weiermair 2007). Thus, it is important to improve the quality of the tourist resources and services by adding new and attractive features, improving technology and productivity and applying the effective use of capital such as human and financial sources (Novelli, Schmitz and Spencer 2006; Hjalager 2010). In the context of destination-based innovation, Goodall (1990) also mentions the importance of innovation, improvement and extension of transport networks and new and revised legislation as impacting on the comparative advantage of destinations. Font and Ahjem (1998) underline that tourist destinations need to find out what they are good at (strengths) rather than simply increasing their supply. They can control supply in order to provide better service. Table 7.1 provides a brief summary of the most common factors that lead to new and innovative products and processes for tourist destinations.

7.8. DESTINATION LOYALTY

In general, a considerable amount of research has been carried out dealing with customer loyalty and its link with marketing strategies (e.g. Cronin and Taylor 1992; Selnes 1993; Bloemer and Ruyter 1998; Sivadas and Baker-Prewitt 2000). However, research into customer loyalty has focused primarily on 'brand loyalty', whereas loyalty to tourist destinations has remained underexposed. The tourism literature is about to pay much attention to reports of research investigating loyalty to specific tourist destinations (Oppermann 1998, 1999; Kozak 2001b; Huan, Beaman and Kozak 2003; Kozak and Beaman 2006). The extent to which the frequent visitors can be accepted as loyal or non-loyal has not been clearly identified either. Even though there are some practical attempts to categorize the frequency of repeat visits, they did not explain the number of visits which qualified for each category.

Of these, Gitelson and Crompton (1984) subdivide the frequency of repeat visitation into three categories such as 'infrequent', 'frequent' and 'very frequent'. In accordance with these subgroups, Oppermann (1999) suggests a conceptual typology of destination loyalty as a function of

Table 7.1 Common Factors Leading to Innovative Products

No	Factors	Consequences
1	Technological change	Can induce innovativeness and create the opportunity to achieve competitive advantage. In tourism, when the industry shifted from mechanical to electronic technology, the opportunity was created for such destinations as Las Vegas, Dubai and Paris to take the leadership.
2	New or shifting buyer needs	Can create competitive advantage if the destination moves faster than competitors or if competitors fail to respond to the opportunity. When consumers around the world begin to favor convenience and consistency in the food industry, destinations offering traditional local restaurants may fail to respond effectively (e.g. France, Italy, India, Japan etc.).
3	The emergence or observance of a new market segment	Can be a source of competitive advantage, although this may not always require producing new products. Modifications to existing products may be sufficient to reach these new segments. Mediterranean destinations revising their current products such as new facilities and green areas can be given as an example.
4	Shifts in the cost or availability of factors of production	Can create competitive advantage for a destination if it moves faster than its competitors in optimizing its systems and resources based on the new conditions. For example, when relative wage levels rose in leading destinations, the developing destinations enjoyed competitive advantage due to their relatively lower costs of labor (e.g. China, Thailand, Turkey).
5	Sudden changes in government regulations	Those involving product standards, environmental controls or trade barriers can create the opportunity for competitive advantage if the destination has the flexibility to quickly adapt to the new conditions and induce innovation (e.g. members of EU).
6	Changes in managerial styles	Can create competite advantage by developing collaboration and networks among multi-level organizations taking place within the management and marketing of destinations (e.g. local tourism businesses, local governments, local Chambers of Commerce and research institutions).

multiple visits. Infrequent visitors are regarded as 'somewhat loyal', regular visitors 'loyal' and annual and biannual visitors 'very loyal'. This typology has several weaknesses because no one can expect loyalty for particular destinations to be as high as it is for individual organizations. In other words, for example, it is unlikely to witness those who visit the same destination at least twice a year on a regular basis.

In a further attempt to identify repeat visitation cycle of tourist destinations, Oppermann (1999) suggests several criteria: undivided loyalty (AAAA), divided loyalty (ABAA), unstable loyalty (AABB) and irregular sequences (ABCA). The term 'undivided loyalty' refers to those people who return to a particular destination year after year. The rest of the terms indicate visitors who visited the destination in question, whereas at the same time are visiting other destinations in the given period. However, Oppermann's proposed model of destination loyalty underestimates the existence of a group of customers who never go on holiday in the intermediate periods. Depending upon the structure of this categorisation, Oppermann (2000) argues that first-time tourists are homogeneous as repeat tourists are not because the first group has no experience of the destination. The second group has the experience but in different periods. For example, repeat visitor A visits destination X, whereas repeat visitor B visits destination Y in the summer of year XYZ. Therefore, this group is assumed to be heterogeneous in terms of repeat visit behavior.

Hanefors and Mossberg (1999) suggest a variety of loyalty types in the tourism context such as travel agency loyalty, hotel loyalty, tour operator loyalty and destination loyalty. It may sometimes be impossible to expect a visitor to keep loyalty to all these elements of tourism at the same time. The visitor may switch to another tour operator or hotel while still visiting a particular destination. Or some visitors may tend to look for new experiences with new destinations but keep their loyalty to their travel agency. This could be due to the fact that changing brands or destinations in tourism does not cost the customer as much as it does in other industries such as health, education and insurance.

Table 7.2 shows the findings relating to the pattern of loyalty to Turkey and some other particular countries as summer destinations. The first letter in the first column represents the presence of the absence of visits in 1995 and the last one in 1999. The term '0' refers to the absence of the visit in that particular year as the term 'A' refers to the presence of a visit. According to criterion reported above (Oppermann 1998, 1999), the presence of only one visit in the last five years is regarded as infrequent visits (somewhat loyal). It is regarded as frequent visits (loyal) if tourists have had two or three visits in the last five years and as very frequent (very loyal) if they had four or five travels to Turkey.

As Table 7.2 shows, the majority of tourists have had their first visits to Turkey in the last five years (infrequent tourists). With its second highest proportion, the category of frequent tourists scattered into different years. The proportion of very frequent tourists remained at a very low level. Although those visiting Turkey four times in the period of five years has been considered as very loyal tourists in this study, there is one point which limits this view because these tourists had a break once in the middle (divided loyalty). Although the number of those in the category of 'AAAAA', which means one visit in summer every year, is not at the desired level to support the presence of very loyal customers and undivided loyalty to destinations, it might be a good example of destination loyalty. Thus, it appears to suggest that loyalty for tourist destinations is very weak. However, those in the category of '000AA', '00AAA', '0A0AA', 'AA0AA' and 'A00AA' have

Table 7.2 Frequency of Visits by Summer Destinations (Turkey)

Frequency	n=91	%
One Visit	(63)	(69.2)
0000A	63	69.2
Two Visits	(14)	(15.4)
A000A	3	3.3
0A00A	1	1.1
00A0A	3	3.3
000AA	7	7.7
Three Visits	(8)	(8.8)
A00AA	1	1.1
AA00A	1	1.1
0A0AA	2	2.2
0AA0A	2	2.2
00AAA	2	2.2
Four Visits	(3)	(3.3)
AA0AA	1	1.1
AAA0A	2	2.2
Five Visits	(3)	(3.3)
AAAAA	3	3.3
Total Visits	139	100

the potential to become very frequent tourists for the Turkish destinations, provided that they continue to come back in the succeeding years.

7.9. SWOT ANALYSIS

SWOT analysis is an acronym of strengths, weaknesses, opportunities and threats. Strengths are associated with those attractions, facilities and operations which match up to the customer's needs. Weaknesses refer to the lack of those attractions, facilities and operations which match up o the customer's needs. Opportunities arise from both elements under the control of the industry and changes in external factors which can be credited to the organization's advantage. Threats arise from both internal and external factors (e.g. political unrest, economic corruption, mass tourism etc.).

In recent years, tourism has become a highly competitive market. For this reason it is important that destinations are able to measure their competitiveness in order to identify their strengths and weaknesses and thereby develop their future strategies. A Chinese proverb attributed to Sun Tzu, a Chinese General in 500 BC has gained a respectful response from benchmarking researchers: 'If you know your enemy and know yourself, you need not fear the results of a hundred battles' (Camp 1989, p. 253). This means that if the destination knows itself and its competitors, it can take steps to ensure its competitive position is maintained. On the other hand, if competitors are believed to be particularly strong, it is important to take action. Battles could be over both internal and external barriers affecting the success of the destination and its competitiveness in the marketplace. When tourist destinations are considered as an element of the marketing mix (place), the importance of their performance levels seems clear.

An action plan containing future goals and recommendations might consist of how to keep up strengths and minimize weaknesses and threats in order to cope with the new applications and developments. Depending on the outcome, destination managers may wish to change their marketing policies or market segments. It may also be possible to attract similar groups of tourists by preserving the current image and improving the existing performance. The measurement of one's own performance indicates its current strengths and weaknesses as well as opportunities and threats for the future. Their comparison to other similar destinations may identify how competitive the destination is in various areas and any possible areas needing improvement (Table 7.3).

Table 7.3   SWOT Analysis for Mallorca and Turkey

| | Mallorca | | Turkey | |
	British	German	British	German
S	Sea, sun and sand	Sea, sun and sand	Sea, sun and sand	Sea, sun and sand
T	Nature	Nature	Culture, nature	Culture, nature
R	Frequent loyalty-	Level of language	and history	and history
E	Hospitality	communication	Hospitality	Accommodation
N	Level of language	Frequent loyalty	Level of prices	services
G	communication	High level of trip	Good value for	Local transport
T	Cater for families	satisfaction	money	services
H	High level of trip	High level of inten-	Level of language	Level of prices
S	satisfaction	tion to come back	communication	Cleanliness and
	High level of inten-	and recommend	Local transport	hygiene
	tion to come back	Attractive in winter	services	High level of trip
	and recommend	season	New accommoda-	satisfaction
	Attractive in	Good airport	tion	High intention to
	winter season	facilities	High level of trip	come back and
	Good airport facili-	Cater for families	satisfaction	recommend
	ties		High level of inten-	Frequent loyalty
			tion to come back	
			and recommend	

continued

Table 7.3 continued

WEAKNESSES	Old accommodation High level of prices Poor cleanliness Negative attitude of shopkeepers	Poor sports facilities and activities Poor quality of accommodation Poor food High level of prices Lack of cleanliness	Harassment Lack of cleanliness Poor signposting Poor airport facilities and services Poor air-conditioning	Harassment Poor language communication Lack of cleanliness Poor signposting Poor air-conditioning
OPPORTUNITIES	Level of prices Repositioning and improvement of resorts A brand-new airport Attractive in winter season Shorter flight Special programs for people who return	Repositioning and improvement of resorts Attractive in winter season A brand-new airport Shorter flight Special programs for people who return	Young destination	Young destination
THREATS	Commercialization and overdevelopment Noise Mixture of family and young individual tourists Heavily dependent on British market	Level of prices Quality of accommodation Overcommercialization & overdevelopment Heavily dependent on German market	Harassment Overcommercialization & overdevelopment Poor cleanliness of sea and beaches Poor hygiene and sanitation Poor road and traffic conditions	Harassment Overcommercialization & overdevelopment Dependent on German market
COMPETITIVE LEVEL	Easy access to the market (shorter flight time) Caters for families Variety of leisure facilities and activities Relaxed atmosphere (no hassle) A brand-new airport Mature (experienced) destination Attractive for winter tourism	Easy access to the market (shorter flight time) Caters for families A brand-new airport Relaxed atmosphere (no hassle) Mature and experienced destination Attractive for winter tourism	Culture and history Hospitality Level of prices (Good value for money) Local transport services Young destination Good shopping possibilities	Culture and history Hospitality Level of prices (Good value for money) Accommodation services Variety of water-sport activities Young destination

Source: Kozak (2000).

7.11. SUMMARY

It is possible to suggest that monitoring competitors on a regular basis will enable one destination management to reinforce the analysis of the market and identify its own strengths and weaknesses and the potential marketing opportunity. This sort of analysis, in the end, may help to develop the correct positioning strategy. Both cost leadership and positioning strategies can be considered within the Porter's focus strategy (e.g. offering cheaper services to those with low income levels or attracting explorer tourists for adventure tourism). In this case, the destination is expected to perform at an above-average level.

* * *

CASE STUDY: LAS VEGAS—A DIVERSIFIED DESTINATION

Written by Terry Jicinsky *(Las Vegas Convetion and Visitors Authority, USA)* **and Seyhmus Baloglu** *(UNLV, USA)*

Las Vegas has been a destination of constant change and evolution, constantly reinventing itself. Whereas the continuous diversification and addition of available product offerings is the most obvious and tangible evidence of this reinvention, the evolution of the Las Vegas brand has been just as apparent. Originally identified almost exclusively as a gambling destination, today's Las Vegas has emerged as one of the most recognizable destination brands in the world.

Throughout the destination's lifecycle, visitors to Las Vegas have come to expect a one-of-a-kind experience that is seldom, if ever, duplicated anywhere else in the world. Whereas the specifics of these experiences have certainly changed over the years, there are threads of consistency in what has become known as the Las Vegas brand.

Over the years, the image of Las Vegas has evolved from the "underworld of the mob" to "family destination" and to "glitz, glamour and adult entertainment." It was in January 2003 that Las Vegas' current, and notably most successful, branding campaign was released. "What Happens Here, Stays Here" hit the market with a response and outcome that few could have anticipated. In a 2005 consumer poll, the *USA Today* newspaper released a survey which found the Las Vegas brand to be the fifth most recognizable brand in America.

The campaign slogan itself has quickly become very popular nationwide. Countless TV shows, movies, stand-up comedians, journalists and celebrities incorporate the slogan into their own work. The research results show that the campaign connection with the targeted consumer is deeply rooted in the core element of "adult freedom". Brand testing and focus groups sessions conducted by the organization consistently report findings which represent the brand personality as exciting, sexy, living the unexpressed live, playfully mischievous, sensual and confidently defiant. The same research demonstrated that the campaign resonates with and motivates a wide rage of people of different ages, incomes, cultures and, most importantly, different perceptions, images and assumptions about the destination. The simple fact is that every visitor to Las Vegas generates their own personal story about their experience in the city. This is very consistent with the current belief that today's tourists are not asking 'what can we do on holiday?', but 'who can we be on holiday?'

The Las Vegas economy is heavily reliant on the hotel, gaming and the convention industry. The Las Vegas Convention and Visitors Authority (LVCVA) is the official destination marketing organization of Las Vegas. The LVCVA is responsible for marketing Southern Nevada as a tourism and convention destination worldwide as well as operating convention and event centers. The founders of the LVCVA established a model that created a "Perpetual Tourism Circle" that provides its own economic stimulus to the benefit of Las Vegas. In this self-perpetuating cycle, demand (visitor volume) drives the new investment in room and convention facility supply.

With rising room inventory and average daily room rates comes increased room tax revenue. A portion of this revenue is used for branding and marketing of the destination to the actual and potential visitors because the ability to create demand is critical to continuing the success of the cycle and entire economy. Maintaining high occupancy rates also allows increased room tax revenue to be used by local government to fund infrastructure needs such as roads, schools and parks. This business model has helped both the community and the destination to benefit and maintain occupancy rates, on average, 25 percent above the national average which revolves around 65 percent. Approximately 53 percent of all room tax paid by visitors goes back into the community, translating into hundreds of millions of dollars distributed among community agencies to build roads, parks, schools and other government programs that benefit residents.

In 2007, approximately 39.3 million people visited Las Vegas. In the same year, the total room tax generated was approximately $398 million, $192 million of which was used by the LVCVA for operating the convention centers, branding and marketing of Las Vegas and hosting special events. The remaining $206 million was distributed for community support. Despite the increasing number of room inventory, hotel occupancy rates in Las Vegas remain around 90 percent over the years. Any increase in the number of visitors has a corresponding effect on increased room tax collected.

Major events generate economic impact resulting from economic factors such as hotel accommodations, food and beverage expenditures, tourist attractions, entertainment events, gasoline and various shopping purchases. Events or facilities increase a local community's tax revenues and the visibility and enhanced images of a community. "Event tourism" in Las Vegas consists of highly diversified large and small events, including conventions meetings, exhibitions, sport and arts events, concerts, shows, festivals, celebrity visits and private parties.

Las Vegas has more than 9.7 million square feet of exhibit space and is home to three of the country's 10 largest convention venues: the Mandalay Bay Convention Center, a 1.5 million-square-foot center on the south Strip, the 1.9 million-square-foot Sands Expo and Convention Center adjacent to the Venetian and the 2.3 million-square-foot Las Vegas Convention Center.

The Las Vegas Convention Center (LVCC) is currently undergoing an US$890 million enhancement program to continue to attract conventions and add more convention and meeting space. In 2006, Las Vegas was home of 45 of the largest 200 trade shows in North America. The LVCC funds the Convention Center Area Command (Metropolitan Police command center) on the grounds of the center and is giving away a portion of its property to the Clark County Fire Department for a homeland security fire station.

In 2007, tourism's economic impact was US$41.6 billion based on 39.3 million visitors; 23,847 conventions were held, and 6.2 million convention delegates visited. Conventions' non-gaming impact was US$8.4 billion. Las Vegas gaming revenue was US$8.4 billion. The number of room nights for convention represents 30 percent of all rooms sold in 2007. Eleven percent of visitors indicated convention/corporate meeting as their primary purpose of trip to Vegas, whereas 5 percent visited for special events.

According to a 2008 Las Vegas Visitor Profile study, convention visitors were most likely to be male (54 percent), employed (91 percent), college graduates (66 percent), under 50 years

old (65 percent) and earning an annual household income higher than other visitors (64 percent earn US$80,000 or more per year).

Hosting major sports events such as NASCAR, the Las Vegas Bowl and the National Finals Rodeo influences daily life, livelihood and exhibits a significant group in travel and tourism industry because of their substantial potential for quality of life and economic impact in the community. The attendees spend more on lodging and non-gaming activities than on gaming. During the years 2002 to 2006, on the average, NASCAR had a total of 95,900 out-of-town visitors per year, which constituted 93 percent of the total visitors. The Las Vegas Bowl had an average of 22,975 out-of-town visitors (94 percent), and National Finals Rodeo had an average 40,375 out-of-town visitors (90 percent).

As far as the economic impact is concerned, NASCAR has had the most dramatic impact on the Las Vegas economy. Each year the economic impact increased, reaching US$200 million in 2006. The NFR had a steady impact of around US$71 million with the exception of 2004 which was at US$55 million. The Las Vegas Bowl had the lowest economic impact of the three events with a low of US$14.6 million in 2003 and a high of just over US$20 million in 2004. In Las Vegas, the event tourism help the destination build the brand image, increase the occupancy and tourism revenue and contribute to the quality of life of the residents.

8　Destination Branding

Most destinations today have excellent facilities and attractions, and every destination claims and promotes a unique culture and heritage, beautiful landscape, excellent facilities and very friendly locals. Therefore, creating a differentiated brand image is more critical (Morgan and Pritchard 1999). Success depends on essentially two dimensions: (1) the management of the tourism system as a system of networks and channels, and (2) the management of brand attributes, their dissemination and consistency (Gnoth 2002). Destination branding should be managed strategically by destination marketing organizations to articulate and communicate a destination identity. This chapter provides concepts, tools and approaches of developing brands in travel and tourism to help destination marketers implement sound brand strategies and tactics.

8.1. DEFINITION OF DESTINATION AND BRAND

Before one can effectively speak of destination branding in tourism, one needs to define "destination" and "brand". Tourism destinations consist of distinct and interrelated products and services under a brand name and generally are considered a geographical area. Kerr (2006) indicated that destination brand has focused only on tourism product and has called for a more holistic perspective, location or place brand, taking into account all aspects of a location (i.e. the economic, social, political and cultural development of cities, regions or countries). This definition still points out that geographical boundaries of "destination", "location" or "place" may range from cities to countries. Perhaps a good distinction in destination branding would be small- and large-scale environments (those environments cannot be perceived directly) (Baloglu and Brinberg 1997).

A common definition of destination is a geographical region perceived as a whole entity by the visitors and consumed under the brand name of the entity. Istanbul or Amsterdam would be the destinations for a European traveler, whereas Europe would be the destination for an Asian tourist who will visit multiple European cities and towns. For a German tourist on an all-inclusive tour to Antalya, the all-inclusive resort would be the destination. For an American tourist taking a Mediterranean cruise, the ports of the trip would be the destinations. "Often destinations are artificially divided by geographical and political barriers, which fail to take into consideration consumer preferences or tourism industry functions. An example of that is the Alps shared by France, Austria, Switzerland, Italy by often perceived and consumed as part of the same product by skiers" (Buhalis 2000, p. 97).

Tourism destinations as a geographical region are a combination of products, services, and experiences. Therefore, branding opportunities for destinations exist at country, city and town levels (umbrella and sub-brands), attractions (historical, cultural, natural, man-made, museums, theme parks etc.), events (mega-events, festivals etc.) and lifestyle travel packages (packages developed and sold by tour operators and travel agents). *When it comes to branding, one needs to define the "destination" from traveler (demand) perspective, not the destination planner/marketer (supply) perspective.*

Many brand definitions exist in the literature. Most, if not all, studies of brand or branding cite the definition of Aaker (1991) or the American Marketing Association (AMA) which is "a name, term, sign, symbol, or design, or a combination of them, intended to identify the goods and services of one seller or group of sellers and to differentiate them from those of competitors." Further definitions have been proposed by various authors. For example, a review of brand definitions has revealed six groups of definitions: visual, perceptual, positioning, added value, image and personality (Hankinson and Cowking 1995).

A brand reflects all the destination products and services and the accumulation of characteristics that form a destination's image and identity. It is a promise and a set of strong associations people have with a place, which form their expectations. A brand needs to have unique elements, which differentiate it from its competitors and establish an image in the mind of the consumer (Kaplanidou and Vogt 2003, p. 1). A review of branding definitions by de Chernatony and Riley (1998) reveals that there are at least 12 different ways of defining the brand: "it is a legal instrument, a logo, a shorthand, a com- pany, a risk reducer, a value system, an image in consumer's mind, a personality, a relationship, a value enhancer, an identity system and evolving entity" (p. 421).

A destination brand is defined as "perceptions about a place as reflected by the associations held in tourist memory" (Cai 2002, p. 273). Building on Aaker's (1991) definition and incorporating visitor experience into the definition, Ritchie and Ritchie (1998) defined *destination brand* as a "name, symbol, logo, word or other graphic that both identifies and differentiates the destination; furthermore, it conveys the promise of a memorable travel experience that is uniquely associated with the destination; it also serves to consolidate and reinforce the recollection of pleasurable memories of destination experience."

An integrative framework that identifies four main streams of brand conceptualization that can be applied to place branding has been proposed by Hankinson (2004, pp. 110–111). His proposed framework is built around the concept of brand networks in which place branding performs four main functions: (1) *brands as communicators*, where brands "represent a mark of ownership, and a means of product differentiation manifested in legally protected names, logos, and trademarks"; (2) *brands as perceptual entities*, which appeal to the consumer senses, reasons, and emotions (functional, symbolic, and experiential); (3) *brands as value enhancers*, which has led to the concept of brand equity; and (4) *brands as relationships*, where the brand is construed as having a personality which enables it to form a relationship with the consumer. This relationship will be based on congruity with the consumer's self-image.

8.2. DESTINATION BRAND DEVELOPMENT CHALLENGES

Branding a destination is more than just designing a logo and slogan and more complex than branding a product. A tourist destination consists of diverse products, services, people and processes. It includes attractions, transportation, facilities, tours, activities and non-tourism-related services such as banks, telecommunication, health services and so on. Destination branding is the set of marketing activities that (1) support the creation of a name, symbol, logo, word mark or other graphic that readily identifies and differentiates a destination; (2) consistently convey the expectation of a memorable travel experience that is uniquely associated with the destination; (3) serve to consolidate and reinforce the emotional connection between the visitor and the destination; and (4) reduce consumer search costs and perceived risk. Collectively, these activities serve to create a destination image that positively influences consumer destination choice (Blain, Levy and Ritchie 2005).

Pike (2005) argued that destination branding is more complex than other products and services for several reasons. First, destinations consist of multidimensional and more diverse offerings, which also make it difficult to create a slogan because they tend to cover everything. Second, there are many players, and the politics of decision making among the destination organizations (DMOs) rely on government funding and distribution channel members. For instance, the chance of success for a country's tourism brand campaign would be significantly influenced and even cancelled by the highly influential intermediaries, say European tour wholesalers, if it does not fit their offerings, as happened to Morocco according to Pike (2005). Third, there would be a possible lack of support from local community or non-agreement on the desired image between country and city DMOs or between state and regional tourism organizations. Fourth, it is undoubtedly difficult to apply relationship marketing or loyalty developing strategies because it is impossible for DMOs to stay in touch with hundreds of thousands or millions of previous visitors. Finally, the funding problem may prevail because a successful brand campaign does not lead to increased revenue for the DMO.

It should be noted that the last point mentioned by Pike (2005) would not apply to all destinations because the Las Vegas Convention and Visitors Authority (LVCVB) has a very effective funding system in place relying on room taxes. Therefore, branding campaign success directly influences the operational and marketing budget of the Authority. According to Morgan and Pritchard (2004), the challenges are diverse tourism products and agencies on which a DMO has no control, limited budget resources of DMOs and vulnerability of tourism industry to volatile external environment such as pandemic diseases, economic downturns, political instability, natural disasters and terrorism. Some other challenges could be added. The major one is, with many players and attractions, the difficulty of controlling delivery to be consistent across tourist experiences. Also, the fact that a destination brand has different competitors in different markets introduces more challenges in designing and communicating a brand positioning strategy.

Aaker (1996a, 1996b) states that brand builders should understand barriers and challenges in general because it is difficult to build any brand in today's competitive world. They are short-term pressures, pressure to compete on price, short-term brand strategies, proliferation of competitors and fragmenting media and markets. These brand development challenges equally apply to tourist destinations as well. Most tourist destinations are forced to compete on price because of economic priorities and value being narrowly defined in monetary terms. Albeit, a sustainable tourism strategy is slowly gaining a momentum to consider the triple bottom-line: economic, environmental and social sustainability.

In applying short-term brand strategies, or frequent changes in brand identity and/or implementation), destinations have a common problem of changing their brand strategies often mostly because of internal pressures or habit before they reach their potential. For example, the "What Happens in Las Vegas Stays in Las Vegas" campaign has been very successful, and LVCVA did not change it despite the internal pressures. Aaker (1999) points out two critical elements of brand-building success: (1) to understand how to build brand identity, know what it stands for and communicate the identity; and (2) manage internal forces and pressures.

When discussing re-imaging Croatia, Hall (2002) mentioned that branding confronts at least three major constraints: (1) a lack of adequate finance to support appropriate marketing campaigns and lack of appropriate expertise, (2) pressure to return short-term results when long-term investment is required to build a consistent brand and (3) limited coordination of local, regional and national interests, where instead a coordinated action among government, the tourism sector and other stakeholders to project clear, positive national, regional and place images. Competition in tourism industry is complex, and different product classes add levels of competition. It is getting increasingly difficult to find a niche position because of the number of players in the marketplace. This also contributes to price competition and copying the competition.

Media options today offer a vast array of alternatives such as broadcast and print media, Internet, database and direct marketing, event sponsorship, publicity, public relations and so on. Coordination and an integrated communication strategy to deliver consistent brand message or customized messages are becoming more difficult and challenging. When advertising, promotions, direct marketing, public relations and trade shows are handled by many separate entities, conflicting brand messages may occur. In addition, destinations generally have multiple target markets and attempt to reach them with specialized media and distribution channels to develop multiple brand identities for the same brand. Travelers will be more likely to be exposed to more than one message, which might lead to customer and brand image confusion.

In some cases, sub-brands or umbrella (family) brands would cause such confusion. For example, in mid-1990s, Las Vegas suffered from a brand image confusion of "sin-city" or "family destination." LVCVA never promoted or sent a message to the consumer to build a family destination image. The problem emanated from the practice of a few Strip properties to develop family attractions to target families, among others, and position themselves as a family resort. So, this "innocent" diversification growth strategy has created a brand dilution for Las Vegas.

8.3. BRAND BUILDING PROCESS

Needless to say, brand building is challenging, but practices out there show that it is doable and destinations do not have much choice but to build, maintain and manage their brand identities. The future success will emanate from the battle of the brands. As Morgan, Pritchard and Piggott (2002) puts it, 'the most powerful marketing weapon available to contemporary destination marketers' due to 'increasing product parity, substitutability and competition' (p. 335). In the context of tourism, a geographic location or product class should be considered for brand development efforts at the destination level because a geographic location or destination product (museums, theme parks etc.) can be branded.

The literature review indicated that most tourism scholars agree on the brand-building process for destinations (Morgan and Pritchard 2004; Hudson and Ritchie 2009). Hudson and Ritchie (2009) proposed a four-step process of building a "destination brand experience": (1) assessing the destination brand's current situation (2) developing a brand identity and brand promise, (3) communicating the brand promise and (4) measuring effectiveness of the brand-building exercise. However, their labeling of the process was confusing because it did not include any experiential component or designing visitor experiences.

The brand-building process should take a strategic approach when an official organization body (CVB or DMO) plans to develop, enhance or transform a brand. Figure 8.1 shows the stages of a strategic brand-building process for destinations (Aaker 1996a, 1996b; Morgan and Pritchard 2004). It is essential that destination stakeholders be involved in the early stages of the brand-building process to be successful. The first stage in the brand-building process is a comprehensive brand SWOT analysis or destination audit to evaluate and reveal the strengths and weaknesses of the brand as well as the current and future opportunities and threats. The analysis includes four key areas: environment, product, market and competitor analysis.

Environmental analysis helps to identify the trends and opportunities in multiple environments such as economic, social, cultural, technological and political. Product analysis is highly important to examine the core destination product and other components and resources available. Because core, supporting and augmented products are examined, the product analysis should not be limited to functional attributes only. Aaker (1996a, 1996b) points out that a common pitfall in branding strategy is to focus on brand attributes, namely functional and tangible attributes. Tourist analysis consists of understanding tourist experiences, perceived destination personality in current and potential target markets and customer-based brand equity dimensions to identify tourist self-image and destination image congruity, brand awareness and recognition and brand loyalty.

Competitor analysis, to a great extent, includes comparative product and tourist analyses because the core of a brand strategy is positioning and differentiation from the competition. Aaker (2003, p.83) uses an analogy that "differentiation is the engine of brand train, if the engine stops so does the train." The differentiation must be sustainable and relevant. This stage would not be effective without the participation of relevant stakeholders. They would include but not be limited to local businesses, DMO members, tour operators, travel agents and meeting planners. This practice was evident in successful destination branding campaigns such as New Zealand (100% Pure), Las Vegas (What Happens in Vegas Stays in Vegas), Wales (The Real Alternative) and Canada (Keep Exploring) (Morgan, Pritchard and Piggott 2002; Knapp and Sherwin 2005; Hudson and Ritchie 2009).

The essence of a SWOT analysis is to compare and contrast destination brand strengths and weaknesses, revealing how destinations stack up against one another. It also elucidates how well destinations use branding to exploit their assets to their full potential, whether they are under-performing or over-performing relative to their assets and resources.

The next stage, based on the information from the SWOT analysis, is to define a vision for the organization's branding efforts, brand identity system and value propositions (functional, affective and symbolic) for each

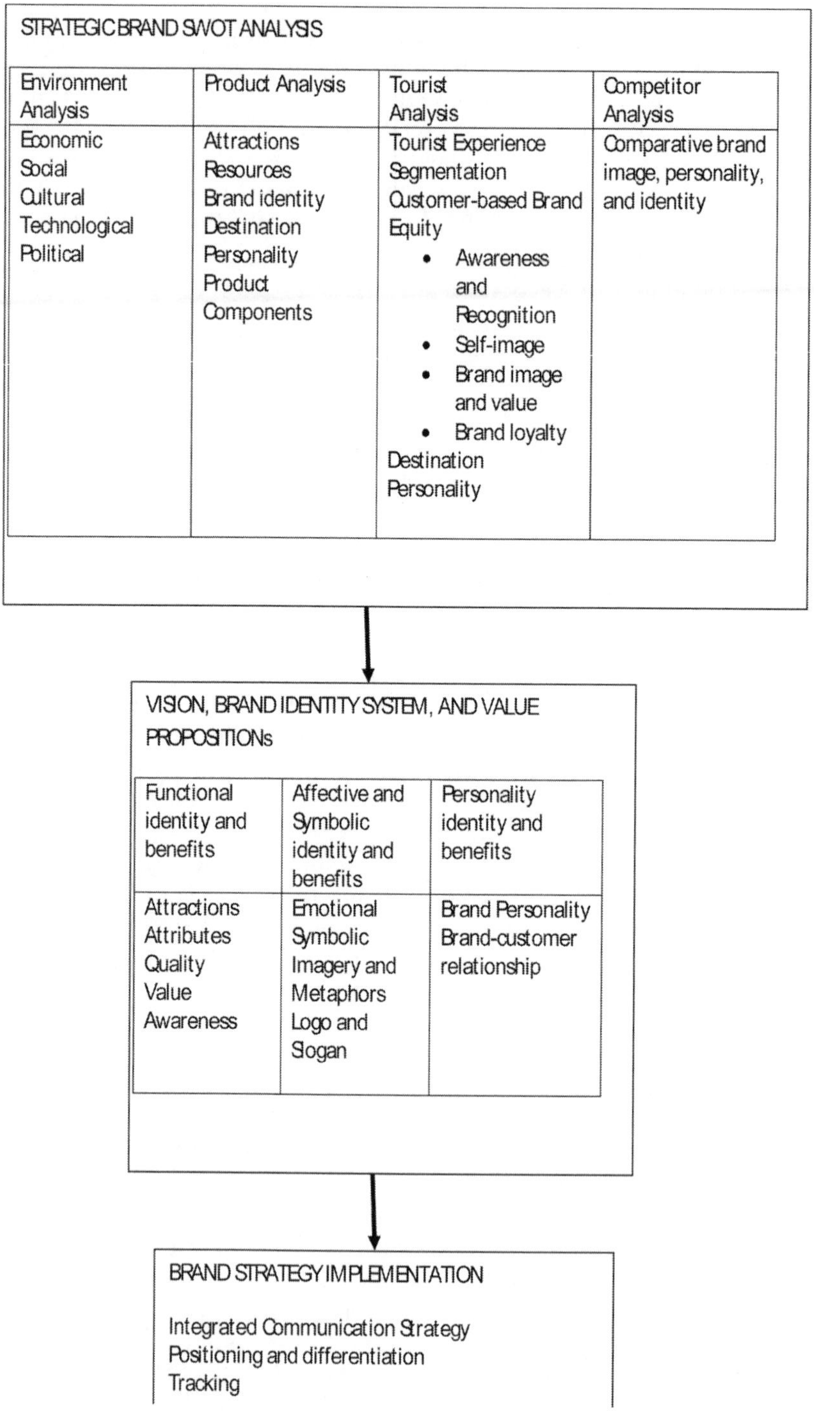

STRATEGIC BRAND SWOT ANALYSIS

Environment Analysis	Product Analysis	Tourist Analysis	Competitor Analysis
Economic Social Cultural Technological Political	Attractions Resources Brand identity Destination Personality Product Components	Tourist Experience Segmentation Customer-based Brand Equity • Awareness and Recognition • Self-image • Brand image and value • Brand loyalty Destination Personality	Comparative brand image, personality, and identity

VISION, BRAND IDENTITY SYSTEM, AND VALUE PROPOSITIONs

Functional identity and benefits	Affective and Symbolic identity and benefits	Personality identity and benefits
Attractions Attributes Quality Value Awareness	Emotional Symbolic Imagery and Metaphors Logo and Slogan	Brand Personality Brand-customer relationship

BRAND STRATEGY IMPLEMENTATION

Integrated Communication Strategy
Positioning and differentiation
Tracking

Figure 8.1   Strategic brand-building process.

target market. At this stage, slogan and logos, positioning and differentiation and communication strategy to convey the brand identity will also be formulated. Critical to the creation of a durable destination brand is the identification of the brand's values, the translation of those into a suitably emotionally appealing personality and the targeted and efficient delivery of that message. This brand identity is central to the direction, purpose and meaning for the brand, and it 'should help establish a relationship between the brand and the customer by generating a value proposition involving functional, emotional or self-expressive benefits' (Aaker 1996a, p. 68).

The last stage is implementing the strategy and tactics developed in the previous stage. After selecting target markets, the positioning, the differentiation strategy and the communication strategy should be implemented. This stage also includes monitoring and tracking brand image, personality and equity in the minds of travelers to assess the gap, if any, between brand identity and brand image.

8.4. BRAND IDENTITY SYSTEM AND IMAGE

Brand literature distinguishes between brand identity and image (Nandan 2004). The branding efforts of the destination, the brand image and position articulated and communicated to the targeted visitors (Konecnik and Go 2008), have been discussed in the literature under *brand identity*. Brand

---

Morgan, Pritchard and Piggott (2004) outlined the following features of the "New Zealand, 100% Pure" successful branding campaign: (1) Developing a unique, compelling, and simple message; (2) Researching the brand values—The first stage in the process of positioning or repositioning any destination brand is to establish the core values and images of the destination and its brand; (3) Positioning the brand—The next phase in defining New Zealand's positioning was to define what the country represents and determine how this should be translated into head and heart of brand personality. Its head refers to the logical brand features, whereas its heart refers to its emotional benefits and associations; (4) Harnessing the Web and non-traditional media—Successful branding is not realized by advertising alone. For all destinations, interactive media, direct marketing and events capitalization will do more for a country than an advertising campaign ever can. These vehicles cannot be ignored because they engage visitors more closely before their visit.

Box 8.1   Stages of Branding for New Zealand.

identity is how brand strategists want the brand to be perceived. It is the supplier's (destination) version of the brand associations and personality. On the other hand, brand image relates to the consumer's perceptions of the brand (demand side). Consumers ascribe a persona or an image to the brand based on subjective perceptions of a set of associations that they have about the brand (Nandan 2004).

Brand identity "is a unique set of brand associations that the brand strategist aspires to create or maintain. These associations represent what the brand stands for and imply a promise to customers. . . . Brand identity should help establish a relationship between the brand and the customer by generating a value proposition involving functional, emotional or self-expressive benefits" (Aaker 1996a, p. 68). Particularly for destinations, a broader scope of brand identity would be necessary because of diverse offerings, target markets, and potential umbrella and sub-brands. Brand identity includes core and extended identity (Aaker 1996a). The core identity is the central and timeless essence of the brand and remains constant as the brand travels to new markets and products. The extended identity complements the core identity. Box 8.2 is an example of brand identity for Las Vegas. The core identity will not change in a short period. The extended identity and the communication strategies may change. The core identity should include elements that will contribute to brand uniqueness and value propositions. It is more global evaluation and soul of the brand.

Brand personality is a part of extended identity, not core identity (Aaker 1996a). Strong and effective brands have the identity elements connected cohesively and meaningfully and have strong links among core and extended identities. The importance of a brand's image in its long-term success necessitates having a framework for strategically managing the image over the long term (Bhat and Reddy 1998). Park, Jaworski and MacInnis (1986) proposed a framework for strategic brand image (identity) management, termed brand concept management (BCM), based on three types of consumer need: functional, symbolic and experiential. Functional needs are utilitarian needs.

To tap into these two different types of needs, Park, Jaworski and MacInnis (1986) proposed that all brands should have a "brand concept", which is an overall meaning that identifies a brand or simply brand identity. A brand with a functional concept is designed to solve externally generated consumption needs. Symbolic needs are desires that satisfy internal needs such as self-enhancement, role position, social identification, group membership or ego-identification. A brand with a symbolic concept is designed to associate the individual with a desired group, role or self-image, and to facilitate the communication of symbolic meaning to the individual and to others. A brand with an experiential concept is designed to fulfill an internally generated need such as sensory pleasure and/or variety seeking. The authors argued that despite the fact that many brands offer a mixture

Core Identity
  Entertainment
  Gaming
  Value for Money
Extended Identity
  Travel Experience: do nothing or do everything, you create your experience
  Personality: Playfully mischievous, Slightly stimulating, Energetic, Somewhat exciting, Randomly thrilling, Safely dangerous
  Slogan: What Happens in Vegas Stays in Vegas
  Logo: "Only Vegas"
  Product Scope: complete resort destination, anything and everything
Value Proposition
  Functional Benefits: value, man-made attractions, shows, shopping, dining
  Emotional Benefits: exciting, arousing, fun
  Self-expressive (symbolic) benefits: young, adult, sexy, be what you want to be

Box 8.2　Destination Brand Identity of Las Vegas

of symbolic, functional, and experiential benefits, managing such a brand would be highly difficult; therefore, only one of the brand concepts (identities) should be selected.

1. A brand with multiple concepts may be more difficult to manage because it competes against more brands (e.g. those with purely functional, experiential or symbolic concepts).
2. A brand with multiple concepts may be less effective in establishing an image/position because it may confuse consumers about the brand's basic meaning.

Bhat and Reddy (1998) studied symbolic and functional positioning of brands and provided some evidence that functionality and symbolism are distinct concepts and not really two ends of a brand identity continuum. Caldwell and Freire (2004) break destination brands into two dimensions: representational and functional. The representational dimension includes those attributes that are "linked to the individuals self-expression" (Caldwell and Freire 2004, p. 52), whereas the functional dimension includes those related to the "utilitarian aspects of the destinations—sun, reefs, sky, culture, and so on" (Caldwell and Freire 2004, p. 52).

Gnoth (2002) applied these concepts to tourist destinations and presented them as different options of branding in tourist destinations: (1) functional, emphasizing the destination's problem-solving capabilities such as accessibility and reliability; (2) symbolic, emphasizing the destination's ego-enhancing attributes such as family and affiliations with celebrities; and (3) experiential, emphasizing the destination's cognitive or affective attributes such as relaxation and learning. The functional and emotional attributes underlie the concept of brand promise or values, in which destinations must communicate to potential and current visitors the benefits and experiences that they can expect from the destination. Whereas the functional level is the easiest to copy by competitors, the experiential and symbolic levels offer opportunities for diversification and uniqueness.

Aaker (1996a) proposed four components of brand value proposition: functional benefits, emotional benefits, self-expressive benefits and relative price. Functional benefits are product attributes that provide functional utility to the consumer, which often fail to differentiate and are easy to imitate. The strongest brand identities have both functional and emotional benefits. Emotional benefits are positive feelings about the brand. Self-expressive benefits are symbolic meaning to communicate his/her self-image. *In this respect, Aaker's self-expressive benefits reflect the match between self-image and destination personality.* A traveler may define himself as adventurous, sophisticated, successful, frugal, competent and so on. When a destination brand provides self-expressive benefits, the connection between the brand and the traveler is likely to be heightened. Aaker (1996a, 1996b) points out that emotional and self-expressive benefits may be mixed, but self-expressive benefits usually focus on self, aspiration and the future, the permanent (not transitory), the act of using the product (not the consequence of using it).

The price is also important because it is directly related to the other benefits: "Within a brand's competitive set, a high relative price signals a higher quality and a low relative price signals a lower quality or value position" (Aaker 1996b, p. 102). The real issue is whether the value proposition is driven by benefits or by price. "The goal of identity creation is usually to focus on benefits not price" (Aaker 1996b, p. 102). If the price is an important part of the identity, one approach is to note explicitly that the brand has a lower price although superior or comparable to others in its set.

Brand Image Components

A brand image is how the brand is perceived by the consumers (Aaker 1996a, 1996b). Brand image is a vital component of brand equity models (Konecnik and Gartner 2007; Boo, Busser and Baloglu 2009). A destination brand image is a set of associations that travelers have with a place. These associations will be perceived as brand promises and form the expectations. A common pitfall in branding strategy is to focus on brand attributes

(Aaker 1996a, 1996b). The battle among tourist destinations will be in minds and hearts (Morgan and Pritchard 1999). Choice of vacation destination has become a significant lifestyle indicator for today's consumers, and places should be emotionally appealing and of high conversational and celebrity value. The key to success and brand differentiation is to develop an emotional relationship between the destination and potential visitors (Morgan and Pritchard 2004).

After a comprehensive literature review of brand image in geography, environmental psychology, consumer behavior and travel and tourism, Baloglu and McCleary (1999) disaggregated the image concept into perceptual/cognitive, affective and overall image components. Perceptual or cognitive evaluation refers to beliefs and knowledge about an object (evaluation of attributes of the object), whereas affective evaluation refers to feelings about the object. Places also have an overall (global) image. This global image is usually formed as a result of both perceptual/cognitive and affective evaluations of the place (Russel and Pratt 1980; Dobni and Zinkhan 1990; Stern and Krakover 1993; Gartner 1993; Echtner and Ritchie 1993), which may be similar to or different from their cognitive or affective perceptions. This resembles the functional, emotional and symbolic brand components in branding literature.

Brand Personality

Gardner and Levy (1955), in their classic article, proposed that brands may have a symbolic personality that may be more important to the consumer than functional attributes. *Similar to a human being, a brand can be described by demographics, lifestyle or human personality traits.* Both product-related attributes, which are primary drivers of brand personality, and non-product-related characteristics, such as advertising style, country-of-origin and celebrity endorsers, can influence brand personality. Other non-product-related brand personality drivers are user imagery, special events and symbols (logo). User imagery may include multiple dimensions such as typical users (travelers you see using the brand) and ideal users (usually shown in advertising). This can be a powerful driver of brand personality because users have personalities as well.

Destination personality would be a useful concept for destinations because:

1. The personality metaphor enriches understanding of the perceptions and images of the destinations.
2. It helps differentiate the brand, particularly in those cases where brands are similar in terms of the functional attributes (attractions, seasonality, etc.).
3. It relates travelers to the brand more effectively in communication strategy. Travelers express their identities (actual and ideal) and

lifestyle by visiting a destination. It may also serve to define a traveler's social identity.

Brand image and brand personality are often used interchangeably in travel and tourism literature. Destination brand personality has been defined as the set of personality traits or characteristics associated with a tourism destination (Ekinci, Sirakaya-Turk and Baloglu 2007). The nature of the relationship between brand image and brand personality is ambiguous. The ambiguity results from the different viewpoints, whether image and destination personality are distinct concepts or brand personality is a component of the brand image. According to prominent branding scholar Aaker (1996a, 1996b), brand personality is part of an extended identity, not the core identity. Hosany, Ekinci and Uysal (2006) indicated that brand personality and brand image are related concepts, and also suggested that brand personality is more related to the affective component of brand image. According to Morgan et al. (2003), a brand's personality has both a head and a heart: its 'head' is its logical features, whereas its 'heart' is its emotional benefits and associations.

It is possible to have brands that have both functional and symbolic meanings for consumers. There was also evidence that brand symbolism is a multidimensional concept and may actually comprise two sub-dimensions that were labeled "Prestige" and "Personality expression" (Bhat and Reddy 1998). This suggests that brand personality is a component of symbolic image. Brand personality, as a component of brand image, serves as a symbolic function and projects a brand's typical user. Initial measures of brand personality included "This brand has personality", "This brand is interesting" and "I have a clear image of the type of person who would use the brand" (Aaker 1996b, p. 118). A destination brand image then is made up of personality characteristics, affective and cognitive image (Murphy, Benckendorff and Moscardo 2007; Gnoth, Baloglu, Ekinci and Sirakaya-Turk 2007).

One element of brand associations/differentiation is brand personality which is based on the brand-as-person perspective (Aaker 1996b). When brands have only minor differences, brand personality is an effective differentiator and can provide a link to emotional and self-expressive benefits, customer-brand relationship and differentiation. As a cautionary note, *using personality as brands strength would be misleading and distortion if the brand image or positioning is built upon functional advantages and value* (Aaker 1996b, pp. 112–113).

From a comprehensive list of personality traits, Aaker (1997) developed a scale, called the Brand Personality Scale (BPS), to measure brand personality across product categories. The 42-item BPS consisted of five personality dimensions: "sincerity", "excitement", "competence", "sophistication" and "ruggedness". These dimensions are derived from 15 personality facets of brands. Ekinci and Hosany (2006) examined the applicability and validity of Aaker's (1997) brand personality framework in the context of tourism destinations. The author(s) found that destination personality consists of three dimensions rather than the original five dimensions: "sincerity", "excitement" and "conviviality." Murphy et al. (2007) examined whether tourists could differentiate the two tourism destinations on the basis of brand personality perceptions. Destination personality was captured using 20 personality traits of BPS (5 dimensions and 15 facets of BPS) and a free elicitation method with open-ended questions. The entire list of the 42-item BPS was not used because of the risk of respondent fatigue. The study found some evidence that brand personality can be used to differentiate tourism destinations.

However, Murphy et al. (2007) suggested that Aaker's (1997) BPS does not directly translate to tourism destinations. In particular, open-ended responses of personality descriptors were not as common as Aaker's (1997) personality traits. Thus, they called further research to develop a brand personality scale that is valid and reliable for tourism destinations. Ekinci, Sirakaya-Turk and Baloglu (2007) found that destination personality was comprised of three salient dimensions, namely sincerity, excitement and conviviality, confirming the findings of Ekinci and Hosany (2006). Ekinci et al. (2007) supported the external validity of the personality dimensions; however, the items did not consistently load on the same dimensions, questioning the items' stability.

It seems that destination personalities are context-specific and should be modified for each destination. Prayag (2007) employed a qualitative methodology to elicit the destination-specific personality characteristics of South Africa and Cape Town. The author used projective methods, such as word association, brand fingerprint, brand personification and in-depth interviews with international tourists. The brand personification technique revealed that Cape Town was perceived as "young" and more "adventurous" than South Africa. The brand personification technique was found effective to elicit the destination-specific traits. Indeed, it revealed personality traits that are quite different from Aaker's (1997) BPS scale.

Multiple Personalities

Aaker (1996a, 1996b) stated that most research on relating actual or ideal self-image with BP found a weak relationship. These studies assume a single traveler personality. One possible explanation of a weak relationship is that people have multiple personalities and only certain parts of a person's personality would surface in different contexts or consumption situations (social gatherings, vacations etc.). For example, Las Vegas marketing efforts encourage doing things one cannot do at home and assuming different roles and personalities when visiting the destination. Tourist destinations should also understand if the destination brand personality changes in different visit contexts to have a good grasp of the destination brand personality profile. Another reason is that destinations are visited by many users, and therefore user imagery and BP may indicate a weak relationship without controlling background characteristics.

Self-image and Destination Image (Personality) Congruency

Self-congruity theory proposes that part of consumer behavior is determined by a matching between consumer self-concept and product/brand image (Sirgy et al. 1997). Sirgy and Su (2000) applied the self-congruity theory to the tourism field and developed a theoretical study to explain the relationships among tourists' self-concept, destination image, self-congruity, functional congruity and travel behavior. They defined self-congruity as the match between the destination visitor image and tourists' self-concept (actual, ideal, social and ideal social self-image).

Additionally, Sirgy and Su (2000) proposed that tourists not only evaluate a destination based on the symbolic attributes but also on the destination's functional and utilitarian attributes such as price, service quality, aesthetics of the destination, variety of activities and accessibility. In line with this view, the authors defined functional congruity as the match between the destination's utilitarian attributes and the tourists' expectations of those attributes. More recently, Beerli et al. (2007), using a modified version of Malhotra's (1981) scale, tested the role of self-congruity for tourist destinations. The study revealed that the greater the match between the destination image and one's actual and ideal self-concept, the greater the tendency for the tourists to visit that destination. However, if the tourist has already visited the destination, both actual and ideal self-congruity lose its power in influencing a tourist's destination choice behavior.

Brand image refers to both functional and symbolic benefits of a brand (Low and Lamb 2000). Brand personality only refers to the symbolic function of a brand (Keller 1993). According to Aaker (1999), the main point of self-congruity is that consumers prefer brands with a set of personality traits congruent with their own. Brand personality refers to a set of human characteristics associated with a brand, which is indeed an expression of consumer self-images through the use of the brand (Aaker 1997, p. 347). Therefore, brand personality may have a closer link to consumer self-concept than brand image because it focuses on personality traits associated with a brand. So, rather than a cognitive or an affective component, brand personality would provide more valid implications for tourist destinations.

8.5. BRAND POSITIONING—BRAND IDENTITY IMPLEMENTATION

Positioning is the process of establishing a distinctive place for a destination in the minds of the travelers in the targeted markets (Crompton,

Fakeye and Lue 1992; Kotler, Haider and Rein 1993; Echtner and Ritchie 1993; Baloglu and McCleary 1999). A brand position "is the part of the brand identity and value proposition that is to be actively communicated to the target audience and that demonstrates an advantage over competing brands" (Aaker 1996, p. 176). The whole purpose is to create a brand image differentiated from the competition that is important and meaningful to the target market.

To develop an effective positioning strategy in a fierce competitive environment, destination marketers should have a sound understanding of travelers' brand images of their own destinations and competing destinations. Potential travelers' images of the destination relative to its competitors provide useful insights into the development of a positioning strategy. This information also enables the destination to see if perceptions (demand side) are compatible with the destination's resources and market offerings (supply side). If any discrepancy exists, destination marketers and planners should either alter image perceptions and positioning or improve and develop tourism products and services, or both (Baloglu and McCleary 1999)

Relative images of tourist destinations can be determined by comparisons across several competing destinations. This process will result in identifying destinations' strengths and weaknesses, competitive advantages and distinctive competencies for each destination relative to other potential sites. The development of a positioning strategy includes (1) identifying a target market segment's images of a destination, (2) comparing these images with those of competitors and (3) selecting destination differentiators that meet the needs and wants of travelers and differentiate a destination from its competitors (Aaker and Shansby 1982; Javalgi, Thomas and Rao 1992; Crompton, Fakeye and Lue 1992). If a destination is differentiated from similar destinations, then the likelihood of being considered and chosen in the travel decision process is increased.

One particular interest of destination image studies has been to identify image strengths and weaknesses of tourism destinations relative to other destinations based on perceived destination attributes, affective evaluations and/or the perceived similarities between destinations with no reference to particular destination attributes (Mayo 1973; Anderssen and Colberg 1973; Goodrich 1978; Haahti 1986; Fenton and Pearce 1988; Gartner 1989; Crompton, Fakeye and Lue 1992; Baloglu and Brinberg 1997; Baloglu and McCleary 1999). They indicated that the most common positioning strategy in tourism is based on functional (cognitive) attributes and price. Typically, a destination claims that it is superior on a functional benefit for a user category. Or it positions against a close competitor based on the functional benefits and at the same time claim to be better than or as good as the competitor at a lower price.

Positioning strategy should not be limited to functional attributes only because many destinations claim to have the best attractions, facilities, services and friendly local people. Destinations can also position themselves based on affective images (emotional benefits) (Baloglu and Brinberg 1997) and brand personality (Bhat and Reddy 1998). Baloglu and McCleary (1999) pointed out that both image components and global images should be measured, as they provide different angles, to develop an effective positioning strategy. The authors found significant differences in these image components for both visitors and non-visitors segments, revealing perceived strengths and weaknesses of the destinations included in their study (Table 8.1).

The three areas to look at to choose the elements of identity to include in the brand position are core identity, points of leverage and the value proposition (Aaker 1996a, 1996b). The brand position should include the core identity which reflects the most unique and important aspects of the brand. A brand position can be based on a point of leverage not part of the core identity (i.e. personality symbol). Brand position can be changed without changing the identity or value proposition. For the brand "New Zealand", the brand essence is "landscape" and the positioning tagline is "New Pacific Freedom' (Morgan, Pritchard and Piggott 2002). For the brand name "Las Vegas", the brand essence is entertainment and the tagline is "What Happens in Vegas Stays in Vegas" to emphasize an adventurous destination and adult freedom.

In developing brand position, a practical step is to compare the brand identity and the brand image on a variety of dimensions to identify the gaps between the two to take specific actions and implement communication tasks (Aaker 1996a, 1996b; Govers and Go 2004). A destination may find it necessary to communicate what a brand is, not if the current perceptions are not there. What a brand is is equally important as what a brand is not.

Multiple Brand Identities

In some situations, the brand identity would be very persuasive and universal that it may be consistently applied across markets. Las Vegas, for example, would use its gambling or entertainment identity in many markets without much adaptation. In many cases, however, it is seldom that a brand identity would equally be used and it needs to be adapted to diverse markets (segments or different set of competitors). So, the same brand may have multiple identities. Branding experts suggest that even if multiple identities are used, one still needs to have a common set of associations, probably the core identity, to have consistency. This can be accomplished by promoting the same identity but stressing different value propositions. In one market brand personality would be emphasized, whereas in another market the functional attributes would be in the forefront (Aaker 1996a, 1996b).

Media Execution of Positioning Strategy

The execution of the positioning strategy should include both traditional media (advertising, memorable icons and logos) and non-traditional

Table 8.1 Strengths and Weaknesses of Destination Pairs

Turkey versus Italy
Visitors

Turkey's strengths/Good value for money/Great beaches/water sports/ Unpolluted/unspoiled environment/ Interesting historical attractions/Interesting and friendly people	Italy's strengths/Appealing local food (cuisine)/Quality of infrastructure/Good nightlife and entertainment/Standard hygiene and cleanliness

Non-visitors

Good value for money/Great beaches/ water sports/Unpolluted/unspoiled environment	Suitable accommodations/Appealing local food (cuisine)/Quality of infra-structure/Good nightlife and entertainment/Standard hygiene and cleanliness

Turkey versus Greece
Visitors

Turkey's strengths	*Greece's strengths*
Good value for money/Beautiful scenery/ natural attractionsUnpolluted/unspoiled environment/Interesting and friendly people/Pleasant/Exciting/Overall image	Great beaches/water sports/Good nightlife and entertainment/Standard hygiene and cleanliness

Non-visitors

Good value for money/Good nightlife and entertainment/Standard hygiene and cleanliness	Great beaches/water sports

Greece versus Italy
Visitors

Greece's strengths	*Italy's strengths*
Good value for money/Great beaches/ water sports/Pleasant/Overall image	Appealing local food (cuisine)/Quality of infrastructure

Non-visitors

Good value for money/Great beaches/ water sports/Unpolluted/unspoiled environment	Suitable accommodations/Appealing local food (cuisine)

Source: Baloglu, Seyhmus and McCleary, "U.S. International Pleasure Travelers' Images of Four Mediterranean Destinations: A Comparison of Visitors and Nonvisitors." Journal of Travel Research (Vol 37, issue 2) p. 9. Copyright © 1999 by Sage Publications. Reprinted by Permission of SAGE Publications.

media (event sponsorship, public relations, movies and social media). Both quantitative and qualitative measures must be used to monitor the brand position. Turkey's brand and tourism industry suffered significantly because of the biased film *Midnight Express* (Kotler and Gertner 2004).

Slogans

A slogan is part of brand identity articulated to position a product. However, slogans were also criticized for not accomplishing the role of intended differentiation. One reason is that destinations consisted of diverse offerings, which also make it difficult to create a slogan because they tend to cover everything (e.g. nature, culture, attractions, activities etc.) (Pike 2005). Blain et al. (2005) explain that a key component of destination branding is a destination logo, where logos are generally developed to reflect the image and attributes of the destination, to be flexible for different market mediums and to be memorable. Blain et al. (2005) found that although the vast majority of DMOs have developed and used logos, they have not involved local businesses and visitors in the logo design process.

A slogan is a short phrase that communicates descriptive or persuasive information about a brand. Effective slogans contribute to the development of both brand image and brand awareness, improving the 'top-of-mind position' of the brand (Keller 1993; Supphellen and Nygaardsvik 2002). In this respect, it is a vehicle to build brand equity, communicate the meaning of the brand and facilitate brand differentiation (Keller 1993). To aid in this process, slogans should focus on core identity and some of the most important associations reflecting brand benefits: functional, hedonic or experiential and symbolic benefits. Hedonic or symbolic benefits are more relevant for countries (Supphellen and Nygaardsvik 2002); therefore, they would serve better if they connect emotionally or symbolically with the customers.

For tourist destinations, functional benefits refer to destination attributes such as attractions, safety and accessibility. Hedonic or experiential benefits refer to the sensory pleasure or cognitive stimulation associated with a brand (e.g. the pleasure of a warm climate or the fun and excitement of its big city nightlife). Supphellen and Nygaardsvik (2002) pointed out that hedonic benefits are often prominent in country brand slogans and gave the example of the tourism slogan "Amazing Thailand" to promote Thailand as a tourist destination. Other slogans include, "I love New York" and "Turkey welcomes you". Finally, symbolic benefits signal status or lifestyle of the brand users. Travelers will prefer destinations congruent with their self-concept. The slogan "Only Vegas" would be a symbolic benefit, indicating everything or anything is possible (adult freedom).

R&R Advertising, the advertising agency in long partnership with Las Vegas Visitors and Convention Authority (LVCVA), develops and execute Las Vegas branding campaigns. Following the terror attacks of Sept. 11, 2001 Las Vegas realized that it could position itself as a center of guilt-free indulgence and "adult freedom" which turned out successful. Later, the prominent "What happens here, stays here" ad campaign were created. The campaign was a shift from amenities message to one with an emotional connection and to resonate with a wide array of target markets. The new tagline was tested online and before live groups in different markets, with and without of the umbrella tagline "Only Vegas." Feedbacks were favorable and there was no conflict.

The campaign did have opponents, mostly locals, who complained that "Vegas Stories" depicted their community as too sleazy. Corporate headhunters offered anecdotes about how the Sin City image made the recruitment of executives for non-gaming businesses a hard sell. Even hotel meeting planners contended that CEOs might be reticent to take sales people away from their spouses for a meeting in the city where what happens there, stays there. Sherrif complained that ads are encouraging people to lose their inhibitions and cause problems for police. A 2006 Poll by News3 TV Channel asked following question: Las Vegas has a slogan "What happens in Vegas, stays in Vegas" Do you think the slogan is good for Las Vegas or bad for Las Vegas? The results were: 58% Good, 38% Bad, and 4% Not Sure. R&R hired an independent research firm to test the spots after their first run. Seventy-three percent of consumers polled said they were more likely to visit Las Vegas after seeing the ads and an equally proportionate number of business people said they were favorably disposed to the destination.

To attract more visitors, in 2008, Las Vegas launched a new marketing campaign—titled "Your Vegas Is Showing. The new campaign is aimed at keeping the destination's winning slogan "What Happens Here Stays Here" intact and to create a new message to highlight cultivated features Vegas: high fashion, extravagant shows and gourmet dining. The marketing campaign is meant to complement the "What Happens Here" ads, not to replace it. The LVCVA's intent was to just "add on" to the highly successful current slogan. It points out that Las Vegas actually has several lesser slogans aimed at narrow audiences, including "Not business as usual," aimed at meeting planners; "Overtime guaranteed," to promote special events; and "A world of entertainment," for international audiences.

continued

Box 8.3 Las Vegas Branding Slogans. Sources: Audi (2008); Wilkening (2007).

Research has long shown that people behave differently in Vegas, allowing themselves the money and permission to do things they would never do at home, marketers say. For years, few non-gambling tourists set foot in Las Vegas. Even the cheap or free meals and accommodations were aimed at driving traffic to the casinos. But in recent years, to broaden the city's appeal, Las Vegas has spent billions of dollars to bring in splashy shows, designer stores and big-name chefs. The strategy has begun to pay off: For a growing number of tourists, the gambling is now an incidental attraction.

The new ad campaign is a bid to exploit that slow shift. After conducting surveys asking respondents what they knew about Las Vegas dining, shows and shopping brands, R&R developed so-called Vegas IQ scores for various cities to help determine where the new campaign should run in the heaviest rotation. Los Angeles, for example, has the highest Vegas IQ in the nation, with a score of 117. But other markets, such as St. Louis, Philadelphia, Boston, Baltimore, Atlanta and Dallas scored lower, in the 80s and 90s. Educating such markets about Las Vegas's full offerings is a reflection of the destination's move even further away from its identity as a gambling destination, and toward the image of full-blown vacation destination. According to Nevada state figures, 59.6% of Las Vegas revenue now comes from nongambling activities versus 40.4% from gambling.

What will be the next campaign for Las Vegas? Billy Vassiliadis, the CEO of R&R advertising states that the key is to let visitors paint their experience and "come here to be free, act free and feel unburdened will always be the core of the messaging."

Box 8.3 continued

8.6. DESTINATION BRAND SYSTEM

Destinations must excel at managing a system of brands' multiple brand identities largely because of the nature of the tourism product and fragmentation of the whole market. The same brand may have multiple identities or multiple brands may form the encompassing brand or umbrella brand. Destination branding can occur at different levels (see Table 8.2).

Destinations must move from the management of brand to management of brand portfolios: Each brand may play a different role in the system. Branding a tour package is overlooked in branding destinations. This would also augment the brand strength. How about using travelers to design an adventure tour package and using the tagline "Designed by adventurers for adventure traveler." This would be a practice similar to

Table 8.2 Destination Brand Hierarchies

Continent	Europe
Region	Mediterranean
Country	Turkey
Brand range	Sun & Sea, Winter
Sub-brands	Istanbul, Bodrum and Cappadocia
Sub-brands	Wine Tourism in Cappadoccia, Historical Tour of Istanbul and Nightlife of Bodrum

Marriott Courtyard's "Designed by business travelers for business traveler." Caldwell and Freire (2004) found that the factors that influence the image of a country are different from the factors that affect a region and city. When imagining a country, people will tend to visualize its functional characteristics. In the case of a region or city, however, people might visualize the representational aspects, such as the types of people who visit the region and how they themselves would be perceived if they went to that destination (self-image), and so on. Cities are 'products', which tend to be consumed more erratically than countries; they depend on specific promotions and events and are more dependent on the trends in the market, whereas countries have a more stable and enduring image. Regions and cities fulfill more self-expression needs when compared to countries.

Leveraging the destination brand: Destination brands could be leveraged by various practices such as brand extensions and co-branding. Offering new products in a different product class or diversification growth strategies to target new markets with new products would extend the brand. For example, Las Vegas targeted upscale travelers by building luxurious resorts such as Bellagio and Wynn, and City Center to extend the Las Vegas brand. Co-branding may take different forms, but perhaps the most applicable one is bundling of two brands to provide an enhanced travel benefit, value for money and/or experience. Destinations should look for opportunities to partner with other destinations and distribution channel organizations. Cruise companies have already been co-branding destinations. Cai (2002) showed that cooperative branding results in building stronger brand associations for a region than for individual communities. A destination brand can be leveraged through co-branding with another destination brand that receives more exposure and receives greater brand awareness.

Stakeholders: Brand-building efforts also require internal strategy: coordination across the destination, across media and across markets. Every destination should communicate the identity to the residents and other stakeholders. They should know what the brand stands for. At any one time, organizations at national, regional and local levels are actively engaged in presenting and promoting place identity in order to attract tourists and increase market share. The drive to establish distinct destination identity in the tourism marketplace is derived from a range of complex and competing interests manifested at global and local scales (Dredge and Jenkins 2003). The involvement of the stakeholders is essential in building a successful brand to coordinate brand strategy across all businesses. A destination usually has various constituents such as transportation, local businesses, airports, information centers and interest groups.

8.7. BRAND EQUITY

The concept of the brand as a value enhancer has led to the development of the concept of brand equity, which developed multiple meanings like the concept of brand (Wood 2000; Hankinson 2004). Brand equity has been approached from two major perspectives: financial and customer-based brand equity. Financial brand equity is the value of the brand to the owners or destination, whereas customer-based approach denotes the value of the brand for the tourists (Keller 1993; Simon and Sullivan 1993; Kim, Kim and An 2003). The latter is about indicators of future income, such as relative price, brand loyalty, distribution and awareness levels (Hankinson 2004).

Customer-based brand equity is more applicable to the tourist destination setting. Adapting the definition from Aaker (1996a), Destination Brand Equity (DBE) could be defined as a set of assets (and liabilities) linked to a brand's name and symbol that adds to (or subtracts from) the value provided by a destination to its potential and actual travelers and stakeholders. Brand equity creates value for visitors as well as other stakeholders. For example, a destination needs to be concerned with its brand image not only held by the travelers, but also tour operators and travel agents (and other stakeholders). The major asset categories are: (1) brand awareness, (2) brand loyalty, (3) perceived quality and (4) brand associations (Aaker 1996a, pp. 7–8).

Only a few studies applied customer-based brand equity to tourist destinations. Konecnik and Gartner (2007) proposed and tested four dimensions of a destination's brand (i.e. awareness, image, quality and loyalty) and found a positive relationship among the variables. Their conclusion was that destination image is central to brand evaluation and brand equity, but that the other dimensions are also necessary to truly measure customer-based brand equity. Boo, Busser and Baloglu (2009) extended the brand equity model by including perceived value and testing it for multiple destinations. They conceptualized and measured the destination brand equity consisting of concepts such as destination awareness, brand image, brand quality, brand value and brand loyalty. Their model posited that destination awareness, image and quality influence the perceived value. Then, destination image, perceived quality and value have impact on destination loyalty. They tested the model for two destinations, Atlantic City and Las Vegas, and for both the findings suggested a revised model in which destination image and perceived quality could be combined to reflect the destination brand experience. The major finding of the study was the mediating role of perceived value between destination brand experience and brand loyalty.

Brand Awareness

Brand awareness is the strength of a brand's presence in the traveler's mind. It must be assessed by multiple measures such as brand recognition, brand recall and top-of-mind awareness. Brand recognition is the familiarity with or exposure to the destination. Familiarity with a destination is a significant concept for tourist destinations because of its vital role in the tourist destination selection process. It represents a key marketing variable in segmenting and targeting certain groups and developing a marketing action plan, including product, distribution, pricing and promotion decisions. Therefore, it is necessary for tourist destinations to use a reliable and valid measure of familiarity with their destinations. Given the importance of the concept, one particular stream of marketing studies in the travel and tourism literature has centered on the relationship between familiarity and destination image. Particularly, for large-scale environments such as tourist destination countries, the destination cannot be wholly experienced at first couple of visits.

Therefore, the traveler would still have an informational image of destination offerings not experienced at earlier visit(s). Baloglu (2001) argued that familiarity with a destination is a multidimensional concept, including both previous experience (experiential familiarity) and amount of information used (informational familiarity). The author developed a familiarity index as a composite of both dimensions. The perceptual/cognitive, affective and overall image of Turkey showed variations due to U.S. travelers' familiarity level with the destination, the higher the familiarity, the more positive the image. The results particularly suggested that Turkey should utilize sales promotion techniques and conduct public relations/publicity activities rather than rely mostly on mass media advertising. The index can be used as a categorical or continuous variable or dependent or independent variable to examine the correlates with destination familiarity.

It was found that the low familiarity group mostly used commercial information sources such as brochures/travel guides, advertisements, tour operators and travel agents. On the other hand, high and medium familiarity groups were exposed to Turkey not only through commercial sources, but also through non-commercial sources such as articles/news, books/ movies and word-of-mouth. The results clearly illustrated the importance of non-commercial or autonomous information sources in image development efforts. Turkey should focus its efforts on public relations and publicity activities to increase the informational familiarity of travelers with the destination.

According to Morgan and Pritchard (2004), the emotional pull and conversation (celebrity) value of the destination are two critical dimensions of a positioning map, and the brand winners will be those who are high on the emotional meaning relations with travelers and have great conversation value. Celebrity value is similar to Aaker's (1996a, 1996b) brand recognition concept as those destinations will be on most travelers' shopping list (consideration set) and considered a must-see place. If a brand comes to travelers' minds when its product class (i.e. ski or sun and sea destination) or push motivation benefit (excitement, relaxation, adventure etc.) is mentioned, the brand will have recall. This is critical to be in the traveler's shopping list or consideration set. A destination that is recalled first will have top-of-mind awareness advantage.

Getting travelers to recognize and recall the destination brand can significantly augment brand equity. "The strongest brands are managed not for general awareness, but for *strategic* awareness. It is one thing to be remembered; it is quite another to be remembered for the right reasons (and to avoid being remembered for the wrong reasons" (Aaker 1996a, p. 17). Saffron Brand Consultants recently examined the strength of European cities' brands and how well cities use branding to exploit their assets. The study has used four factors (see Table 8.3) to assess brand recognition and strength (Hildreth 2009).

Brand Associations

Brand associations are defined as anything linked in memory to a brand (Aaker 1991; Low and Lamb 2000). Associations may be based on product experience, product attributes, positioning of the brand in promotional communications, price information, packaging, perceived typical user imagery or other sources. A set of brand associations which is organized

Table 8.3   Factors to Assess Brand Recognition and Strength

1	Pictorially recognized	Could many people recognize the city from a postcard without having to read the description on the back?
2	Quantity/strength of positive/attractive qualities	What prompted and unprompted associations do people have of the city?
3	Conversational value	How interesting would it be at a cocktail party to say, "Hey, I just got back from _____"?
4	Media recognition	How many times is the brand covered in the media in a given period?

in some meaningful way constitutes a brand image. A differentiating association can be a point of competitive advantage (Dean 2004). Brand associations would encompass several key marketing concepts such as image, personality, quality and perceived value. The pivotal and central concept, however, is the brand image. The perceived quality is a significant measure of brand equity (Aaker 1996b). It is often a key positioning basis and point of differentiation. Perceived quality is also a key dimension of brand equity and highly related to functional benefits and experience. Good value for the money (among comparable brands or among brands with which it competes) is a critical measure of destination brand equity.

Because a brand will provide functional, emotional and self-expressive or symbolic benefits, the brand image will have hierarchical components (i.e. brand image pyramid where upper levels are formed based on the lower levels). The first level is a cognitive image involving functional attributes. The second level, affective image, relates to emotional benefits and associations built upon cognitive perceptions. The third level is the symbolic or value expressive images such as global image and brand personality.

Brand Loyalty (Word-of-Mouth)

Often times the brand loyalty has not been included in the conceptualization of brand equity. It is a valid indicator of brand equity measures such as awareness, quality and value. "A focus on loyalty segmentation provides strategic and tactical insights that will assist in building strong brands" (Aaker 1996a, p. 22). A destination can enhance brand loyalty by ensuring that there is congruence between brand identity and brand image (Nandan 2004). A market can be divided into non-visitors, first-time visitors and repeat visitors. This is the most commonly used segmentation based on behavioral loyalty (Kotler, Bowen and Makens 2009). Destination loyalty is a multi-dimensional construct that includes both behavioral and attitudinal dimensions (Day 1969; Backman and Crompton 1991; Pritchard and Howard 1997; Baloglu 2001). Previous studies on brand loyalty have developed a four-cell loyalty typology based on attitudinal and behavioral dimensions (i.e. Day 1969; Dick and Basu 1994), and several studies in travel and tourism provided empirical support for the typology with respect to certain behavioral situations such as recreation, hotel, resort and airline patronage (Backman and Crompton 1991; Pritchard and Howard 1997; Baloglu 2001).

The cross-classification of attitude and behavior dimensions results in four distinct types of loyalty: high (true), spurious, latent and low (no) loyalty. The typology is illustrated in Figure 8.2. The high or "true" loyalty group is characterized by a strong preference or attitude and high repeat patronage. The latent loyalty group exhibits low patronage, although their preference for or attitude toward a company's brand is high. Their low patronage can be explained by several factors on the demand and supply sides. They may not have enough resources to increase their patronage, or the price, accessibility or distribution strategy of the company may not be stimulating repeat patronage. The spurious loyalty group, unlike "latent loyals," purchases frequently (high repeat patronage) despite a weak level of attitudes. They may be buying habitually or are influenced by price incentives and situational factors.

Baloglu (2001) applied the typology to loyalty for international destinations to assess its usefulness of this typology for international tourist destination behavior with respect to behavioral (actual visit and intentional loyalty) and attitudinal (cognition and affect) dimensions. The results revealed four distinct loyalty levels: high loyalty, latent loyalty and low loyalty, which included two distinct levels (natural switchers and experiential switchers), whereas the spurious loyalty group was not supported (Baloglu 2001). From both theoretical and practical standpoints, this makes sense because it would be unrealistic to expect a traveler to demonstrate a high repeat visitation behavior toward an international destination (high-involvement and high-risk product class) if that traveler does not have a strong and positive attitude or image toward that destination.

It is shown that the low loyalty type could further be sub-segmented into natural switchers (variety seekers) and experiential switchers (Baloglu 2001).

The loyalty groups provide attractive segments that can be targeted with different marketing strategies tailored to their attitudinal and/or behavioral loyalty levels. The Natural Switchers are possibly variety seekers or price-sensitive travelers. Therefore, value-based pricing strategy and usage of opinion leaders are more likely to influence their decisions. They can also be targeted by emphasizing destination attractions other than those they have experienced. Experiential Switchers, like the Natural Switchers, mostly consist of first-time visitors. They have somehow developed

	Repeat Behavior	
	High	**Low**
Attitude — High	"True" Loyalty	Latent Loyalty
Attitude — Low	Spurious Loyalty	Low Loyalty

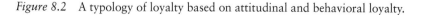

Figure 8.2   A typology of loyalty based on attitudinal and behavioral loyalty.

comparatively negative images as result of their experiences and demonstrated the weakest intentional loyalty. For that reason, this segment can best be targeted by product/service development and improvement efforts rather than a persuasive communication strategy because their attitudes were developed based on an actual experience (Baloglu 2001).

The loyalty research in travel and tourism should also take multi-destination loyalty into consideration. Given the number and variety of international destinations, it would make more sense to focus on multi-destination loyalty as well rather than single destination loyalty alone. The multi-destination loyalty has marketing implications in terms of positioning and developing strategic alliances with other destinations. Tourist destinations in the multi-brand loyal group should first identify the destination(s) visited by more travelers and should minimize the comparability between that destination and themselves. In as much as the destinations should position themselves aiming at the "leader," efforts should be expended to develop joint tourism packages with the "leader" if possible (Baloglu 2001).

It is very important to include brand advocacy or word-of-mouth behavior in the measurement of customer-based brand equity for tourist destinations. If travelers seek variety, they will not exhibit a repeat visitation. Therefore, the repeat behavior would not be a valid measure. Word-of-mouth behavior is a critical measure of brand equity for international destinations. To enhance loyalty for small-scale destinations, attractions, parks and museums, frequent buying programs and customer clubs could be used. "The customer club provides a vehicle by which the customer can identify with the brand, express his/her brand perceptions and attitude, and experience the sharing of a brand relationship with like-minded people" (Aaker 1996a, p. 24). It should also be noted that brand loyalty would be less important if a destination, like Las Vegas, wants to increase first-time visitors to have a healthy balance. In that case, perhaps proportions of first-time and repeat visitors would be a better measure.

* * *

CASE STUDY: BRANDING DESTINATIONS WITH UNIQUE SELLING PROPOSITIONS

Written by Mark M. Miller *(University of Southern Mississippi, USA)* **and Tony L. Henthorne** *(University of Nevada, Las Vegas, USA)*

Do tourism destinations use "unique selling propositions" in their marketing campaigns? That is, do destinations try to distinguish themselves from their competitors in terms of distinctive attractions, strategies, price levels, culture, history, landscape, music, cuisine or other attributes? Or, do most destinations employ similar, generic—albeit enticing—images to attract visitors?

The concept of the "unique selling propositions" (USP) and its application to advertising is generally credited to Reeves (1961). Richardson and Cohen operationalized and tested the USP concept in their 1990 comparative study of tourism marketing campaigns for U.S. states. Richardson and Cohen developed a hierarchical scale for analyzing states' marketing slogans, which ranged from "Level 0: No proposition" through "Level 4b: Unique selling proposition" (p. 95).

In an earlier published study—"In search of competitive advantage in Caribbean tourism websites: revisiting the Unique Selling Proposition"— Miller and Henthorne (2006) expanded the USP concept to an international tourism context while also updating the analysis to 21st-century Web-based marketing technology. In that paper, we argued for the appropriateness of the USP concept in international tourism in general and the Caribbean as a study region in particular:

> The intense competitiveness of the global tourism industry increasingly demands of destinations the most effective possible marketing, including product development, image creation, and promotional strategy. This necessity is nowhere more evident than for the Caribbean region: itself a highly fractured and intra-competitive collection of small destinations, which also must compete with a world of increasingly aggressive and expanding tourism alternatives.

We concluded in our analysis that the marketing campaigns of international tourism destinations such as Caribbean countries could be classified in a meaningful and useful manner according to Richardson and Cohen's USP hierarchy. On the other hand, we also concluded that tourism marketing based on the USP was rarely implemented, even more than four decades past the concept's introduction. Based on the data (collected in November and December 2004), most Caribbean destinations competed head-on against one another in their Web-based marketing campaigns based on similar and highly generic slogans and imagery. Standard beach images predominated, along with "one-size-fits-all" slogans such as Anguilla's "Tranquility Wrapped in Blue." Destinations with non-unique selling propositions then included several of the region's major tourism players: Bermuda, Cuba, Puerto Rico, the Bahamas, Jamaica and the Dominican Republic.

At the same time, however, a few highly creative campaigns did demonstrate the potential for inventing truly USPs for tourism destinations—and implementing these USP-based campaigns on the Web. These creative websites included some of the smallest players in the region, such as:

- Dominica: "The nature island of the Caribbean." No beaches shown.

- Guyana: Website presents several rotating slogans with accompanying images. Technologically sophisticated site. No tourists or tourism facilities shown.
- Suriname: "The Beating Heart of the Amazon." No beach images shown. (Miller and Henthorne 2006)

Perhaps, we speculated then, the relatively new technology of Web-based marketing opened up a more level playing field among the big-budget and small-budget destinations, and we might reward the more creative campaigns that made use of uniquely compelling images and slogans.

This study returns to the Caribbean for an updated analysis of tourism campaigns by the same destinations. As Web-based marketing continues to mature in the tourism industry, our research question here is: Is there a trend toward these Caribbean countries adopting USP-based campaigns for their tourism marketing?

Richardson and Cohen (1993) created the following hierarchical categorization of marketing slogans for their analysis of tourism campaigns by U.S. states:

- Level 0: No proposition
- Level 1: Proposition equivalent to "Buy our product"
- Level 2: Proposition equivalent to "Our product is good"
- Level 3a: Proposition gives a product attribute, but virtually any [tourism destination] could claim the same attribute
- Level 3b: Proposition gives a product attribute, but many [tourism destinations] claim the same attribute
- Level 4a: Proposition gives a unique product attribute which is not a product benefit (i.e., does not "sell")
- Level 4b: Unique selling proposition (Richardson and Cohen 1993, p. 95)

In our own analysis of marketing slogans for Caribbean destinations, we added one additional category, "Level X," indicating no slogan or proposition offered at all other than the destination's name, which was true of several of the study destinations involved.

We analyzed the marketing slogans of all members of the Caribbean Tourism Organization (CTO a, CTO b), based both on the destinations' slogans and images on their own "official" tourism marketing websites. For the weaker sites, we also gave them the benefit of the doubt by considering the slogan and images used on the CTO's promotional website for that destination (CTO a). Our data "snapshot" was taken in November and December 2004, generally considered as the beginning of the "high season" for Caribbean tourism. Data analysis included both text slogans and visual images (usually photographic) on the destinations' websites. Textual analysis followed, as closely as possible, Richardson and Cohen's "liberal" (generous) interpretation of uniqueness. Visual analysis focused primarily on the extent to which employed stereotypical and generic images of "sun & sand" tourism—sunny weather and sand beaches being fairly ubiquitous commodities across the Caribbean region.

The analysis for this updated study employs comparable data collected five years later, in November 2009, using much the same methodology as the earlier study. Our only modification this time is to put greater emphasis on imagery, compared with text slogans—recognizing the growing importance of visual images in our new media age.

As we allowed in our original paper, readers may well argue with our exact classifications of the following destinations. But we hope that you, the reader, will find this to be a meaningful, useful—and fun—exercise in destination branding.

Level X: No slogan or other proposition offered

Cuba

None. (CTO: none)
The state of Cuban tourism Web marketing in 2009 is very disappointing, to say the least. The country's tourism Web address listed by the CTO (http://www.cubatravel.cu/) was dead throughout November and well into December. The CTO site included a few standard Cuban images, but no slogan. A Web search returned a Canadian site (*http://www.gocuba.ca/en/index.asp*), with the pitiful slogan of "Viva Cuba."

St. Lucia

"St. Lucia" (CTO: "Simply Beautiful")
    2004: level 3b; slogan, "Simply Beautiful"
Imagery rotates through panning views of aerial island shots, beaches, water sports, golfing and concerts. Disappointing, as St. Lucia had developed a strong reputation as a highly focused eco-tourism destination.
    http://www.stlucia.org

Level 0: No proposition

No websites in 2009 fit this classification, in which a destination offers a simple slogan that makes no proposition (such as 2004's "The islands of the Bahamas").

Level 1: Proposition Equivalent to "Buy our product"

Cayman Islands

"Your Cayman Islands. Discover our Islands"

2004: level 3b; slogan, "Close to home. Far from expected."
The site's opening slideshow features almost entirely beach and related scenes.
http://www.caymanislands.ky/

Guyana

"Travel Guyana"
2004: level 4b; no slogan, but website presented several rotating slogans with accompanying images
Perhaps the greatest disappointment of all the website changes since 2004. Guyana's was our favorite site of 2004. Visual images now consist of mainly of a single picture, of two green tree frogs on a red stem. No beach pictures. The website now appears to be geared to tourism professionals, with calendar of events, reports on activities, and a blog which requires a subscription to log in. A very unappealing website for tourists. The CTO site includes two small images: Kaieteu Falls and (quite unusual for the Caribbean) a rodeo.
http://guyana-tourism.com/

Level 2: Our Product is Good

Bahamas

"It's better in the Bahamas"
2004: level 0; slogan, "The islands of Bahamas," (CTO: "It just keep getting better")
The site opens to a clickable, animated map of multi-colored islands. Beaches are shown in the backdrop, but are not the main focus of the imagery.
http://www.bahamas.com/

Bermuda

"Feel the Love"
2004: level X; slogan, (CTO only) "Out of the Blue"
The site opens with an animation, turning the globe upside down from an urban "your world" to a beach-fringed "our world." A subtle image of Bermuda shorts accompanies the slogan.
http://www.bermudatourism.com

Haiti

"Experience Haiti: It is unique and fascinating, it has personality" (CTO: "Part French, Part African, Part Caribbean—100% Unforgettable")

2004: level X; slogan, (CTO only) "Part French, Part African, Part Caribbean—100% Unforgettable"
The only image on the Haiti's site is a pair of Chica shoes. The site is a sad commentary on the deterioration of this beautiful country. The CTO website at least provides pictures of a waterfall and a port. There are no beach pictures on either of the sites.
http://www.haititourisme.com/

Level 3a: Virtually any Country could Claim the Same Attribute

Anguilla

"Feeling is Believing"
2004: level 3a; slogan, "Tranquility wrapped in blue"
The site rotates through a series of images within three picture frames, emphasizing beach imagery without much distinctiveness.
http://www.anguilla-vacation.com

Antigua & Barbuda

"The beach is just the beginning"
2004: level 2; slogan, "The Caribbean you've always imagined"
Most of the images on the website are of beaches. The CTO site adds pictures of sailboats and golfers. Whereas Antigua & Barbuda's website boasts of 25 reasons to travel to their destination, none of the reasons are unique.
http://www.antigua-barbuda.org/

British Virgin Islands

"Nature's Little Secrets"
2004: level 3b; slogan,"Nature's Little Secret—over 60 Caribbean islands to explore"
A single picture on the homepage rotates through a series of very conventional Caribbean—predominantly beach—images. The site is neither distinctive nor impressive. Not much imagery in support of the nature theme of the slogan.
http://www.bvitourism.com

St. Barths

"The Art of Being an Island" (CTO: "The Island for EXCELLENCE")
2004: level X; slogan, intended message perhaps: if you have to ask you can't afford it

This site opens with a stunning full-page aerial view of the island, revealing beaches, coastal cliffs and mountainous terrain. Beach images on the site are not typical sun & sand shots. Striking, even if not unique.
http://www.saintbarth-tourisme.com/

St. Eustatius

"The Caribbean's Hidden Treasure"
2004: level 3b; slogan, "The Caribbean's Hidden Treasure"
The header of the site scrolls through images of diving and palm tree-lined shores. The website is not very technically advanced, nor unique in its representations. *http://www.statiatourism.com/*

St. Vincent & The Grenadines

"The Caribbean You're Looking for"
2004: level 3b; slogan, "Jewels of the Caribbean"
The very colorful homepage presents a slideshow at the top of the page featuring mainly beach imagery.
discoversvg.com

Turks and Caicos Islands

"Beautiful by Nature"
2004: level 3a; slogan, "The everything island"
Web imagery is very tropical, colorful and stylized. The site manages to work a beach into the background of almost every picture on the slide show and subtly into the background of most portions of the site.
http://www.turksandcaicostourism.com/

Level 3b: Many Countries Claim the Same Attribute

Aruba

"90,000 friends you haven't met yet"
2004: level 2; slogan, "Where happiness lives"
Visitors to the site can click on a series of tabs for different attractions, each featuring a single, related photo image. Beach imagery is minimal, in favor of more distinctive—if not unique—images.
www.aruba.com

Dominican Republic

"DR endless. Has it all"

2004: level 1; slogan,"Experience our Caribbean"
Most pictures on the homepage are associated with the beach and ocean. At the bottom of the page, four tabs highlight distinctive characteristics of the Dominican Republic; beaches, golf, eco-tourism and cigars—although none are unique to the DR. Beaches and water activities are stressed throughout the website.
www.godominicanrepublic.com

Guadeloupe

"Archipelago of Discoveries"
2004: level X; slogan, (CTO only) "Decidedly French. Undeniably Caribbean."
In the French language version of the site, a very attractively animated slideshow of photos includes images of children sitting in a hammock, adventure sports, and local foods. Beaches are not displayed; cultural and adventure activities receive full attention. A very distinctive site, even if not entirely unique. Rather bizarrely, the English language version of the site is completely different and very conventional.
http://www.lesilesdeguadeloupe.com

Martinique

"Color Me Martinique"
2004: level 3a; slogan,"So much MORE than just an Island"
Three frames of photos labeled "Discovery," "Activities" and "Beaches" rotate a series of images that are very attractive & intriguing, but not strikingly unique.
http://www.martinique.org/

Puerto Rico

"Explore beyond the shore"
2004: level X; slogan,"The Shining Star" (CTO)
The site grabs attention with a flashy slide show of images ranging from downtown areas to snorkeling. The beach imagery complements other possible tourism locations of the island—some unusual, although none entirely unique to PR.
http://www.gotopuertorico.com/

St. Kitts

"An Experience Like No Other"
2004: level X; slogan, (CTO only) "Two Islands. One Paradise"

The slideshow images on this website feature beaches among a wide variety of other images: natural, architectural, cultural and recreational. Many of the photos are of beaches, but also golf courses and hotels.
http://www.stkittstourism.kn/

St. Martin

"The Friendly Island"
2004: level 3b; slogan,"Friendly Caribbean. French Caribbean"
The website opens with a striking series of interesting, artistic images, only some involving beaches, but none fully projecting a uniqueness for the destination.
http://www.st-martin.org/

Trinidad & Tobago

"The True Caribbean"
2004: level X; slogan, (CTO only) "Come to life"
Only two main pictures represent Trinidad & Tobago on the homepage of this site: a woman in festival dress and a scuba diver. Much smaller thumbnail images—divided between the two major islands of the country—emphasize the great diversity of attractions, although not the destinations' uniqueness in the region.
http://www.gotrinidadandtobago.com/

Level 4a: Unique Product Attribute which is not a Product Benefit

Grenada

"The Spice of the Caribbean"
2004: level 4a; slogan, "The Spice of the Caribbean"
The site features a slideshow of various tropical beaches and water-related activities. Beaches and water activities are featured prominently. The slogan is apparently a play on the island's unique dependence on allspice production: not exactly a benefit to tourists.
http://www.grenadagrenadines.com/

Montserrat

"A Caribbean Treasure—Spectacular by Nature"
2004: level 2; slogan, "One Hundred Thousand Welcomes"
A banner features pictures of the island's volcano fronted by a cute little girl holding a yellow flower. Banners for all the other pages have various

Montserrat images, with no beaches shown. The volcano appears to be the unique asset that Montserrat has used to sell the island—although given the volcano's violent, destructive history, this is not necessarily a product benefit.
www.visitmontserrat.com

St. Maarten

"Maagical St. Maartin"
2004: level 3b; slogan, "A little European a lot Caribbean"
A very splashy, colorful, appealing site with a variety of images including beaches, casino and nightlife. The text features memorable plays on the spelling of "Maartin," such as "Plaayful"—resulting in a memorable maarketing campaign.
http://www.st-martin.org/

Level 4b: Unique Selling Proposition

Barbados

"Welcome to Barbados: the official ambassadors of how to live life"
2004: level 2; slogan, "Just beyond your imagination"
The site opens immediately with a short, musical, well-produced video, featuring beach scenes but also images of local culture, architecture, and local residents. Residents also speak directly to the viewer. A very immediate, appealing site, with much that portrays a unique spirit of the country.
www.visitbarbados.org

Belize

"Mother Nature's Best Kept Secret"
2004: level 3b; slogan,"Mother Nature's Best Kept Secret"
Beach scenes are included in the slideshow, but are very much secondary to other attractions: Exploration of natural tropical settings, scuba diving, and Mayan ruins Mayan ruins. The site emphasizes a very unusually active sort of travel experience: similar to the 2004, but stepped up in terms of uniqueness.
http://www.travelbelize.org/

Bonaire

"Once a Visitor Always a Friend" (CTO: "Once a Visitor Always a Friend")
2004: level 3b; slogan, "Divers (sic) Paradise"

A single homepage image features a middle-aged woman in traditional dress, saying (in a text caption) "'Kon ta bai'," is "how are you" in Papiamentu, our native language on Bonaire. It's a common greeting heard on our friendly island in the Dutch Caribbean." The uniqueness (except for the other two Dutch destinations) and distinctive marketing approach of Bonaire is readily apparent.

http://www.tourismbonaire.com/

Curaçao

No text slogan, although site emphasizes "The Curaçao difference"
    2004: level 3a; slogan, "In the Southern Caribbean. Real. Different."
Although no slogan is presented, the top tab on the site is labeled "The Curaçao difference"—emphasizing the elements that distinguish this destination from other islands of the Caribbean. Imagery includes beaches, but emphasizes culture, architecture and nature.

http://www.curacao.com/

Dominica

"Defy the Everyday. Dominica. The Nature Island"
    2004: level 4b; slogan, "The Nature Island of the Caribbean"
The slideshow includes very little beach imagery, in favor of scenes of natural beauty, Scuba diving, and culture. Overall, the website emphasizes Dominica's particularly strong focus on eco-tourism—in 2009, seemingly uniquely so.

http://www.dominica.dm/site/index.cfm

Jamaica

"Once you go, you know"
    2004: level 1; slogan,"Explore Jamaica", "Come. Feel Alright" (CTO)
Perhaps no promotional website in the Caribbean has developed further in five years than Jamaica's—in many ways, the best of all the sites today. The technical level of the site is stunning, but is consistent with, rather than overpowering the marketing concept. A catchy reggae promotional song bursts out, and you can slide across a scale of attraction images that range between "ritzy" and "roadside." The overall effect of the site is distinctively Jamaican—and very compelling. We are tempted to stop writing right now and start checking out airfare rates to Jamaica.

http://www.visitjamaica.com/

Nevis

"Naturally" (CTO: "Naturally")

2004: level 3a; slogan, "Nevis . . . Naturally"
The images on this site open with a stunning aerial photo of the entire island. Photos feature both beaches and other aspects of natural beauty. The site opens with the video image and locally-accented voice of a local woman, welcoming us to Nevis and explaining the uniqueness of the island.
http://www.nevisisland.com/

Suriname

"The Beating Heart of the Amazon"
2004: level 4b; slogan, "The Beating Heart of the Amazon"
The site's images are not likely to be confused with any other Caribbean destination, strongly emphasizing the people, nature and culture of the nation's South American interior. There are no beach images on the homepage.
http://www.suriname-tourism.org/

U.S. Virgin Islands

"America's Caribbean"
2004: level 4b; slogan, "America's Caribbean"
The same emphasis on "America's Caribbean," and "No passport required" as 2004 has grown rather stale. With the exception of Puerto Rico, however, this remains a unique selling proposition. The site has little else distinctive to offer, however, other than a slideshow of fairly typical Caribbean scenery and attractions.
http://www.usvitourism.vi/
We found many striking changes—and overall, we think, advancements—between the 2004 and 2009 data. Based on text slogans and images, we classified nine destinations in 2009 in the highest, 4b, Unique Selling Proposition category—up from only four in 2004. On the other end of the spectrum, we assigned only seven destinations to the lowest categories in 2009: levels X—2. In 2004, we assigned 15 destinations to these categories.

Some of this upward shift is due to our greater emphasis on images, rather than just text slogans, but on the other hand the websites are now using much better and, we believe, more sophisticated use of imagery. Technical advancements in video, animation and use of aerial photography technologies are particularly striking between 2004 and 2009. The appropriate application of this technology in support of the marketing message is also very impressive; we found no instances in which the technology distracted from the selling proposition.

As in 2004, several of the Caribbean's smaller destinations put their creativity to work to earn the highest ranking in this classification. Unlike

2004, on the other hand, one of the region's largest destinations—Jamaica—has leapfrogged into the top rank category, as well.

Clearly, the race is on in terms of advancements of marketing technology. Websites that would have been impressive in 2004 fall into the background of 2009 website-based marketing. Substandard or unavailable websites—such as those of Haiti and Cuba, respectively—now represent stunning market failures.

Overall, we conclude that the destinations of the Caribbean are indeed placing greater emphasis on using Unique Selling Propositions in their tourism marketing. We expect this trend only to expand further, over the next five years, as at least nine destinations have raised the bar and provide exceptional examples of USP-based marketing for other destinations across the Caribbean and beyond. We believe that our implications from the original study still stand firmly:

The USP approach may help grow the overall tourism "pie" in the Caribbean region. Smaller destinations could grow their tourism industries by identifying and attracting new niche markets, rather than simply diverting traditional markets from their larger and more established neighbors. Working cooperatively in this way, rather than competing against one another, the many Caribbean countries could more effectively promote this endlessly fascinating region as a whole. Tourists could be encouraged to make more repeat visits, as well, to experience other clearly differentiated destinations within this region. If successful, the Caribbean region and the CTO could serve as models for strengthening the competitive advantage of developing tourism regions worldwide (Miller and Henthorne 2006).

Acknowledgments: 2009 data collected and analyzed by masters and doctoral students in Miller's Fall 2009 Tourism & Service Industry Development, Department of Economic & Community Development, the University of Southern Mississippi: Robert Hales, Shelia Jackson, Matthew McWhorter, Tyler Moore, Hana Prudilova, John Scott, Louis Whittington and James Wilcox. UNLV graduate student Kasra Ghaharian assisted with formatting the data analysis.

9 From Traditional Marketing to "IT" Marketing

Practical evidence indicates that the traditional travel distribution system is going through a very dramatic change. Therefore, this chapter aims to examine the present and potential impact of Information Technology (IT) on the tourism industry, tourism marketing and management and destination competitiveness. The first part provides basic knowledge about current applications of IT and its future predictions. The second part revisits the main features of distribution channels in tourism and travel marketing. The third part is devoted to several discussions examining the extent to which developments in IT will reshape the distribution channels in the tourism and travel industry. The fourth part examines major differences between traditional tourism and travel marketing and Internet marketing (cyber marketing). The link between developments in IT and destination competitiveness is discussed in the final part.

9.1. IMPORTANCE OF "IT"

Over the past two decades, IT has become increasingly vital for the efficient and effective management of operations and managing the distribution of products and services with the tourism and travel industry (Buhalis 1998; Stamboulis and Skayannis 2003; Buhalis and Law 2008; Alford and Clarke 2009). Everything from information centers to check out processes can potentially be integrated. Businesses seem highly ambitious to set up new IT applications which will enable customers to manage their own information-gathering and booking arrangements. The evidence seems to be that many users find such facilities valuable, and the volume of business transacted through them is growing substantially. Changes in the distribution of services as a result of such developments potentially impact the structure of the tourism and travel industry. Individual businesses as well as their broader authorities such as DMOs involved in both direct and indirect marketing need to take into these changes and the opportunities, threats and uncertainties which they represent.

Commencing from the early 1990s, a number of studies have explored the importance of technology in the tourism and travel industry (Stipanuk 1993; Hope, Hope and Tavridou 1996; Ortega and Rodríguez 2007; Tanrisevdi and Hancer 2008; Law, Qi and Buhalis 2010) and have also attempted to indicate IT as a source of competitive advantage (e.g. Rimmington and Kozak 1997; Cho and Olsen 1998; Kozak, Andreu and Bigne 2005; Eraqi 2006; Pikkemaat and Weiermair 2007). In general, most people are well aware of the importance of IT to their destinations or customers because IT has the capability of (1) strengthening the bargaining power between suppliers and users, (2) improving efficiency in production and distribution of products and services for lower costs and (3) adding value to such products and services for differentiation.

Thus, avoiding the use of IT may keep one destination behind its competitors. Using it may help to keep the gap between competitors narrow, but trying to increase its capability and spread its functionality may help to distinguish it from others and bring competitive advantage over them. Competitive advantage gained through the use of IT will be acquired mostly over businesses or destinations that do not use it widely or do not have access to it.

The travel and transportation industry worldwide spends billions of dollars on technology per annum, and technological innovation has been ranked as the top priority in the next years of the tourism industry. Managers of large businesses believe that technology plays a vital role in improving the effectiveness of their operations and enhancing consumer satisfaction (Hoof, Verbeeten and Combrink 1996). However, high staff turnover rates, lack of proper training and limited financial resources were listed in the same survey as the main barriers affecting the use of technology in a productive manner. It was also suggested that multimedia technology such as interactive TV, on-line networks and multimedia kiosks present new opportunities for communicating with end users (Bennett 1996; Ortega and Rodríguez 2007).

Being a part of software technology, IT is the most recent development in the electronic and communication technologies used for the acquisition, processing, analysis, storage, dissemination and application of information among its potential or actual users (Poon 1993). Hence, it is regarded as a powerful tool for maintaining and sustaining competitive advantage in the international business arena (Hamill 1997). The travel and tourism industry has used IT extensively for more than 20 years. The Internet (together with email and intranet), virtual reality, electronic shopping channels, smart cards, digital cash, personal digital assistants, DVDs, travel blogs and social media are the evidence of developments in IT and of its applications within destination marketing and management. Each of these applications has the potential to be taken into consideration as a main topic of separate papers. This chapter, therefore, focuses mainly on the application of IT as a marketing tool and its potential impact on destination competitiveness.

9.2. DISTRIBUTION CHANNELS IN TOURISM

The AMA defines marketing in general as "the performance of business activities that direct the flow of goods and services from the producer to the consumer or user" (Coltman 1989, p. 11). Although this definition does not give us any clue how products or services will be moved from the producer to the end user or vice versa, it is widely known that either direct (from the producer to the end user) or indirect distribution channels (the sale to the end user through an intermediary) are widely used in practice, depending upon what benefits each provides.

Instead of a physical distribution system, the tourism and travel industry includes several intermediaries within the distribution channels due to characteristics of services such as intangibility, inseparability, variability (heterogeneity) and perishable (Rust, Zahonik and Keiningham 1996). This situation is significant particularly for the distribution channel system of accommodation facilities as well as tourist destinations when they are mostly marketed at the international level. From this point of view, the distribution channel in tourism is to be considered as a total system of linkages between actual and potential visitors and the suppliers of tourism services. As this statement implies, the challenge is how to get the end user to the consumption site (retailer). This unique feature raises the need for a different kind of distribution system in tourism. Nevertheless, the primary purpose of distribution channels is to sell a business's products and services (Holloway and Plant 1988). Businesses therefore care more about the amount of financial figures they expect than about how they sell.

The major features of distribution channels in the tourism and travel industry could be highlighted as below. First, intermediaries have a pivotal role in directing tourism demand through a destination or an accommodation facility, particularly in mass tourism. Second, there are several intermediaries taking part in the pipeline of the distribution channel in tourism and travel at the time interval between when end users start and end their travel or vacations. Third, there is no need to transfer any physical product in tourism and travel. The only item that needs to be moved is consumers (end users). Therefore, the circulation of information on the network is the most remarkable aspect of tourism and travel. The barrier in any part of the chain will possibly make organizations and people unable to complete the circle or the tourism product.

Recent arguments on the topic have focused on whether, or to what extent, IT may have an impact on the distribution system of tourism and travel marketing in the future. One group says that future developments in IT will never influence the structure of distribution channels in tourism and travel, whereas another takes the opposite view. Therefore, this chapter considers both views in the succeeding paragraphs.

The first group of commentators supports the view that changes in the technological environment of tourism and travel have led to the reorganization of the distribution channels (Steiner and Dufour 1998; Schuster 1998). Similarly, much emphasis has been given to the importance of information in tourism and travel, a sector where the main purpose of distribution channels is to bring information to the end user and to get feedback from him or her in return. Developments in IT therefore surely impact upon the structure of distribution channels in this sector. Having reviewed developments in technology and its impact on advertising strategies over the last 40 years, Rust and Oliver (1994) examined the possible future of technology as an advertisement tool in the 21st century. These authors expect technology will bring a revolution in the marketing of goods and services as well as in academia. Benjamin and Wigard (1995) strongly believe that as traditional marketing procedures will be replaced by IT, there will be no need to gather consumers in a specific place or bring consumers and producers (or retailers) together. This means that a new version of marketing policy will possibly exist.

Because IT possibly has an opportunity to bring demand and supply on the virtual market together, the definition of "the tourism market" concept needs to be reconsidered. Whereas the main element of tourism demand as being the consumer who needs to satisfy his leisure requirements remains the same, computers could serve as suppliers or have the responsibility of suppliers. In addition to the specific feature of the accommodation industry being open for 24 hours a day, computers may improve the non-stop services offered by the tourism and travel industry generally. Major hotel and airlines businesses have launched their websites on the Internet and are about to activate them as a two-way communication channels (e.g. Hilton, Sheraton, British Midland and American Airlines). An Internet user can search for the hotel and the flight company or the destination where he wants to spend his holiday and complete reservations simply by giving details such as name, address and credit card number or other payment options. Once the reservation is accepted, the ticket is delivered to the user in a couple of days, and the booking fare is transferred from the users' account into the business's account.

Hamil (1997) agrees with the statement that the Internet is likely to have an impact on international marketing in the near future and to reduce the importance of intermediaries which are expected to change their roles and services. In parallel with this statement, there could be grounds to argue that travel agents could take a place within the tourism market as consultant agencies providing information about any activity, product or service (e.g. looking after mailings, gardening and home security). According to the opposite view, in terms of direct and indirect tourism and travel marketing, consumer–producer linkages may increase, but this may not cause intermediaries to disappear. There can always be a role for both traditional and new types of intermediaries (Sarkar, Butler and Steinfield 1995). Intermediaries will be likely to preserve their importance in the marketing of tourism products and services because:

- They help end users determine their needs.
- They inform end users about the existence and main features of products.
- They do marketing research studies and inform producers about the result.
- End users do not always have perfect information, so there is a risk they may not be satisfied.

One series of studies suggests that although IT will facilitate the transformation of tourism and travel marketing, it is unlikely to bypass the travel agent (e.g. Walle 1996; Mayr and Zins 2009). However, travellers may gather information through the Internet and negotiate better deals, and lower profit margins could appear in the operations of travel agents. Moreover, Lin (1998) claims that it is not clear how service providers such as travel agents or tour operators will take their place in the emerging distribution channels of the tourism and travel industry, although it is expected that the technological environment will change the existing marketing strategies (e.g. releasing advertisement campaigns on cyberspace, redesigning products, services, offers and brand recognition).

Another view (Sarkar, Butler and Steinfield 1995) centers on the importance of intermediaries as representing multiple producers such as a travel agent who sells the products of a wide variety of tour operators, hotels and transport businesses. This view believes that a producer cannot be expected to meet the full range of end-user needs as a direct result of specialization in service production and marketing. Although this view stresses the importance of intermediaries as a business providing consultancy services, it is not clear how this will work because users are likely to have an opportunity to be informed about the products and the services of different producers on the Internet.

Moreover, although users need to find suppliers or intermediaries rather than vice versa, it is also true that suppliers or intermediaries need to reach potential users via computers or other advertising tools to make them more aware of their products or services provided on the screen (Berthon, Pitt and Watson 1996). Therefore, it should be necessary to redefine the role of intermediaries as "cybermediaries" (or artificial agents) and the concept of marketing as "cybermarketing" (Schuster 1998). Cybermediaries or artificial agents have been introduced into cyber tourism and travel marketing as a bridge that interacts information between the end user and the producer

(Schuster 1998). Cybermediaries seem to be the competitors of traditional intermediaries in tourism and travel. A traditional intermediary is defined as "any third party or organisation between producer and consumer that facilitates purchases, the transfer of title to the buyer, and sales revenue to the producer" (Middleton 1994, p. 203). There appear to be no reasons that cybermediaries are not accepted as intermediaries because both concepts' tasks fit into each other.

Hoffman (1994) claims that traditional travel agents could never be replaced due to the fact that the majority of the potential market is Internet illiterate. These non-trained users always need help sorting out prices and options. It is assumed that these individuals will continue to want and need personal contact with a travel agent or consultant despite developments in the marketing of goods and services. This view is shared by several authors (e.g. Connolly, Olsen and Moore 1998). These authors state that those individuals who do not have access to the Internet or who are not familiar with technology could continue to visit travel agents. Considering developments in IT and arguments made relating to the possibility of altering the current marketing structure of the tourism and travel industry, the distribution channel of destination marketing can be revised as in Figure 9.1 (see also Table 9.1).

1. Traditional direct tourism and travel marketing where suppliers and/or tour operators traditionally reach end users without using any intermediaries.
2. Traditional indirect tourism and travel marketing where suppliers reach end users via travel agents or vice versa. Indirect tourism and travel marketing via CRSs where suppliers provide their products and services via intermediaries by using CRSs.
3. Traditional indirect tourism and travel marketing where suppliers reach end users via tour operators (e.g. package tours).
4. Traditional indirect tourism and travel marketing where suppliers reach end users via package tours designed by tour operators and sold by travel agents.
5. Direct tourism and travel marketing via the Internet where suppliers and tour operators have the opportunity to reach their end users directly on the Internet or vice versa. Travel agents can take place as consultants.
6. Indirect tourism and travel marketing via IT where negotiations between suppliers and intermediaries can be seen. Intermediaries can launch their own websites by bringing products and services from suppliers to end users. They can promote hotels that have no access to the Internet. They can also make bookings on behalf of those individuals who do not have their own computers and are technology illiterate.

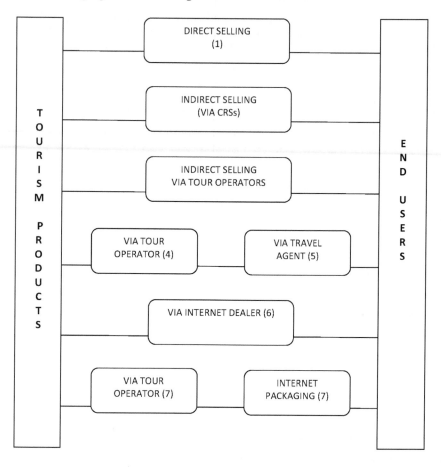

Figure 9.1   The distribution channels of tourism and travel marketing. Source: Own elaboration

Table 9.1 Examples of Various Tourism Marketing Channels

Channels	Details of Marketing Approaches
1	Rooms or seats can be sold directly to the end user.
2	Rooms or seats can be sold to the end user via travel agents by paying commission.
3	Rooms or seats can be sold in bulk via tour operators who use these rooms and seats to create package tours.
4–5	Rooms and seats are transformed into a package tour. A package tour can be sold via travel agents. However, this type of distribution channel is mainly related to mass tourism activities as the majority of inclusive tours are sold through travel agents.
6	Direct selling via the Internet to reach end users. Businesses can design their own websites including all the material required to obtain information about the product and make reservation and payments on the screen.
7	Hotels that have no access to the Internet can be promoted. Bookings can also be made on behalf of those individuals who do not have their own computers and are technology illiterate.

Source: Own elaboration.

The preference for a distribution channel varies from one user to another and from one organization to another when considering market segment represented, accommodation required and purpose of travel or vacation (Connolly, Olsen and Moore 1998). The structure of distribution channels in the marketing of inclusive tours differs from that of the city or business and convention hotels. Hotels dealing with inclusive tours have a longer distribution channel compared to what others have. The main objective of inclusive tours is to bring tourism products and services together, rename and offer them to end users with reasonable prices (at a specific inclusive price).

Individual and business travellers benefit from IT much more than other segments do. For instance, booking a resort hotel and a flight separately would be much more expensive than buying a package deal including the same hotel and the same flight. However, there would not be much difference in price if a city or convention hotel is booked either individually or through an intermediary. Resort hotels are not allowed to promote themselves because they are widely dominated by tour operators. Therefore, there is no ground to argue that IT will change the marketing of resort hotels in the international market. Nevertheless, the place where IT is effectively used and impacts on the distribution channel will be city and business or convention hotels that market themselves either individually or through an intermediary but are not dependent on them so largely.

The view that tour operators intend to create consumer loyalty to themselves rather than to tourist destinations should not be under-estimated (Carey, Gountas and Gilbert 1997). Hence, potential developments in the number of travel agents and horizontal integration force tour operators to come up with new marketing strategies to maintain their existing share of the market. It can be claimed that the use of IT is a significant tool for tour operators to help themselves bypass travel agents and sell their products directly to end users. This strategy could shorten the amount of time spent on the chain. Moreover, it is also expected that the use of CRSs and GDSs for booking reservations will diminish in the future. This means that users do not have to call at travel agents and wait for minutes in the queue and travel agents will be at risk to lose some part of commissions they get from suppliers (i.e. tour operators or accommodation facilities).

9.3. TRADITIONAL VERSUS INTERNET MARKETING

Advertising and promotion are the two main features of the Internet. The Internet has the potential to be a 'virtual shopping and learning centre' in the future by moving all department stores, banks, schools, travel agencies, hotels and entertainment facilities and activities onto the screen. Internet users show high interest in booking travel and making their travel plans via computers. Consumers in tourism and travel are becoming more experienced and knowledgeable about what they should expect from organizations, facilities or destinations and what they are offered in return. Similarly, the demographic and economic profiles of Internet users show them to be highly educated and members of middle or upper income groups. One could assume that future users will be much more Internet literate if trends follow the predicted path.

The Internet has therefore a potential to become an essential tool for successful international tourism and travel marketing. In comparison with the domains of traditional marketing, international tourism and travel marketing through the Internet provides benefits to service providers and users (Walle 1996; Hamil 1997; Connolly, Olsen and Moore 1998; Buhalis 2000; Diaz, Martin-Consuegra, Esteban and Blazquez 2009) because it is:

- faster as it removes barriers of communication with actual and potential consumers, suppliers and partners around the world by eliminating problems created by geographical distance, time zones and location. Internet may enable users to make bookings at their home or office in a short time without having to wait in the office of travel agents. Users are not forced to make their reservations during the daytime; they can use computers 24 hours a day. Transaction with credit cards is another opportunity of saving time.

- less expensive because it reduces marketing and promotion costs and the efforts of businesses (suppliers), which are required to directly reach end users around the world. It also reduces the importance of intermediaries who are expected to revisit their roles and services. Similarly, the Internet is likely to reduce the cost and efforts of end users to have access to information as a result of the short distance between suppliers and end users appearing on the screen. Users do not have to wait until information is prepared and sent by producers (or suppliers and intermediaries); rather they will have a great opportunity to seek information from all competitors operating in the same market, not only one. Furthermore, it may reduce the prices of goods or services because businesses may have an opportunity to decrease their production and marketing costs which could be reflected to end users as discounts in return.

- more global because it is easy to reach potential end users around the world via the Internet. It also increases the standardization of prices across borders as end users become more aware of prices in different countries or businesses. This feature has the potential to make IT service providers offer equal opportunities for all players on the Internet. The share of voice is essentially uniform and more flexible as it takes a short time to update information taking place on the Internet. It is also available for the dissemination of time-sensitive information or products (e.g. research findings, speeches and brochures). Therefore, no player can drown out others due to variations in price levels or information sources.

- more bi-directional because it provides an opportunity for direct tourism and travel marketing to gain two-way communication. The Internet also provides the opportunity to obtain feedback from end users in a short time. This can result in improved consumer relations and relationship marketing. As known, the spread of negative word-of-mouth communication will be much faster via the Internet; therefore, businesses will need to keep both their actual and potential consumers well informed and will be sensitive and responsive to consumer complaints.

- more likely to offer wider and deeper material because it helps organizations and people to access a wide range of information sources. For instance, the user does not need to make a telephone call with the independent or the hotel restaurant in order to learn the contents of the menu to be served in the evening or during the week and to book a place. Marketing promotions can be designed on the Internet (i.e. providing hotel discount programs or giving bonus points to users making reservations on their computers). The Internet can also generate a wealth of information on market trends and developments in the industry and other related industries worldwide.

- more likely to offer an opportunity to gather more information about facilities and services provided by other businesses. This can be very useful to make a product and service comparison with others. End users may have an opportunity to compare all items and choose what they desire by looking at colorful pictures of attractions and facilities, checking the availability of hotel rooms and seats and fares of more than one business or destination on the screen. This could be helpful for users to enhance their tourism experiences by stabilizing the gap between expectations and perceptions of real holidays. This would also facilitate competitiveness among businesses. As a result, end users will be provided with enough information prior to commencing either their virtual holidays on the computer or their actual holidays in the final destination.
- more environmentally friendly because everything is sent via computers and so reducing the distribution of brochures, letters and bureaucracy. The traditional marketing efforts have created several problems regarding natural resources and their use for the purpose of making profits. It is expected that developments in IT will make a contribution to the quality of environmental management. The idea of becoming an environmentally friendly tourism industry has been currently accepted by a large number of academics and practitioners.
- more competitive in the international arena because the above-mentioned features will enable businesses to offer goods and services that users need and demand and improve the effectiveness of marketing and promotion strategies and operations within the organization. Direct marketing could provide service providers beneficial means to better understand their market segments by analyzing detailed consumer records. The use of IT spreads the recognition of an organization's brand to a wider audience, which means gaining access to broader markets. The contribution of IT in enhancing consumer satisfaction, loyalty and profitability is also noteworthy and indicates the extent to which IT would be vital for enhanced competitiveness.

Although such advantages are listed and the relative communication effectiveness of both advertising and personal selling has been identified as being from high to low levels, the position of the Web or Internet within tourism and travel marketing still seems unclear because the Internet could be regarded as "a complementary tool to the direct selling by industrial marketers and a supplementary tool to advertising by end-user marketers" (Berthorn, Pitt and Watson 1996). It appears that end users must find the marketer rather than vice versa. However, it is true that marketers sometimes need to reach end users via computers or other advertising tools to make them aware of products and services provided on the screen.

IT appears to change the shape of the tourism and travel industry in the near future by developing new types of products and services. Therefore, new marketing strategies will need to be established in accordance with developments in both the tourism industry and IT. For instance, it is expected that new businesses will be added to the distribution chain in tourism and travel such as *IT Marketing Service* (center) or *IT Consumer Service* that will be responsible for assisting technologically non-trained hoteliers, agents or users. This could expand the chain (see the channel marked as 4 on Figure 9.1).

9.4. DEVELOPMENTS IN IT AND DESTINATION COMPETITIVENESS

Taking the advantage of new opportunities available in the external environment, the technological change has become a key factor in achieving success for destination competitiveness (Diaz, Martin-Consuegra, Esteban and Blazquez 2009). Industrial change was the prerequisite for tourism demand in the 19th century, providing new production methods in manufacturing which could stop for public holidays and steam motive power for mass transport by rail and sea. In the 20th century, transport technology for air and road vehicles allowed the spread of mass tourism to widespread destinations, rather than being limited to those reachable by rail and ship (Bull 1995). Suppliers of tourist attractions have quickly adopted technical advances in such areas as gaming machines, theme parks or exhibits and synthetic tourist experiences which may simulate wilderness or subaquatic (underwater sports) environments, saving the originals (Bull 1995).

Beyond the hardware technology, IT is also making travel and tourism markets more competitive. It is believed that the future competitiveness of tourist destinations will largely depend on the range of new telecommunication technologies being used and the extent to which destinations have access to the marketing and promotion opportunity via such technologies (Buhalis and Cooper 1998). Inequality in gaining access to IT may possibly create first- and second-class tourist destinations, organizations and customer groups. Such an imbalance between developed and developing countries or tourist destinations could be the direct consequence of IT for international tourism and travel marketing. Tourist destinations and their organizations with undeveloped telecommunication structures could be less suitable for Internet marketing as being slower, weaker and more expensive.

Distribution channels in tourism and travel are undergoing a dramatic change. Whereas large or international businesses have welcomed new developments in IT, seeing them as opportunities to be more competitive in the market, small and medium-sized businesses are forced to adapt themselves into the new business environment. Despite the benefits of the Internet, small tourism organizations may not be able to afford it. Thus, large organizations will be able to preserve their leadership by dominating

Internet marketing activities. However, the question as to how to investigate the extent to which the competition (or balance) between developed and developing countries, or destinations, will be affected by such developments in IT still remains unanswered.

Does this mean that businesses in developing countries cannot sell their tourism products on the Internet because they do not have ready access to IT as in many developed countries? Or do tour operators still have a catalyst role in keeping both types of countries in balance? Trends demonstrate that developing countries such as eastern Mediterranean, eastern Europe and the Far East are significantly becoming popular for both individual and mass tourism activities. They are also considered culturally and naturally attractive, exotic and up-market destinations. It is difficult to predict if this will continue when the use of IT spreads. Such an imbalance between developed and developing countries or tourist destinations could be the direct consequence of IT for the international tourism and travel marketing.

Schertler (1994) classifies the impact of IT on the tourism and travel industry using five points produced by Porter (1980) to determine the strength of competitive forces and the impact on industry profitability:

- Competition among existing businesses and their destinations (new distribution channels)
- Threat of new entrants (new distribution channels and new competitor destinations)
- Bargaining power of customers (access to prices, highly experienced customers)
- Bargaining power of suppliers (direct selling of accommodation stocks and subsequently destinations)
- Threat of substitute products and services (new distribution systems and virtual reality)

Many businesses and destinations are attempting to secure competitive advantage by adopting both direct and/or indirect tourism marketing methods in order to reach customers. Direct tourism marketing strategies, utilizing electronic information and reservation systems via IT, include the provision of information about products, services, events and destinations, and the opportunity to purchase and sell travel, accommodation, leisure services and events. An extensive bulk of tourism establishments and even destination organizations in the industry has recently produced their own websites as pioneers of such services.

IT could be a source of developing effective strategies for maintaining, sustaining and improving the competitive position of tourism, travel and hospitality businesses and tourist destinations. Practical observations as well as related literature prove that businesses using high-technology equipment and up-to-date management and marketing strategies are more likely to be competitive than those who do not. Major determinants of competitive advantage can be summarized as enhancing competitive pricing, decreasing supply and distribution costs and maintaining closer relationships with suppliers and users. It is argued that businesses should carry out a benefit-cost analysis because the deployment of IT applications such as the Internet might not make any contribution to revenue enhancement but also could make a negative impact on the cost side (Buhalis 1998).

Therefore, it is recommended to initially establish a distribution strategy that fits into the purpose of the business for the use of delivering its products and services and then to use IT as a support (Connolly, Olsen and Moore 1998). Otherwise, there could be a waste of time and financial resources. Thus, IT could be used as a complementary part of the pull channel strategy if the business intends to sell itself directly because IT is expected to make a significant contribution to attracting end users or directing their interest toward the business.

IT potentially reduces per transaction communication costs and efforts (Schertler 1994; Buhalis 2000; Diaz, Martin-Consuegra, Esteban and Blazquez 2009). It provides inexpensive delivery of information in that it enablers suppliers to communicate directly with existing and potential customers and differentiate their products by considering customers' needs and wants. There may be rather less requirements to attend expensive international tourism fairs, open international offices and produce expensive hard copy publicity materials. It could also be a powerful tool to overcome bureaucracy.

Tourism information systems can be categorized as computerized (low technology), basic computerized (middle-range technology) and advanced computerized (high technology) systems (Kingsley and Fesenmaier 1995). The tourism industry is currently experiencing advanced computerized systems such as CRSs, the Internet and virtual reality. These recent developments in IT may also help to create first- and second-class tourism providers. For large multi-national businesses, there does not seem to be a problem. In fact, exciting new opportunities are opening up through IT-linked strategic alliances.

However, small and medium independent groups are likely to face challenges because of their reduced IT resource capacity. Some of the greatest threats to these businesses are the potential barriers in marketing. Even if such businesses access IT distribution channels, they may find that unless they enter into alliances through consortia, their individual efforts will lack impact and be ineffective. When customers tend to access web information provided by well-known brand leaders, such negative impacts may make these businesses unable to compete in the international arena and maintain their market share. Tourism boards and authorities will surely play an important role in counterbalancing this, but they will need higher levels of resources if they are to adequately support small independent businesses.

Difficulties faced by small businesses may also be experienced by less-established destinations. Although newly established network systems may in some respects lower a destination country's marketing and publicity expenditures, they also require additional investment and ongoing payments to maintain a full membership of the system. This is a challenge for developing tourism destinations. They will be unable to compete in international tourism and gain full benefits unless they can enter IT systems. Use of IT intermediaries and IT alliances will be crucial. Otherwise, a second tier of first- and second-class tourism destinations may result. A division of customer groups into first and second class may also be created, reflecting an increased social and technological inequality between groups of the population worldwide. The first-class customer group represents people who have high disposable income, high purchasing power and technological literacy. They will be able to experience first-class destinations, have unlimited choices and enjoy good terms of business. A second-class customer group that is technologically illiterate and lacking high levels of disposable income may not have access to either enhanced information or good prices.

Competitive reasons alone present a strong case for improving the quality of websites an ongoing basis. Because online marketing seems to help one user save money and time, it will play a pivotal role in shaping international marketing strategies in the future. It is important to integrate the key elements of the tourist experience. So, web-based promotion may make the consumer's tourism plans easier (e.g. what to see, how to travel etc.). It is also important to use the web-promotion campaigns integrated in the general advertising campaign, public relations and tourism fairs and include the web address in destination booklet or tourism guides. Independently of the tourism governments' policy (party) the tourism promotions should be continued because it can reinforce the destination image. Otherwise, confusion could be generated among users. Because customer relationship management (CRM) practices in tourism destinations are still under-developed, the integration of web-promotion practices and a CRM perspective is synergetic.

The website of a tourist destination can give a competitive advantage especially toward the main tourist-generating countries, where people become more technology literate. One needs to bear in mind that the quality of websites may help individual organizations or destinations take full advantage of direct marketing. There would be no problem if any end user or the person seeking information is provided with the opportunity to obtain what they seek. Feeling happy or unhappy with what has been obtained as a result of a search on the website may also encourage the potential customer (end user) to use this information as a "benchmark" or "best-practice" in order to make a comparison with the quality of websites established or the context of information provided by other national tourism authorities. The results to be obtained through such a comparison may be helpful to assess one's own position among its competitors. It also should be noted that the quality of websites both from the perspective of mapping and the availability of online services may influence how one perceives the image of this country or destination (see Table 9.2 for a list of websites).

Table 9.2   List of Websites for Selected Countries

No	Country	Official Website	Name of the official tourism authority
1	Albania	www.albaniatourism.com	Access is temporarily lifted
2	Algeria	www.algeria-tourism.org	Access is temporarily lifted
3	Cyprus	www.cyprustourism.org	Cyprus Tourism Organization
4	Egypt	www.touregypt.net	Tourism Office
5	France	www.tourisme.fr	Tourist Office
6	Greece	www.gnto.gr	Ministry of Tourism
7	Israel	www.goisrael.com	Ministry of Tourism
8	Italy	www.enit.it	State Tourist Board
9	Jordan	www.mota.gov.jo	Ministry of Tourism and Antiquities
10	Lebanon	www.lebanon-tourism.gov.lb	Ministry of Tourism
11	Malta	www.tourism.org.mt	Malta Tourism Authority
12	Morocco	www.tourism-in-morocco.com	Ministry of Tourism
13	Palestine	www.visit-palestine.com	Ministry of Tourism and Antiquities
14	Portugal	www.visitportugal.pt	Department of Investment, Trade and Tourism
15	Spain	www.tourspain.es	Ministry of Tourism, Industry and Trade
16	Syria	www.syriatourism.org	Ministry of Tourism
17	Tunisia	www.tourismtunusia.com	National Tourism Office
18	Turkey	www.kultur.gov.tr	Ministry of Culture and Tourism
19	Croatia	www.croatia.hr	National Tourist Organisation

Source: Own elaboration.

In summary, developing or launching a website is not enough on its own for having an active marketing activity in either an organization or in a tourist destination if one experiences difficulties with accessibility to the site (Kozak, Andreu and Bigne 2005). Accessibility problems usually appear as a result of a poor technical quality and language barriers. For example, bearing in mind the homogeneous structure of the potential market through globalization, there is evidence that some UK- and Germany-based tourism businesses provide additional languages to their actual ones (Williams, Rattray and Stork 2004). In addition, the website of destinations should provide useful, complete, and relevant information to potential users. This is because providing useful and relevant information on the web directly is an important feature that affects online users' intention to purchase. Finally, the design and presentation of the website is also essential in helping users meet their expectations (Kaynama and Black 2000). Thus, what the destination authorities need to consider is that the distribution of pictures, illustrations and headlines should be on balance.

Online Marketing Systems

A destination marketing system (DMS) should be composed *of* four inter-related components: virtual information space (VIS), virtual communication space (VCS), virtual transaction space (VTS) and virtual relationship space (VRS). *The* analysis *of the* applications in *the* four components *of* DMS showed that convention and visitor bureaus (CVBs) are performing well in providing and incorporating information-oriented applications but are weak in applications related to transaction and relationship building (Wang and Russo 2007). The study showed that CVBs are performing well in providing and incorporating information-oriented applications related to attractions, activities and accommodations, and the performance is becoming weaker in relation to applications for communication purposes (Wang and Russo 2007).

It has been observed that all the Mediterranean countries have implemented some kind of official website (an Internet tourism portal) to promote their own destinations along with culture and events. In general, the four best countries regarding the use of IT in their practices of web promotion are Spain, France, Lebanon and Portugal. The first two countries are also the number one and two destinations attracting the highest number of tourists or tourism incomes not only in the Mediterranean area but also around the globe. From this finding, it can be speculated that these countries pay much more attention to keeping the design and content of their websites up-to-date. Other countries, such as Tunisia, Albania, Malta, Palestine and Cyprus, can be regarded among the lower performing countries failing to meet no more than 25 percent of the selected criteria. Based on the analytical content analysis, an index was calculated for each general category to reflect the use of web criteria. High values (near 1) mean that the destination website uses a broad range of criteria to provide customers with more information in the initial page, general information or in an interactive way.

Box 9.1　Official Websites of Selected Mediterranean Destinations. Source: Kozak, Andreu and Bigne (2005).

Internet with current and emerging multimedia features provides ample opportunities and is particularly useful for informational and transactional strategies and to gain a competitive advantage. The research in hospitality and tourism have demonstrated that the website design and Internet marketing features contribute to effective delivery of messages, quality of products and services and brand image (Perdue 2001). The Internet with current and emerging multimedia features provides ample opportunities and is particularly useful for dealing with the intangible nature of the service and transforming marketing mix variables to capitalize on the informational and transactional potential of the Internet (Baloglu and Pekcan 2006).

The Internet contributes to five key functions: promotion, product distribution, communication, management and research (Schmalleger and Carson 2008). To capitalize on the opportunities, tourist destinations design their websites for ease and convenience, personalized appeal and emotional features. They also initiate web campaigns, develop brands and integrate branding strategy on the web, gather traveller information, improve traveller service and streamline content delivery (Baloglu and Pekcan 2006). Site design characteristics include three major categories: interactivity, navigation and functionality (Benckendorff and Black 2000). The dominant role of the website is to communicate and inform users about the place brand identity (Florek, Insch and Gnoth 2006). The goal is to achieve 'positive response action' from users such as downloading content from a site, forwarding it to others, requesting information from the site, making a purchase, remaining on the site for a certain period of time or returning to the site (Sharp 2001).

Destinations have to try to convey a sense of experiencing the place (through web cams, weather updates, music clips, oral histories, collection highlights, virtual tours etc.) and experiencing the brand rather than merely delivering a site encounter (Morgan, Pritchard and Piggott 2002). The online communication might take the form of passive transmission of information (general information about the place, picture gallery and brochures) as well as interactive communication (customized information, consultations, feedback, events calendar, interactive maps, virtual sightseeing and accommodation booking) (Florek, Insch and Gnoth 2006).

A destination web page should be interactive, stimulating and attractive to engage potential visitors in interactive communications and provide a destination experience before their visits have the following features and capabilities. It should also include different links for multiple stakeholders and be further customized to multiple visitor segments. Content can also be tailored to target different audiences through multiple sections and customizable settings to create a favorable image of the place. On the other hand, as an active tool, websites might contribute to building relationships with different kinds of stakeholders (Florek, Insch and Gnoth 2006). With the broad scope of programs that the CVBs or DMOs employ in their branding and marketing efforts, ensuring that all stakeholders are alerted to programs is vital. For this purpose, the Las Vegas Convention and Visitor Authority (LVCVA) decided to develop integrated platforms online for managing contacts and information flow to improve and integrate the communication between the LVCVA and its internal and external stakeholders (LVCVA 2009).

Online Domains

Given the fierce competition for the attention of Internet users, online marketers must secure memorable web names and addresses. Gertner, Berger and Gertner (2006) found that only 20 percent of the world's nations have country name-dot-com websites that are country portals. The authors have pointed out that a potential development for destination branding online has been the recent creation of the "dot-travel" domain, launched in 2005. The new domain made the registration of place names available only to governments or organizations appointed by them.

Travel Blogs

Blogs have several advantages over web-based content. They are relatively easily updated, relatively flexible in structure, encourage interaction between authors and readers and allow people to participate in information exchange who might not otherwise have the opportunity (Schmalleger and Carson 2008). A useful application of travel blogs for destination marketing organizations is monitoring travelers' experiences with and perceptions of the destinations. A study revealed that travel blogs reflect the kaleidoscopic aspects of a visitor's experience at a destination. Travel blogs can also be a useful tool in monitoring the competitive environment of a destination and provide valuable real-time customer feedback (Pan, Maclaurin and Crotts 2007).

Schmalleger and Carson (2008) mention a couple of substantial challenges in effectively employing blogs in the travel and tourism industry, such as regular attention and update and responding to negative or incorrect information posted on third-party hosted blogs. Puhringer and Taylor (2008) argued that travel blogs (T-blogs) provide a range of useful information for DMOs and their members, which includes comparisons and contrasts between individual and groups of destinations, critiquing of activities or attractions at destinations, reviews of accommodation establishments and so on. For DMOs, there are a range of possible applications for traveler-generated content within T-blogs (Puhringer and Taylor 2008, p. 180):

- Identifying and monitoring trends in traveler movements to and from the destination such as previous and future stopover locations
- Specific product evaluations and reviews of service standards
- Event evaluations
- Identification of product or infrastructure gaps

- Performance reviews of associated products (like airlines) or collaborators (such as partnering ventures)
- Competitor analysis

However, the recent developments in technology and social media lessened the importance of travel blogs. They are more interactive and effective in engaging actual and potential travelers in discussion than the T-blogs.

New Technology Applications

Mobile access to the Internet provides various sectors of tourism with considerable innovative opportunities to develop transaction-based and location- and situation-based applications (Katsura and Sheldon 2008). A podcast is a series of digital media files delivered as simple download or streamed webcasts. Xie and Lew (2008) examined the websites of CVBs in U.S. cities to find out their podcasting use practices for tourism marketing. They found limited use but a rapid adoption rate for this new technology. Xie and Lew (2008, p. 174) distinguished among three types of podcasts.

Destination podcasts: These may be sponsored by destination marketing organizations (DMOs) but are more likely to comprise the insights and experiences of an avid booster who lives in, or often frequents, a place. Examples of this type of podcast include: Five Hundy by Midnight—The Original Las Vegas. Podcast (at www.fivehundybymidnight.com) and iPod Traveller Podcast—"The Best in European. Travel" with a focus on budget travel (at www.ipodtraveller.net).

Travel Experience podcasts: These podcasts relate the experience of travel, typically from a personal perspective. They may focus on the logistics of travel, such as trip planning, the flight experience, hotels and meals or descriptions and experiences of a variety of different places. Two examples of this type of podcast include: Travel Commons Podcast—about road warrior (business) travel, "more about the journey than the destination" (at www.travelcommons.com) and Amateur Traveler Podcast—personal travel experiences and destination reviews by the host and interviews with other travelers (at amateurtraveler.com).

Travel and Tourism Industry and Education podcasts: These podcasts are more focused on special areas of travel and tourism. They are less oriented toward the general travel consumer, although they may still generate popular interest. Examples of this type of podcast include: The Home-Based Travel Agent Podcast—how to run a home-based travel service (at hometravelagent.net) and Geography for Travellers Podcast—social science perspectives of travel and tourism (at travelgeography.info). Foreign language learning podcasts are also often "tagged" as travel related.

Over the last decade, the LVCVA's web strategy has evolved from disseminating every message via a single site to using a network of targeted microsites to reach a variety of niche audiences. As the next step in content distribution, the LVCVA plans to distribute its destination information, applications and branding messages via syndication, Really Simple Syndication (RSS) feeds and social networks allowing external audiences—meeting planners, members of the travel trade and other "Vegas enthusiasts"—to share the Las Vegas experience with their own web users and help sell and promote Las Vegas (LVCVA 2009).

As the capabilities, performance and technology of personal computers, cell phones and Personal Digital Assistance (PDAs) continue to merge, the LVCVA plan to expand the range of destination content published online and via these "smart" devices to further the Las Vegas brand by sharing photo and video resources via applications on personal computers and a wide range of mobile devices (LVCVA 2009).

Social Media

In the coming years, tourist destinations may find it necessary to expand their social media efforts significantly because social media will play a large role in all future marketing endeavors. The LVCVA plan to employ social media programs across market segment and seek to exploit technologies that allow users to "pull" compelling Las Vegas content into their own social networks and help distribute key messages virally (LVCVA 2009). Destinations today need to have both word-of-mouth and word-of-mouse. Possible uses of social media:

- Build brand equity and manage the brand online
- Develop/improve products/services
- Showcase heritage, attractions, music, art, cuisine, events & festivals and people
- Trip planning—Connect potential visitors before, during and after the experience
- Host community involvement is critical in tourism. Social media also help to get the community and employees involved.

Social media are creating a new world of storytelling and idea sharing. The new social media content uses the latest Internet technology to showcase product offerings and destinations in digital world. Tourist destinations need to work to expand their social media efforts significantly and exploit the new technologies available. Destinations now distribute their information, applications and branding messages via syndication "Reach Site Summary" (RSS or Really Simple Syndication) and social networks, allowing distribution channels (meeting planners, travel agents, trade magazines and others) to share destination experience with their own web users and help sell and promote the destination.

Marketing has changed dramatically for DMOs because of the latest technology developments and adoption of online techniques. Significant improvements have been achieved through the integration of social media with more traditional forms of online marketing as well as with cooperative promotional initiatives that support partner organizations (Green 2009a). According to a study conducted by Green (2009a), the most common online marketing strategies adopted by DMOs included (1) designing an interactive website that conveys the image of the destination and supports the community, (2) outreaching and engaging travelers to interact with the destination through the DMO's database with emails and social media and (3) engaging the destination community via social media and getting them involved actively in becoming advocates of the destination.

While the motivations of adopting social media may vary, enhancing top-of-mind awareness, stimulating visitor demand, or branding, a strategy with clear objectives and plan should be designed before allocating resources and developing tactics. This plan should be integrated into the annual marketing plan to supplement overall media strategy. For example, contests and games are effective ways of interacting with consumers and building brand equity online. They can include photo and video contest submissions, destination experience competition and drawings in the social media arena. The popular social media tools and applications are listed in Box 9.2.

As such, IT could be a source of developing effective strategies for maintaining, sustaining and improving the competitive position of tourism, travel and hospitality businesses and tourist destinations. Practical observations as well as related literature prove that businesses using high-technology equipment and up-to-date management and marketing strategies are more likely to be competitive than those who do not. Major determinants of competitive advantage can be summarized as enhancing competitive pricing, decreasing supply and distribution costs and maintaining closer relationships with suppliers and users. It is argued that businesses should carry out a benefit-cost analysis because the deployment of IT applications such as the Internet might not make any contribution to revenue enhancement but also could make a negative impact on the cost side (Buhalis 1998). Thus, the Internet (or IT) could be used as a complementary part of the pull channel strategy if the DMOs intend to sell itself directly because IT is expected to attract end users or direct their interests toward the destination.

However, the majority of current websites provide only brochures with little attention in attracting the attention of users on an ongoing basis. The Internet is currently used to gather information and send emails rather than make transactions. Lack of opportunity to see the products, security concerns and traditional marketing habits are the main reasons for not extending the potential use of the IT applications. It is a fact that, in the existing type of distribution channels of the tourism and travel industry, services are either supplier- or intermediary-based, meaning that users still need to contact a representative of the accommodation facilities or the travel agencies in some way. But in the future, such marketing services are expected to be mostly consumer-based.

YouTube (Online Video)—it is a video sharing website. Green (2009a) found that those DMOs with a highly developed use of online video have used it to share information and have not only focused on the use of it on their site, but also the syndication or sharing of their content on other sites, called RSS (Really Simple Syndication).

Twitter—It is a social networking and micro-blogging service that enables its users to send and read messages known as tweets. Tweets are text-based posts of up to 140 characters displayed on the destination profile page and delivered to the destination's subscribers known as followers. In other words, it is targeted toward "twibes." This would be a more appropriate tool to target intermediaries and distribution channels as well as niche segments to promote events and special deals and to provide real-time customer service. Green (2009a) found that some DMOs or CVBs use it for culinary and wine groups, and some opened a "Twisitor Center" to give tips and answer questions of the visitors.

Facebook—It is a global social networking website that is operated and privately owned by Facebook, Inc. Destinations can develop their profiles, add friends, send messages and establish networks. It is a vehicle to feature information, photos, videos, events and discussions.

Blogging—One of the earliest forms of social media to convey information about the destination, not to engage the visitors in discussion. It is mainly used in the travel industry to supplement destination information, develop destination images and reach out to niche markets.

Photo Sharing (Flickr)—It is an online image- and video-hosting website that enables visitors to upload their own pictures and videos and to present their own destination experience. Green (2009b) found that many DMOs invite visitors and partners to share personal photos on their site. This would be an appropriate tool to have best photo contests for brand recognition and illustrate type of activities in a given destination.

Box 9.2   List of Popular Social Media Tools.

9.5. SUMMARY

This chapter has examined the nature, structure and characteristics of distribution channels for tourism and travel service providers alongside the implications of the IT as a new management and marketing instrument. This chapter has further presented theoretical knowledge to examine developments in IT. It reported on how IT's current and potential use as a tourism marketing tool impacts upon the competitiveness of tourism and travel businesses in particular and tourist destinations in general. Therefore, it is recommended to initially establish a distribution strategy that fits into the purpose of destinations for the use of delivering their products and services and then use IT as a support. Otherwise, there could be a waste of time and financial resources.

* * *

CASE STUDY: NEW ZEALAND—NEW MEDIA MODEL

New Zealand was one of the first countries in the world to use the Internet as an integral part of its marketing. In 1999, New Zealand launched its first comprehensive website, www.purenz.com. The campaign worked to push the concept of New Zealand as 'The Youngest Country' on earth. The campaign combined advertising, international media work, events and work with trade around the world to promote New Zealand as a unique, compelling destination that appeals to New Zealand's target market. The consumer website www.newzealand.com provides up-to-date and inspiring information on tourism product, transport, regions and much more on destination New Zealand for visitors. Total users sessions on www.newzealand.com have gone from 1.4 million in 2002 to 10 million a year in 2008.

Tourism New Zealand has identified an ideal visitor as someone who:

- Travels regularly
- Participates in a wide range of tourism experiences
- Actively participates in the natural environment
- Is environmentally and culturally aware
- Seeks authentic and new experiences
- Wants to share them with others.

These travellers are high users of technology (such as the internet) and leaders with liberal attitudes and have a global mindset (http://10yearsyoung.tourismnewzealand.com). The prime targets of the New Zealand brand are so-called 'interactive travellers'—people young in body or heart who love travel, seek new experiences and enjoy the challenge of new destinations. The award-winning TNZ website (www.purenz.com) was extensively redesigned, following research on users' preferences and views about the site. The visually attractive website is user friendly and navigable and above all stimulates interest and provokes reactions. For instance, web visitors can send copies of the New Zealand adverts and photographs of natural environments as e-postcards—adding to New Zealand's conversational appeal, celebrity and anticipation value. In the next phase of development, TNZ will be implementing a toll that will enable visitors to plan unique travel itineraries as they move through the site (Morgan, Pritchard and Piggott 2002).

In a new era of 100% Pure New Zealand, Tourism New Zealand is focusing more on talking directly to consumers, embracing new technology and providing content to people conveniently. New Zealand adopts a new media model to adapt to the changing world travel consumers live in and the way they access information on which they base their travel decisions.

When Tourism New Zealand launched the 100% Pure New Zealand, television and print were the key mediums to reach many people. In today's world, people are getting their news and information in many different ways, through iPods, mobile phones, the Internet, blog sites, television, electronic billboards and social sites formats they are using. New media technologies are travel blogs by travel journalists, Google Earth for special New Zealand layer, mobile phones messaging, and a New Zealand page is carrying video clips, mini-documentaries and other content appealing to the YouTube community. The 100% Pure New Zealand branding is moving from expressing New Zealand as a destination to presenting it as an experience (Tourism New Zealand 2007).

References

Aaker, D. A. (1991). *Managing brand equity.* New York: Free Press.

Aaker, D. A. (1996a). *Building strong brands.* New York: The Free Press.

Aaker, D. A. (1996b). Managing brand equity across product and markets. *California Management Review, 38*(3), 102–120.

Aaker, D. A. (2003). The Power of the branded differentiator. *MIT Sloan Management Review, 45*(1), 83–87.

Aaker, D. A., & Shansby, J. G. (1982). Positioning your product. *Business Horizons, 25*(3), 56–62.

Aaker, J. L. (1997). Dimensions of brand personality. *Journal of Marketing Research, 34*(3), 347–356.

Aaker, J. L. (1999). The malleable self: The role of self-expression in persuasion. *Journal of Marketing Research, 36,* 45–57.

Aguas, P., Rita, P., & Costa, J. (2004, May 18–21). *Market share analysis: Tourist destination competitiveness.* Paper presented at the 33rd EMAC Conference, Murcia, Spain.

Ahmed, Z. U., & Krohn, F. B. (1990). Reversing the United States' declining competitiveness in marketing international tourism: A perspective on future policy. *Journal of Travel Research, 29,* 23–29.

Alegre, J., & Garau, J. (2010). Tourist satisfaction and dissatisfaction. *Annals of Tourism Research, 37*(1), 52–73.

Alford, P., & Clarke, S. (2009). Information technology and tourism a theoretical critique. *Technovation, 29*(9), 580–587.

Alsever J. (2006, October 15). Basking on the beach, or maybe on the operating table. *The New York Times* (Late Edition [East Coast]), 3.5.

Anderssen, P., & Colberg, R. T. (1973). *Multivariate analysis in travel research: A tool for travel package design and market segmentation.* Proceedings from the Fourth Annual Conference of Travel and Tourism Research Association (pp. 225–238). Sun Valley, ID: Travel and Tourism Research Association.

Anholt, S. (2009). Branding places and nations. In R. Clifton (Ed.), *Brands and branding* (2nd ed.). New York: Bloomberg Press.

Ashworth, G., & Goodall, B. (1988). Tourist images: Marketing considerations. In B, Goodall & G. Ashworth (Eds.), *Marketing in the tourism industry: The promotion of destination regions.* London: Routledge.

Ashworth, G. J., & Voogd, H. (1990). Marketing of tourism places: What are we doing. In M. Uysal (Ed.), Global tourist behavior (pp. 5–19). New York: The Haworth Press.

Ayala, H. (1996, October). Resort ecotourism: A paradigm for the 21st century. *Cornell Hotel and Restaurant Administration Quarterly,* pp. 46–53.

Aziz, H. (1995). Understanding attacks on tourists in Egypt. *Tourism Management, 16*(2), 81–95.

Backman, S. J., & Crompton, J. L. (1991). Differentiating between high, spurious, latent, and low loyalty participants in two leisure activities. *Journal of Park and Recreation Administration, 9*(2), 1–17.

Bahar, O., & Kozak, M. (2006). Potential impacts of Euro on destination choice, *TOURISM: An Interdisciplinary Journal, 54*(3), 245–253.

Bahar, O., & Kozak, M. (2007). Advancing destination competitiveness research: comparison between tourists and service providers. *Journal of Tourism and Travel Marketing. 22*(2): 61–71.

Bahar, O., & Kozak, M. (2008). *Tourism economics: Concepts and operations.* New York: Nova Sciences.

Baker, D. A., & Crompton, J. L. (2000). Quality, satisfaction and behavioural intentions. *Annals of Tourism Research, 27*(3), 785–803.

Balm, G. J. (1992). *Benchmarking: A practitioner's gGuide for becoming and staying best of the best* (2nd ed.). Quality and Productivity Management Association, Illinois.

Baloglu, S. (2001). Image variations of Turkey by familiarity index: Informational and experiential dimensions. *Tourism Management, 22*(2), 127–133.

Baloglu, S., & Brinberg, D. (1997). Affective images of tourism destinations. *Journal of Travel Research, 35*(4), 11–15.

Baloglu, S., & Love, C. (2005). Association meeting planners' perceptions and intentions for five major convention cities. *Tourism Management, 26,* 743–752

Baloglu, ., & Mangalo lu, M. (2001). Tourism destination images of Turkey, Egypt, Greece, and Italy as perceived by US-based tour operators and travel agents. *Tourism Management, 22,* 1–9.

Baloglu, S., & McCleary, K. W. (1999). U.S. International pleasure travelers' image of four Mediterranean destinations: A comparison of visitors and non-visitors. *Journal of Travel Research, 38*(2), 144–152.

Baloglu, S., & Pekcan, A. (2006). The website design and the internet site marketing practices of upscale and luxury hotels in Turkey. *Tourism Management, 27,* 171–176.

Baloglu, S., Pekcan, A., Chen, S. L., & Santos, J. (2004). The relationship between destination performance, overall satisfaction, and behavioral intention for distinct segments. *Journal of Quality Assurance in Hospitality & Tourism, 4*(3/4), 149–165.

Barksy, J. D. (1992). Customer satisfaction in the hotel industry: Meaning and measurement. *Hospitality Research Journal, 16*(1), 51–73.

Beeho, A. J., & Prentice, R. C. (1997). Conceptualising the experiences of heritage tourists: A case study of new Lanark and world heritage village. *Tourism Management, 18*(2), 75–87.

Beerli, A., & Martin, J. D. (2004). Factors influencing destination image. *Annals of Tourism Research, 31*(3), 657–681.

Beerli, A., Meneses, G. D., & Gil, S. M. (2007). Self-congruity and destination choice. *Annals of Tourism Research, 34*(3), 571–587.

Benckendorff, P. J., & Black, N. L. (2000). Destination marketing on the Internet. A case study of Australian Regional Tourism Authorities. *The Journal of Tourism Studies, 11*(1), 11–21.

Benjamin, R., & Wigard, R. (1995, Winter). Electronic markets and virtual value chains on the information superhighway. *Sloan Management Review,* pp. 62–72.

Bennett, M. M. (1996). Information technology and databases for tourism. In A. V. Seaton & M. M. Bennett (Eds.), *Marketing tourism products* (pp. 421–443). Oxford: International Thomson Business Press.

Berthon, P. R., Pitt, L. F., & Watson, R. T. (1996). The World Wide Web as an advertising medium: Towards an understanding of conversion efficiency. *Journal of Advertising Research, 36*(1), 43–53.

Bhat, S., & Reddy, S. K. (1998). Symbolic and functional positioning of brands. *Journal of Consumer Marketing*, 15(1), 32–43.

Blain, C., Levy, S. E., & Ritchie, J. R. B. (2005). Destination branding: Insights and practices from destination marketing organizations. *Journal of Travel Research*, 43, 328–338.

Blichfeldt, B. S. (2003). Unmanageable tourism destination brands. *IME Working Paper* 47/03. University of Southern Denmark, Esbjerg.

Blichfeldt, B. S. (2008). What to do on our holiday: The case of in situ decision making. *Anatolia*, 19(2), 287–305.

Bloemer, J., & Ruyter, K. (1998). On the relationship between store image, store satisfaction and store loyalty. *European Journal of Marketing*, 32(5/6), 499–513.

Bojanic, D. (1991). The use of advertising in managing destination image. *Tourism Management*, 12(4), 352–355.

Bojanic, D. (1996). Consumer perceptions of price, value and satisfaction in the hotel industry: An exploratory study. *Journal of Hospitality and Leisure Marketing*, 4(1), 5–22.

Boo, S., Busser, J., & Baloglu, S. (2009). A model of customer-based brand equity and its application to multiple destinations. *Tourism Management*, 30, 219–231.

Bookman, M. Z., & Bookman, K. R. (2007). *Medical tourism in developing countries*. New York: Palgrave Macmillan.

Bordas, E. (1994). Competitiveness of tourism destinations in long distance markets. *The Tourist Review*, 47(3), 3–9.

Botha, C., Crompton, J. L., & Kim, S. S. (1999). Developing a revised competitive position for Sun/Lost City, South Africa. *Journal of Travel Research*, 37(2), 341–352.

Boulding, W., Kalra, A., Staeling, R., & Zeithaml, V. A. (1993). A dynamic process model of service quality: From expectations to behavioral intentions. *Journal of Marketing Research*, 30, 7–27.

Bowman, C., & Faulkner, D. (1994). Measuring product advantage using competitive benchmarking and customer perceptions. *Long Range Planning*, 27(1), 119–132.

Bray, R. (1996). The package holiday market in Europe. *Travel and Tourism Analyst*, 4, 51–71.

Brayshaw, D. (1995). Negative publicity about tourism destination: A Florida case study. *EIU Travel and Tourism Analyst*, No. 5.

Briguglio, L., & Vella, L. (1995). The competitiveness of the Maltese Islands in the Mediterranean International Tourism. In M. V. Conlin & T. Baum (Eds.), *Island tourism: Management principles and practice*. Brisbane: John Wiley and Sons.

Buck, M. (1988). The role of travel agent and tour operator. In B. Goodall & G. Ashworth (Eds.), *Marketing in the tourism industry: The promotion of destination regions* (pp. 67–74). London: Routledge.

Buhalis, D. (1998). Strategic use of information technologies in the tourism industry. *Tourism Management*, 19(5), 409–421.

Buhalis, D. (2000). Marketing the competitive destination of the future. *Tourism Management*, 21(1), 97–116.

Buhalis, D., & Cooper, C. (1998). Competition or co-operation: The needs of small and medium sized tourism enterprises at a destination level. In E. Laws, B. Faulkner, & G. Moscardo (Eds.), *Embracing and managing change in tourism*. London: Routledge.

Buhalis, D., & Fletcher, J. (1995). Environmental impacts on tourism destinations: An economic analysis. In H. Coccosis & P. Nijkamp (Eds.), *Sustainable Tourism Development Avebury* (pp. 3–24). England.

Buhalis, D., & Law, R. (2008). Progress in information technology and tourism management: 20 years on and 10 years after the Internet—The state of a tourism research. *Tourism Management*, 29(4), 609–623.

Bull A. (1995). *The economics of travel and tourism.* Melbourne: Longman.

Burton, R. (1995). *Travel geography* (2nd. ed.). London: Pitman

Butler, R. W. (1980). The concept of a tourist area cycle of evolution: Implications for management of resources. *Canadian Geographer, 24*(1), 5–12.

Cai, L. (2002). Cooperative branding for rural destinations. *Annals of Tourism Research, 29*(3), 720–742.

Calantone, R. J., di Benedetto, C. A., Halam & Bojanic, D. C. (1989, Fall). Multiple multinational tourism positioning using correspondence analysis. *Journal of Travel Research, 28,* 25–32.

Caldwell, N., & Freire, J. (2004). The differences between branding a country, a region and a city: Applying the brand box model. *Journal of Brand Management, 12*(1), 50–61.

Camp, R. C. (1989). *Benchmarking: The search for industry best practices that leads to superior performance.* ASQC Quality Press.

Campos-Soria, J., Garcia, L., & Garcia, M. (2005). Service quality and competitiveness in the hospitality sector. *Tourism Economics, 11*(1), 85–102.

Carbone, L. B. (2004). *Clued in: How to keep customers coming back again and again.* Upper Saddle river, NJ: Pearson Education.

Carey, S., Gountas, Y., & Gilbert, D. (1997). Tour operators and destination sustainability. *Tourism Management, 18*(7), 425–431.

Cavlek, N. (2002). Tour operators and destination safety. *Annals of Tourism Research, 29*(2), 478–496.

Cheong, R. (1995). The virtual threat to travel and tourism. *Tourism Management, 16*(6), 417–422.

Chernatony, L., & Riley, D. (1998). Defining a brand: Beyond the literature with expert's interpretations. *Journal of Marketing Management, 14,* 417–443.

Chi, C. G., & Qu, H. (2008). Examining the structural relationships of destination image, tourist satisfaction and destination loyalty: An integrated approach. *Tourism Management, 29*(1), 624–636.

Cho V. (2003). A comparison of three different approaches to tourist arrival forecasting. *Tourism Management, 24*(3), 323–330.

Cho, W., & Olsen, M. D. (1998). A case study approach to understanding the impact of information technology on competitive advantage in the lodging industry. *Journal of Hospitality & Tourism Research, 22*(4), 376–394.

Chon, K., & Mayer, K. J. (1995). Destination competitiveness models in tourism and their application to Las Vegas. *Journal of Tourism Systems and Quality Management, 1*(2/3/4), 227–246.

Churchill, G. A., & Suprenant, C. (1982). An investigation into the determinants of customer satisfaction. *Journal of Marketing Research, 29,* 491–504.

Codling, S. (1992). *Best practice benchmarking: A management guide.* Hampshire: Gower.

Coltman, M. M. (1989). *Tourism marketing.* New York: Van Nostrand Reinhold.

Connell, J. (2006). Medical tourism: Sea, sun, sand and . . . surgery. *Tourism Management, 27,* 1093–1100.

Connolly, D. J., Olsen M. D., & Moore, R. G. (1998). Internet as a distribution channel. *Cornell Hotel and Restaurant Administration Quarterly, 39*(4), 42–54.

Cormany, D. (2008, November). Taking a pulse on potential medical tourism destinations: The hospitality and tourism industries. *Medical Tourism Magazine, 7,* 34–37.

Cormany, D. (2009, January–February). The evolution of the hotel industry with the rise of medical tourism. *Medical Tourism Magazine, 8,* 80–82.

Court, B., & Lupton, R. A. (1997). Customer portfolio development: Modelling destination adopters, inactives and rejecters. *Journal of Travel Research, 36*(1), 35–43.

Crompton, J. L. (1979, Spring). An assessment of the image of Mexico as a vacation destination and the influence of geographical location upon that image. *Journal of Travel Research, 17*(4), 18–23.

Crompton, J. L. (1993). Understanding a business organization's approach to entering a sponsorship partnership. *Festival Management & Event Tourism: An International Journal, 1*(3), 98–109.

Crompton, J. L., Fakeye, P., & Lue, C. (1992). Positioning: The example of the lower Rio Grande Valley in the winter long stay destination market. *Journal of Travel Research, 31*(2), 20–26.

Cronin, J., & Taylor, S. A. (1992). Measuring service quality: A re-examination and extension. *Journal of Marketing, 56*(3), 55–68.

Crouch, G. I. (1995). A meta-analysis of tourism demand. *Annals of Tourism, 22,* 103–118.

Crouch, G. I., & Ritchie, J. R. B. (1999). Tourism, competitiveness and societal prosperity. *Journal of Business Research, 44,* 137–152.

Czepiel, J. A., Rosenberg, L. J., & Akerele, A. (1974). Perspectives on consumer satisfaction. In R. C. Curhan (Ed.), *Combined Proceedings Series No: 36* (pp. 119–123). Chicago, IL: American Marketing Association.

d'Hauteserre, A. M. (2000). Lessons in managed destination competitiveness: The case of foxwoods casino resort. *Tourism Management, 21*(1), 23–32.

Davidson, R. (1998). *Tourism in Europe* (2nd ed.). London, UK: Longman.

Davidson, R., & Maitland, R. (1997). *Tourism destinations.* London: Hodder and Stoughton.

Davies, B., & Mangan, J. (1992). Family expenditure on hotels and holidays. *Annals of Tourism Research, 19*(4), 691–699.

Day, G. S. (1969). A two-dimensional concept of brand loyalty. *Journal of Advertising Research, 9,* 29–35.

de Chernatony, L., & Riley, D. (1998). Defining a brand: Beyond the literature with expert's interpretations. *Journal of Marketing Management, 14,* 417–443.

Dean, D. H. (2004). Evaluating potential brand associations through conjoint analysis and market simulation. *The Journal of Product and Brand Management, 13*(7), 506–513.

Decrop, A. (2010). Destination choice sets: An inductive longitudinal approach. *Annals of Tourism Research, 37*(1), 93–115.

Decrop, A., & Kozak, M. (2009). Decision strategies in tourism evaluation. In M. Kozak & A. Decrop (Eds.), *Handbook of tourist behaviour: Theory & practice* (pp. 67–82). New York: Routledge.

Demicco, F. J., & Cetron, M. (2006). Club medic. *APBN (Association of Pacific Biotech News), 10*(10), 527–531.

Dharmaratne, G. S., & Brathwaite, A. E. (1998). Economic valuation of the coastline for tourism in Barbados. *Journal of Travel Research, 37*(2), 138–144.

Diaz, E., Martin-Consuegra, D., Esteban, A., & Blazquez, J. J. (2009). European tourist destinations in internet search engines: A comparison. In A. Fyall, M. Kozak, L. Andreu, J. Gnoth, & S. Lebe (Eds.), *Marketing innovations for sustainable destinations* (pp. 34–53). Oxford, UK: Goodfellow.

Díaz-Pérez, F. M., Bethencourt-Cejas, M., & Álvarez-González, J. A. (2005). The segmentation of canary island tourism markets by expenditure: Implications for tourism policy. *Tourism Management, 26*(6), 961–964.

Dick, A. S., & Basu, K. (1994). Customer loyalty: Toward an integrated conceptual framework. *Journal of the Academy of Marketing Science, 22*(2), 99–113.

Dickinson, J., Jones, I., & Leask, A. (2007) Event tourism; enhancing destinations and the visitor economy. *International Journal of Tourism Resources, 9*(5), 301–302.

Dieke, P. U. C. (1993). Cross-national development of tourism development: Lessons from Kenya and Gambia. *The Journal of Tourism Studies, 4*(1), 2–18.

Dobni, D., & Zinkhan, G. M. (1990). In search of brand image: A foundation analysis. *Advances in Consumer Research, 17*, 110–119.

Dredge, D., & Jenkins, J. (2003). Destination place identity and regional tourism policy. *Tourism Geographies, 5*(4), 383–407.

Driscoll, A., Lawson, R., & Niven, B. (1994). Measuring tourists' destination perceptions. *Annals of Tourism Research, 21*(3), 499–510.

Dwyer, L., Forsyth, P., & Rao, P. (2000). The price competitiveness of travel and tourism: A comparison of 19 destinations. *Tourism Management, 21*(1), 9–22.

Dwyer, L., Forsyth, P., & Rao, P. (2002). Destination price competitiveness: Exchange rate changes versus domestic inflation. *Journal of Travel Research, 40*(3), 328–336.

Dwyer, L., Forsyth, P., & Spurr, R. (2006). Assessing the economic impacts of events: A computable general equilibrium approach. *Journal of Travel Research, 45*, 59–66.

Echtner, C. M., & Ritchie, J. R. B. (1993). The measurement of destination image: An empirical assessment. *Journal of Travel Research, 31*, 3–13.

Edgett, S., & Snow, K. (1996). Benchmarking measures of customer satisfaction, quality and performance for new financial services products. *Journal of Services Marketing, 6*, 6–16.

Edwards, A. (1993). *Price competitiveness of holiday destinations: Costs from european travellers* (No. 2). London: The Economist Intelligence Unit.

Ekinci, Y., & Hosany, S. (2006, November). Destination personality: An application of brand personality to tourism destinations. *Journal of Travel Research, 45*, 127–139.

Ekinci, Y., Sirakaya-Turk, E., & Baloglu, S. (2007). Host image and destination personality. Tourism Analysis, *12*(5/6), 433–446.

Engel, J., & Blackwell, R. (1982). *Consumer behavior* (4th ed.). Hinsdale: The Dryden Press.

Enright, M., & Newton, J. (2005). Determinants of tourism destination competitiveness in Asia Pacific: Comprehensiveness and universality. *Journal of Travel Research, 43*(2), 339–350.

Enright, M. J., & Newton, J. (2004). Tourism destination competitiveness: A quantitative approach. *Tourism Management, 25*(6), 777–788.

Eraqi, M. I. (2006). IT as a means for enhancing competitive advantage. *Anatolia, 17*(1), 25–42.

Erfurt-Cooper, P., & Cooper, M. (2009). *Health and wellness tourism: Spas and hot springs.* Tonawanda, NY: Channel View Publications.

Fakeye, P. C., & Crompton, J. L. (1991). Image differences between prospective, first-time, and repeat visitors to the lower Rio Grande Valley. *Journal of Travel Research, 30*(2), 10–16.

Faulkner, B., Oppermann, M., & Fredline, E. (1999). Destination competitiveness: An exploratory examination of South Australia's core attractions. *Journal of Vacation Marketing, 5*(2), 125–139.

Faulkner, B., & Vikulov, S. (2001). Katherine, washed out one day, back on track the next: A post-mortem of a tourism disaster. *Tourism Management, 22*, 331–344.

Fenton, M., & Pearce, P. L. (1988). Multidimensional scaling and tourism research. *Annals of Tourism Research, 15*, 236–254.

Florek, M., Insch, A., & Gnoth, J. (2006). City council websites as a means of place brand identity communication. *Place Branding, 2*(4), 276–297.

Font, X. (2002). Environmental certification in tourism and hospitality: Progress, process and prospects. *Tourism Management, 23*(3), 197–205.

Font, X., & Ahjem, T. A. (1998). Searching for a balance in tourism development strategies. *International Journal of Contemporary Hospitality Management, 11*(2/3), 73–77.

Fornell, C. (1992). A national customer satisfaction barometer: The Swedish experience. *Journal of Marketing, 56*(1), 6–21.

Fuchs, G., & Reichel, A. (2006). Correlates of destination risk perception and risk reduction strategies. In M. Kozak & L. Andreu (Eds.), *Progress in tourism marketing* (pp. 161–170). London: Elsevier.

Fuchs, M., & Weiermair, K. (2004). Destination benchmarking: An indicator-system's potential for exploring guest satisfaction. *Journal of Travel Research, 42*(3), 212–225.

Furman, J., Porter, M. E., & Stern, S. (2002). The determinants of national innovative capacity. *Research Policy, 31,* 899–933.

Fyall, A., Callod, C., & Edwards, B. (2003). Relationship marketing: The challenge for destinations. *Annals of Tourism Research, 30*(3), 644–659.

Fyall, A., Fletcher, J., & Spyriadis, T. (2010). Diversity, devolution and disorder: The management of tourism destinations. In M. Kozak, J. Gnoth, & L. Andreu (Eds.), *Advances in tourism destination marketing: Managing network* (pp.15–26). Oxon: Routledge.

Gahlinger, P. (2008). *The medical tourism travel guide.* North Branch, MN: Sunrise River Press.

Gardner, B. B., & Levy, S. J. (1955). The product and the brand. *Harvard Business Review, 33,* 33–39.

Gartner, W. (1993). Image formation process. In M. Uysal & D. R. Fesenmaier (Eds.), *Communication channel systems in tourism marketing* (pp. 191–215). New York: Haworth.

Gartner, W. B. (1989, Fall). Some suggestions for research on entrepreneurial traits and characteristics. *Entrepreneurship: Theory and Practice, 14*(l), 27–38.

Gearing, C. E., Swart, W. W., & Var, T. (1974). Establishing a measure of touristic attractiveness. *Journal of Travel Research, 12*(4), 1–8.

Gertner, R., Berger, K., & Gertner, D. (2006). Country-Dot-Com: Marketing and branding destinations online. *Journal of Travel & Tourism Marketing, 21*(2/3), 105–116.

Gezici, F. (2008). Components of sustainability: Two cases from Turkey. *Annals of Tourism Research, 33*(2), 442–455.

Gitelson, R. J., & Crompton, J. L. (1983, Winter). The planning horizons and source of information used by pleasure vacationers. *Journal of Travel Research,* pp. 2–7.

Gitelson, R. J., & Crompton, J. L. (1984). Insights into the repeat vacation phenomenon. *Annals of Tourism Research, 11*(2), 199–217.

Gnoth, J. (2002). Leveraging export brands through a tourism destination brand. *Journal of Brand Management, 9*(4/5), 262–280.

Gnoth, J., Baloglu, S., Ekinci, Y., & Sirakaya-Turk, E. (2007). Introduction: Building destination brands. . *Tourism Analysis, 12*(5/6), 339–343.

Go, F. (1998).Globalization and emerging tourism education issues. In W, Theobold (Eds.), *Global tourism* (2nd ed., pp. 447–475). London: Butterworth Heinemann.

Go, F. M., & Govers, R. (1999). The Asian perspective: Which international conference destinations in Asia are the most competitive? *Journal of Convention & Exhibition Management, 1*(4), 37–50.

Go, F. M., & Govers, R. (2000). Integrated quality management for tourist destinations: A European perspective on achieving competitiveness. *Tourism Management, 21*(1), 79–88.

Go, F. M., & Williams, A. P. (1993). Competing and co-operating in the changing tourism channel system. *Journal of Travel and Tourism Marketing, 2*(2/3), 229–248.

Gokovali, U., Bahar, O., & Kozak, M. (2007). Determinants of length of stay: A practical application of survival analysis. *Tourism Management, 28*(3), 736–746.

Gomezelj, D. O., & Mihalic, T. (2008). Destination competitiveness—Applying different models, the case of Slovenia. *Tourism Management, 29*(2), 294–307.

Gonzalez, A. M., & Garcia-Falcon, J. M. (2003). Competitive potential of tourism in destinations. *Annals of Tourism Research, 30*(3), 720–740.

Goodall, B. (1988). How tourists choose their holidays: An analytical framework. In B. Goodall & G. Ashworth (Eds.), *Marketing in the tourism industry: The promotion of destination regions* (pp. 1–17). London: Routledge.

Goodall, B. (1990). Opportunity sets as analytical marketing instruments: A destination area view. In G. Ashworth & B. Goodall (Eds.), *Marketing tourism* (pp. 63–84). London: Routledge.

Goodall, B., & Bergsma, J. (1990). Destinations as marketed in tour operators' brochures. In G. Ashworth & B. Goodall (Eds.), *Marketing tourism places* (pp. 170–192). London: Routledge.

Goodrich, J. N. (1977, Summer). Differences in perceived similarity of tourism regions: A spatial analysis. *Journal of Travel Research, 16*, 10–13.

Goodrich, J. N. (1978, Fall). The relationship between preferences for and perceptions of vacation destinations. *Journal of Travel Research, 16*, 8–13.

Govers, R., & Go, F. M. (2004). Cultural identities constructed, imagined and experienced: A 3-gap tourism destination image model. *Tourism, 52*(2), 165–182.

Grabler, K. (1997). Perceptual mapping and positioning of tourist cities. In J. A. Mazanec (Ed.), *International city tourism: Analysis and strategy* (pp. 101–113). London: Pinter.

Green, C. E. (2009a). *Social media and the DMO marketer—Part 1.* Chevy Chase, MD: TIG Global.

Green, C. E. (2009b). *Social media and the DMO marketer—Part 2.* Chevy Chase, MD: TIG Global.

Greenberg, P. (2007). *The complete travel detective.* New York: Rodale.

Grigorous, E., & Siskos, Y. (2004). A survey of customer satisfaction barometers: Some results from the transportation-communications sector. *European Journal of Operational Research, 15*(2), 334–353.

Gronroos, C. (1978). A service-oriented approach to marketing of services. *European Journal of Marketing, 12*(8), 588–601.

Grosspietsch, M. (2006). Perceived and projected images of Rwanda: Visitor and international tour operator perspectives. *Tourism Management, 27*(2), 225–234.

Gunn, C. A. (1997). *Vacationscape: Developing tourist areas* (3rd ed.). Washington, DC: Taylor and Francis.

Gursoy, D., Baloglu, S., & Chi, C. G. (2009). Destination competitiveness of Middle Eastern countries: An examination of relative positioning. *Anatolia, 20*(1), 151–163.

Haahti, A. J. (1986). Finland's competitive position as a destination. *Annals of Tourism Research, 13*, 11–35.

Haahti, A., & Yavas, U. (1983). Tourists' perceptions of Finland and selected European countries as travel destinations. *European Journal of Marketing, 17*(2), 34–42.

Hair, J. F., Anderson, R. E., Tatham, R. L., & Black, W.C. (1995). *Multivariate data analysis with readings* (4th ed.). Englewood Cliffs, NJ: Prentice-Hall.

Hall, C. M. (1994). *Tourism and politics: Policy, power and place.* Chichester, UK: Wiley.

Hall, D. (2002). Brand development, tourism and national identity: The re-imaging of former Yugoslavia. *Journal of Brand Management, 9*(4/5), 323–334.

Hamil, J. (1997). The internet and international marketing. *International Marketing Review, 14*(5), 300–323.

Hanefors, M., & Mossberg, L. L. (1999). Package tourism and customer loyalties. In A. Pizam & Y. Mansfeld (Eds.), *Consumer behavior in travel and tourism* (pp.185–203) New York: Haworth Hospitality Press.

Hankinson, G. (2004). Relational network brands: Towards a conceptual model of place brands. *Journal of Vacation Marketing, 10*(2), 109–121.

Hankinson, G., & Cowking, P. (1995). What do you really mean by a brand? *Journal of Brand Management, 3*(1), 43–50.

Harrill, R. (2005). *Fundamentals of destination management and marketing.* Washington, DC: EIAHL.

Hassan, S. (2000). Determinants of market competitiveness in an environmentally sustainable tourism industry. *Journal of Travel Research, 38*(3), 239–245.

Hawkins, D. E., Leventhal, M., & Oden, W. L. (1996). The virtual tourism environment: Utilisation of information technology to enhance strategic travel marketing. *Progress in Tourism and Hospitality Research, 2,* 223–238.

Heath, E., & Wall, G. (1992). *Marketing tourism destinations: A strategic planning approach.* Canada: Wiley.

Hjalager, A. (2010). A review of innovation research in tourism. *Tourism Management, 31*(1), 1–12.

Hoffman, J. D. (1994). Emerging technologies and their impact on travel distribution. *Journal of Vacation Marketing, 1*(1), 95–103.

Holloway, J. C., & Plant, R. V. (1988). *Marketing for tourism.* London: Pittman

Hoof, H. B. V., Verbeeten, M. J., & Combrink, T. E. (1996, October). Information technology revisited-international lodging-industry technology needs and perception: A comparative study. *Cornell Hotel and Restaurant Administration Quarterly, 37*(6), 86–96.

Hope, C., Hope, R., & Tavridou, L. (1996). The impact of information technology on distribution channels. *Tourism Review, 51*(4), 9–14.

Hosany, S., Ekinci, Y., & Uysal, M. (2006). Destination image and destination personality: An application of branding theories to tourism places. *Journal of Business Research, 59*(5), 638–642.

Hoti, S., McAleer, M., & Shareef, R. (2007). Modelling international tourism and country risk spillovers for Cyprus and Malta. *Tourism Management, 28*(6), 1472–1484.

Howard, J. A., & Sheth, J. N. (1969). *The theory of buyer behavior.* New York: John Wiley.

Hsieh, S., O'Leary, J. T., & Morrison, A. M. (1994). A comparison of package and non-package travelers from the United Kingdom. *Journal of International Consumer Marketing, 6*(3/4), 79–100.

Hsu, C. H. C., Wolfe, K. C., & Kang, S. K. (2004). Image assessment for a destination with limited comparative advantages. *Tourism Management, 25*(1), 121–126.

Huan, T.-C., Beaman, J., & Kozak, M. (2003). Implications of models of repeat travel for the concept of destination loyalty. *Leisure and Society, 26*(1), 183–207.

Huan, T.-C., Beaman, J., & Shelby, L. (2004). No-escape natural disaster: Mitigating impacts on tourism. *Annals of Tourism Research, 31,* 255–273.

Huang, J., & Min, J. (2002). Earthquake devastation and recovery in tourism: The Taiwan case. *Tourism Management, 23,* 145–154.

Hudson, S., & Ritchie, J. R. B. (2009). Branding a memorable destination experience. The case of "Brand Canada." *International Journal of Tourism Research, 11,* 217–228.

Hunter, C. (2002). Sustainable tourism and the touristic ecological footprint. *Environment, Development and Sustainability, 4*(1), 7–20.

Icoz, O., Var, T., & Kozak, M. (1998). Tourism demand in Turkey. *Annals of Tourism Research, 25*(1), 236–239.

Inskeep, E. (1991). *Tourism planning: An integrated and sustainable development approach.* New York: Van Nostrand Reinhold.

Jacobson, D., & Andreosso-O'Callaghan, B. (1996). *Industrial economics and organization: A European perspective.* New York: McGraw-Hill.

Jafari, J. (1983, May). Anatomy of the travel industry. *Cornell Hotel and Restaurant Administration Quarterly, 24,* 71–77.

Javalgi, R. G., Thomas, E. G., & Rao, S. R. (1992). US pleasure travellers' perceptions of selected European destinations. *European Journal of Marketing, 26*(7), 45–64.

Jefferson, A. L., & Lickorish, L. J. (1991). *Marketing tourism* (2nd ed.). London, UK: Longman.

Juaneda, C. (1996). Estimating the probability of return visits using a survey of tourist expenditure in the Balearic Islands. *Tourism Economics, 2*(4), 339–352.

Kale, S. H., & Weir, K. M. (1986, Fall). Marketing third world countries to the western traveller: The case of India. *Journal of Travel Research, 25*(2), 2–7.

Kaplanidou, K., & Vogt, C. (2003). *Destination branding: Concept and measurement.* Department of Park, Recreation and Tourism Resources, Michigan State University.

Karlof, B., & Ostblom, S. (1993). *Benchmarking: A signpost excellence in quality and productivity.* West Sussex: Wiley.

Katsura, T., & Sheldon, P. (2008). Forecasting mobile technology use in Japanese tourism. *Information Technology & Tourism, 10*(3), 201–214.

Kaynama, S., & Black, C. (2000). A proposal to assess the service quality of online travel agencies: An exploratory study. *Journal of Professional Services Marketing, 21*(1), 63–88.

Keller, K. L. (1993). Conceptualising, measuring and managing customer-based brand equity. *Journal of Marketing, 57,* 1–22.

Keller, P., & Smeral, E. (1997, April 9–10). Increased international competition: New challenges for tourism policies in European countries. In *WTO/CEU-ETC Joint Seminar: Faced with Worldwide Competition and Structural Changes, What are the Tourism Responsibilities of European Governments* (pp.1–24). Salzburg, Austria.

Kerr, G. (2006). From destination brand to location brand. *Journal of Brand Management, 13*(4/5), 276–283.

Kim, H., Kim, W. G., & An, J. A. (2003). The effect of consumer-based brand equity on firms' financial performance. *Journal of Consumer Marketing, 20*(4), 335–351.

King, B. (1994). Australian attitudes to domestic and international resort holidays: A comparison of Fiji and Queensland. In A. V. Seaton et al. (Eds.), *Tourism: The state of the art* (pp. 347–358).New York: Wiley.

Kingsley, I., & Fesenmaier, D. R. (1995). Travel information kiosks: An emerging communications channel for the tourism industry. *Journal of Travel & Tourism Marketing, 4*(1), 57–70.

Knapp, D., & Sherwin, G. (2005). *Destination brand science, 22.* Washington DC:

Kneesel, E., Baloglu, S., & Millar, M. (2010). Gaming destination images: Implications for branding. *Journal of Travel Research, 49*(1), 68–78.

Konecnik, M., & Gartner, W. (2007). Customer-based brand equity for a destination. *Annals of Tourism Research, 34*(2), 400–421.

Konecnik, M., & Go, F. (2008). Tourism destination brand identity: The case of Slovenia. *Journal of Brand Management, 15,* 177–189.

Kotler, P. (1994). *Marketing management: Analysis, planning, implementation and control* (8th ed.). Englewood Cliffs, NJ: Prentice-Hall International Editions.

Kotler, P., Armstrong, G., Saunders, J., & Wong, V. (1999). *Principles of marketing* (2nd ed.). Englewood Cliffs, NJ: Prentice-Hall Europe.

Kotler, P., Bowen, J. T., & Makens, J. C. (2009). *Marketing for hospitality and tourism. Englewood Cliffs, NJ:* Prentice-Hall.

Kotler, P., Bowen, J. T., & Makens, J. C. (2010). *Marketing for hospitality and tourism* (5th ed.). Upper Saddle River, NJ: Prentice-Hall.

Kotler, P., & Fox, K. (1985). *Strategic marketing for educational institutions.* Englewood Cliffs, NJ: Prentice-Hall.

Kotler, P., & Gertner, D. (2004). Country as brand, product and beyond. In N. Morgan, A. Pritchard, & R. Pride (Eds.), *Destination branding: Creating the unique destination proposition* (2nd ed., pp. 40–56). Elsevier: Oxford.

Kotler, P., Haider, D. H., & Rein, I. (1993). *Marketing places*. New York: Free Press.

Kozak, K., Baloglu, S., & Bahar, O. (2010) Measuring destintation competitiveness: A comparison between three destinations. *Journal of Hospitality Management and Marketing*, 19(1), 56–71.

Kozak, M. (2000). *Destination benchmarking: Facilities, customer satisfaction and levels of tourist expenditure*. Unpublished doctoral dissertation, Sheffield Hallam University, UK.

Kozak, M. (2001a). Comparative assessment of tourist satisfaction with destinations across two nationalities. *Tourism Management*, 22(3), 391–401.

Kozak, M. (2001b). Repeaters' behavior at two distinct destinations. *Annals of Tourism Research*, 28(3), 785–808.

Kozak, M. (2002a). Comparative analysis of tourist motivations by nationality and destinations. *Tourism Management*, 23(2), 221–232.

Kozak, M. (2002b). Destination benchmarking. *Annals of Tourism Research*, 29(2), 497–519.

Kozak, M. (2002c). An overview of tourism development in Mallorca. *Tourism: An Interdisciplinary Journal*, 50(1), 67–80.

Kozak, M. (2002d). Measuring tourist satisfaction with multiple destination attributes. *Tourism Analysis*, 7(3/4), 229–240.

Kozak, M. (2004a). *Destination benchmarking: Concepts, practices and operations*. Oxon, UK: CAB International.

Kozak, M. (2004b). The practice of destination-based total quality management. *Anatolia*, 15(2), 125–136.

Kozak, M. (2007a, July 16–18). *Cultural heritage management: Economic, social & political perspectives*. Paper presented at the 3rd Tourism Outlook conference, Kuala Lumpur, Malaysia.

Kozak, M. (2007b). Tourist harassment: A marketing perspective. *Annals of Tourism Research*, 34(2), 384–399.

Kozak, M., Andreu, L., & Bigne, E. (2005). Web-based national tourism promotion in the Mediterranean area. *The Tourist Review*, 60(1), 6–11.

Kozak, M., Baloglu, S., & Bahar, O. (2010). Measuring destination competitiveness: A comparison between three destinations. *Journal of Hospitality Management and Marketing*. 19(1), 56–71.

Kozak, M., & Beaman, J. (2006). Relationship between customer satisfaction and loyalty. *Tourism Analysis*, 11(6), 397–409.

Kozak, M., Crotts, J. C., & Law, R. (2007). The impact of the perception of risk on international travellers. *International Journal of Tourism Research*, 9(4), 233–242.

Kozak, M., Gokovali, U., & Bahar, O. (2009). Estimating the determinants of tourist spending: A comparison of four models. *Tourism Analysis*,13,143–155.

Kozak, M., & Nield, K. (2001). An overview of benchmarking literature: Strengths and weaknesses. *Journal of Quality Assurance in Tourism and Hospitality*, 2(3/4), 7–23.

Kozak, M., & Nield, K. (2004). The role of quality and eco-labelling systems in destination benchmarking. *Journal of Sustainable Tourism*, 12(2), 138–148.

Kozak, M., & Rimmington, M. (1998). Benchmarking: Destination attractiveness and small hospitality business performance. *International Journal of Contemporary Hospitality Management*, 10(5), 74–78.

Kozak, M., & Rimmington, M. (1999). Measuring destination competitiveness: conceptual considerations and empirical findings. *International Journal of Hospitality Management*, 18(3), 273–283.

Kozak, M., & Rimmington, M. (2000). Tourist satisfaction with Mallorca, Spain as an off-season holiday destination. *Journal of Travel Research*, 39(3), 260–269.

Kozak, M., & Tasci, A.D.A. (2005). Locals' Perceptions of Foreign Tourists: A Case Study in Turkey. *International Journal of Tourism Research*, 7(4–5): 261–277.

Las Vegas Convention and Visitors Authority. (2009). *Destination Las Vegas: 2010 and beyond*. Las Vegas: Author.

Las Vegas Review Journal. (2009, Sept 20). p. E1.

Law, R., Qi, S., & Buhalis, D. (2010). Progress in tourism management: A review of website evaluation in tourism research. *Tourism Management*, 31(3), 297–313.

Laws, E. (1991). *Tourism marketing: Service and quality management perspectives*. Cheltenham: Stanley Thornes.

Laws, E. (1995). *Tourist destination management: Issues, analysis and policies*. New York: Routledge.

Laws, E., & Cooper, C. (1998). Inclusive tours and commodification: The marketing constraints for mass-market resorts. *Journal of Vacation Marketing*, 4(4), 337–352.

Lee, K. F. (2001). Sustainable tourism destinations: The importance of cleaner production. *Journal of Cleaner Production*, 9(4), 313–323.

Leibrock, C. (2000). *Design details for health: Making the most of interior design's healing potential*. New York: John Wiley.

Lennon, J. J., Smith, H., Cockerell, N., & Trew, J. (2006) Benchmarking national tourism organizations and agencies: Understanding best practice. Oxford: Elsevier.

Lepp, A., & Gibson, H. (2003). Tourist roles, perceived risk and international tourism. *Annals of Tourism Research*, 30(3), 606–624.

Leslie, D. (2001). Serviced accommodation, environmental performance and benchmarks. *Journal of Quality Assurance in Hospitality and Tourism*, 2(3/4), 127–148.

Lewis, B. R., & Owtram, M. (1986). Customer satisfaction with package holidays. In B. Moores (Ed.), *Are they being served?* (pp. 201–213). Oxford: Philip Allan Publishers.

Lin, L. (1998). Computer-based information technologies and their impact on the marketing of international tourism industry. In D. Buhalis, A. M. Tjoa, and J. Jafari (Eds.), *Information and communication technologies in tourism* (pp. 318–327). Wien: Springer-Verlag.

Lopez, E. P., Navarro M. M., & Dominguez, A. R. (2004). A competitive study of two tourism destinations through the application of conjoint analysis techniques: The case of the Canary Islands. *Pasos. Revista de Turismo y Patrimonio Cultural*, 2(2), 163–177.

Low, G. S., & Lamb, C. W. (2000). The measurement and dimensionality of brand associations. *Journal of Product and Brand Management*, 9(6), 350–368.

Lundberg, E. D., Stavenga, M. H., & Krishnamoorthy, M. (1995). *Tourism economics*. New York: John Wiley.

MacLaurin, D. J. (2004). 2003 Annual International Council on Hotel Restaurant and Institutional Education (CHRIE). *Journal of Teaching in Travel and Tourism*, 4(2), 89–92.

Malhotra, S. K. (1981). Systems models for parasite pathways in ichthyoparasitology of the Himalayan riverine ecosystem. *Current Science, 50*, 874–875.

Man, T. W. Y., Lau, T., & Chan, K. F. (2002). The competitiveness of small and medium enterprises a conceptualization with focus on entrepreneurial competencies. *Journal of Business Venturing*, 17(2), 123–142.

Mangion, M. L., Durbarry, R., & Sinclair, M. T. (2005). Tourism competitiveness: Price and quality. *Tourism Economics*, 11(1), 45–68.

Mansfeld, A., & Romaniuk, J. (2002, May 20–23). *How do destinations compete? An application of the duplication of purchase law.* Paper presented at the 32nd EMAC Conference, Glasgow, Scotland.

Marsek, P., & Sharpe, F. (2008). *The complete idiot's guide to medical tourism.* New York: Penguin.

Matzler, K., & Pechlaner, H. (2001). Guest satisfaction barometer and benchmarking: Experiences from Austria. *Journal of Quality Assurance in Hospitality and Tourism, 2*(3/4), 25–48.

Mayo, E. J. (1973). Regional images and regional travel destination. In *Proceedings of the 4th Annual Conference of TTRA* (pp. 211–217). Sun Valley, ID: Travel and Tourism Research Association.

Mayo, E. J., & Jarvis, L. P. (1981). *The psychology of leisure travel: Effective marketing and selling of travel services.* Boston: CBI.

Mayr, T., & Zins, A. H. (2009). Acceptance of online vs traditional travel agencies. *Anatolia, 20*(1), 164–177.

Mazursky, D. (1989). Past experience and future tourism decisions. *Annals of Tourism Research, 16*(3), 333–344.

McDougall, G. H. G., & Munro, H. (1994). Scaling and attitude measurement in travel and tourism research. In J. R. B. Ritchie & C. R. Goeldner (Eds.), *Travel and hospitality research: A handbook for managers and researchers* (2nd ed.). New York: Wiley.

McIntyre, G. (1993). *Sustainable tourism development: Guide for local planners.* Madrid: World Tourism Organisation.

McLellan, R. W., & Fousher, K. D. (1983, Summer). Negative images of the United States as expressed by tour operators from other countries. *Journal of Travel Research, 22*(1), 2–5.

McNair, C. J., & Leibfried, K. H. J. (1992). *Benchmarking: A tool for continuous improvement.* New York: Harper Business.

Melián-González, A., & Garcia- Falcón, J.M. (2003). Competitive potential of tourism in destinations. *Annals of Tourism Research, 30*(3), 720–740.

Middleton V. T. C. (1994). *Marketing in travel and tourism* (2nd ed.). Oxford: Butterworth & Heinemann.

Middleton, V. T. C., & Clarke, J. (2001). *Marketing in travel and tourism.* Oxford: Butterworth-Heinemann.

Middleton, V. T. C., & Clarke, J. (2002). *Marketing in travel and tourism* (3rd ed.). Woburn, MA: Butterworth-Heinemann.

Mihalic, T. (2000). Environmental management of a tourist destination: A factor of tourism competitiveness. *Tourism Management, 21*(1), 65–78.

Mill, R. C., & Morrison, A. M. (1992). *The tourism system: An introductory text* (2nd ed.). Englewood Cliffs, NJ: Prentice-Hall International Editions.

Miller, M. M., & Henthorne, T. L. (2006). In search of competitive advantage in Caribbean tourism websites: Revisiting the unique selling proposition. *Journal of Travel and Tourism Marketing, 21*(2/3), 49–62.

Milman, A., & Pizam, A. (1995). The role of awareness and familiarity with a destination: The central Florida case. *Journal of Travel Research, 33*(3), 21–27.

Min, H., & Min, H. (1997). Benchmarking the quality of hotel services: Managerial perspectives. *International Journal of Quality and Reliability Management, 14*(6), 582–597.

Morgan, N., & Pritchard, A. (1999). Building destination brands: The cases of Wales and Australia. *Journal of Brand Management, 7*(2), 102–119.

Morgan, N., & Pritchard, A. (2004). Meeting the destination branding challenge. In N. Morgan, A. Pritchard, & R. Pride (Eds.), *Destination branding: Creating the unique destination proposition* (pp. 59–78). Oxford, UK: Elsevier.

Morgan, N., Pritchard, A., & Piggott, R. (2002). New Zealand, 100% Pure. The creation of a powerful niche destination brand. *Journal of Brand Management*, 9(4/5), 335–355.

Morgan, N., Pritchard A., & Piggott, R. (2003). Destination branding and the role of the stakeholders: The case of New Zealand. *Journal of Vacation Marketing*, 9(3), 285–299.

Morgan, N., Pritchard, A., & Pride, R. (2004). *Destination branding: Creating the Unique Destination Proposition*. Oxford: Elsevier.

Morrison, A. M. (1989). *Hospitality and travel marketing*. New York: Albany.

Moser, C. A., & Kalton, G. (1971). *Survey methods in social investigation* (2nd ed.). England: Gower.

Mountinho, L. (1987). Consumer behaviour in tourism. *European Journal of Marketing*, 21(10), 2–44.

Mountinho, L., & Trimble, J. (1991). A probability of revisitation model: The case of winter visits to the Grand Canyon. *The Service Industries Journal*, 11(4), 439–457.

MTA. (2008, September). World Medical Tourism & Global Health Congress, 9–12.

Muñoz, T. G. (2006). Inbound international tourism to Canary Islands: A dynamic panel data model. *Tourism Management*, 27(2), 281–291.

Muñoz, T. G. (2007). German demand for tourism in Spain. *Tourism Management*, 28(1), 12–22.

Murdaugh, M. (2005). Marketing. In R. Harrill (Ed.), *Fundamentals of destination management and marketing*. Washington, DC: Educational Institute of the American Hotel and Lodging Association.

Murphy, E. (1997). *Quality management in urban tourism*. New York: Wiley.

Murphy, L., Benckendorff, P., & Moscardo, G. (2007). Linking travel motivation, tourist self- image and destination brand personality. *Journal of Travel and Tourism Marketing*, 22(2), 45–59.

Murphy, P. E., & Pritchard, M. (1997, Winter). Destination price-value perceptions: An examination of origin and seasonal influences. *Journal of Travel Research*, 35, 16–22.

Mykletun, R. J., Crotts, J. C., & Mykletun, A. (2001). Positioning an island destination in the peripheral area of the Baltics: A flexible approach to market segmentation. *Tourism Management*, 22(5), 493–500.

Nadkarni, R. A. (1995, November). A not-so-secret recipe for successful TQM. *Quality Progress*, pp. 91–96.

Nahrstedt, W. (2004). Wellness: A new perspective for leisure centers, health tourism, and spas in Europe on the global health market. In K. Weiermair & C. Mathies (Eds.), *The tourism and leisure industry: Shaping the future* (pp. 181–198). Binghamton, NY: Haworth Hospitality.

Nandan, S. (2004). An exploration of the brand identity–brand image linkage: A communications perspective. *Brand Management*, 12(4), 264–278.

Nicolau, J.L., & Mas, F.J. (2006). The influence of distance and prices on the choice of tourist destinations: The moderating role of motivations. *Tourism Management*, 27(5), 982–996.

Novelli, M., Schmitz, B., & Spencer, T. (2006). Networks, clusters and innovation in tourism: A UK experience. *Tourism Management*, 27(6), 1141–1152.

Oliver, R. L. (1980). A cognitive model for the antecedents and consequences of satisfaction decisions. *Journal of Marketing Research*, 27, 460–469.

Oppermann, M. (1998). Destination threshold potential and the law of repeat visitation. *Journal of Travel Research*, 37(2), 131–137.

Oppermann, M. (1999). Predicting destination choice: A discussion of destination loyalty. *Journal of Vacation Marketing*, 5, 51–65.

Oppermann, M. (2000). Where psychology and geography interface in tourism research and theory. In A. G. Woodside, G. I. Crouch, J. A. Mazanec, M.

Oppermann, & M. Y. Sakai (Eds.), *Consumer psychology of tourism, hospitality and leisure* (pp. 10–37). Oxon: CABI.

Ortega, E., & Rodríguez, B. (2007, February). Information at tourism destinations. Importance and cross-cultural differences between international and domestic tourists. *Journal of Business Research, 60*(2), 146–152.

Ozdemir, G., & Kozak, M. (2009). Event and network management: Application of EFQM for tourist destinations. *International Journal of Tourism Policy, 2*(4), 262–273.

Pan, B., Maclaurin, T., & Crotts, J. C. (2007). Travel blogs and the implications for destination marketing. *Journal of Travel Research, 46*(1), 35–45.

Papatheodorou, A. (2002). Exploring competitiveness in Mediterranean resorts. *Tourism Economics, 8*(2), 133–150.

Paraa-Lopez, E., & Calero-Garcia, F. (2010). Success factors of tourism networks. In M. Kozak, J. Gnoth, & L. Andreu (Eds.), *Advances in tourism destination marketing: Managing network* (pp. 27–39). Oxon: Routledge.

Park, C. W., Jaworski, B. J., & MacInnis, D. J. (1986). Strategic brand concept-image management. *Journal of Marketing, 50*(4), 135–145.

Paskaleva-Shapira, K. A. (2007). New paradigms in city tourism management: Redefining destination promotion. *Journal of Travel Research, 46,* 108–114.

Patterson, T. M., Niccolucci, V., & Marchettini, N. (2008). Adaptive environmental management of tourism in the Province of Siena, Italy using the ecological footprint. *Journal of Environmental Management, 86*(2), 407–418.

Payne, J. W., Bettman, J. R., & Johnson, E. J. (1997). The adaptive decision maker: Effort and accuracy in choice. In W. M. Goldstein & R. M. Hogarth (Eds.), *Research on judgment and decision making: Currents, connections and controversies* (pp. 181–204). Cambridge, UK: Cambridge University Press.

Pearce, D. G. (1997). Competitive destination analysis in Southeast Asia. *Journal of Travel Research,*–(4), 16–24.

Peattie, K., & Peattie S. (1996). Promotional competitions: A winning tool for tourism marketing. *Tourism Management, 17*(6), 433–442.

Perdue, R. R. (2001). Internet site evaluations: The influence of behavioral experience, existing images, and selected website characteristics. *Journal of Travel & Tourism Marketing, 11*(2/3).

Pike, S. (2002). Destination image analysis—A review of 142 papers from 1973 to 2000. *Tourism Management, 23*(5), 541–549.

Pike, S. (2005). Tourism destination branding complexity. *Journal of Product & Brand Management, 14*(4), 258–259.

Pike, S. (2008). *Destination marketing: An integrated marketing communication approach.* Burlington, MA: Butterwork-Heinemann.

Pikkemaat, B., & Weiermair, K. (2007). Innovation through cooperation in destinations: First results of an empirical study in Austria. *Anatolia, 18*(1), 67–84.

Pine, J. B. II., & Gilmore, J. H. (1999). *The experience economy.* Boston: Harvard Business School Press.

Pizam, A. (1999). Life and tourism in the years 2050. *Hospitality Management, 8.*

Pizam, A., Tarlow, P. E., & Bloom, J. (1997). Making tourists feel safe: Whose responsibility is it? *Journal of Travel Research, 36*(1), 23–28.

Plog, S. (1974). Why destination areas rise and fall in popularity? *Cornell HRA Quarterly, 14*(4), 55–58.

Plog, S. (2004). *Leisure travel: A marketing handbook.* Upper Saddle River, NJ: Prentice-Hall.

Poetschke, B. (1995). Key success factors for public/private partnerships in island tourism planning. In M. Conlin & T. Baum (Eds.), *Island tourism: Management principles and practice* (pp. 532–564). Chichester: Wiley.

Poon, A. (1993). *Tourism, technology, and competitive strategies.* Wallingford: CABI.

Poon, A. (1998). All-inclusive tours. *Travel and Tourism Analyst*, 6, 62–77.

Porter, M. (1980). *Competitive strategy: Techniques for analysing industries and competitors*. New York: Free Press.

Porter, M. (1996, November–December). What is strategy? *Harvard Business Review*, 74(6), 61–78.

Porter, M. E. (1985). *Competitive advantage: Creating and sustaining superior performance*. New York: Free Press.

Porter, M. E. (1990). *The competitive advantage of nations*. New York: The Free Press.

Porter, M. E. (1998). *Competitive advantage*. New York: The Free Press.

Prayag, G. (2007, Fall). Exploring the relationship between destination image and brand personality of a tourist destination: An application of projective techniques. *Journal of Travel and Tourism Research*, pp. 111–130.

Prebensen, N. K. (2007). Exploring tourists' images of a distant destination. *Tourism Management*, 28(3), 747–756.

Prideaux, B. (2000). The resort development spectrum. *Tourism Management*, 21(3), 225–241.

Prideaux, B. (2009). Sustainability, change and drivers—Shaping future destinations. In B. Prideaux (Ed.), *Resort destinations: Evolution, management and development* (pp. 255–277). Oxford: Butterworth-Heinemann.

Pritchard, M. P., & Howard, D. R. (1997). The loyal traveler: Examining a typology of service patronage. *Journal of Travel Research*, 35(4), 2–10.

Puhringer, S., & Taylor, A. (2008). A practitioner's report on blogs as a potential source of destination marketing intelligence. *Journal of Vacation Marketing*, 14(2), 177–187.

Pyo, S., Mihalik, B. J., & Uysal, M. (1989). Attraction attributes and motivations: A canonical correlation analysis. *Annals of Tourism Research*, 16, 277–282.

Pyo, S. S., Uysal, M., & McLellan, R. W. (1991). A linear expenditure model for tourism demand. *Annals of Tourism Research*, 18, 443–454.

Reeves, R. (1961). *Reality in advertising*. New York: Knopf.

Reisinger, Y., & Turner, L. W. (2002). Cultural differences between Asian tourist markets and Australian hosts: Part 2. *Journal of Travel Research*, 40(4), 385–395.

Richardson, J., & Cohen, J. (1993). State slogans: The case of the missing USP. *Journal of Travel & Tourism Marketing*, 2(2/3), 91–109.

Rimmington, M., & Kozak, M. (1997). Developments in information technology: Implications for the tourism industry and tourism marketing. *Anatolia: An International Journal of Tourism Hospitality Research*, 8(3), 59–80.

Ritchie, B., & Crouch, G. (1993). *Competitiveness in international tourism: A framework for understanding and analysis*. Paper presented at the annual congress of the International Association of Scientific Experts in Tourism, Bariloche, Argentina.

Ritchie, J. R. B., & Crouch, G. I. (2003). *The competitive destination: A sustainable tourism perspective*. Wallingford: CABI.

Ritchie, J. R. B., & Ritchie, R. J. B. (1998). The branding of tourism destinations: Past achievements and future challenges. In P. Keller (Ed.), *Proceedings of the 1998 Annual Congress of the International Association of Scientific Experts in Tourism, Destination Marketing: Scopes and Limitations* (pp. 89–116). Marrakech, Morocco.

Ritchie, J. R. B., & Crouch, G. I. (2000). The competitive destination: A sustainability perspective. *Tourism Management*, 21, 1–7.

Rodríguez, J. R. O., Parra-López, E., & Yanes-Estévez, V. (2008). The sustainability of island destinations: Tourism area life cycle and teleological perspectives. The case of Tenerife. *Tourism Management*, 29(1), 53–65.

Russel, J. A., & Pratt, G. (1980). A description of affective quality attributed to environment. *Journal of Personality and Social Psychology*, 38(2), 311–322.

Rust, R. T., & Oliver, R. L. (1994). Service quality: Insights and managerial implications from the frontier. In R. T. Rust & R. L. Oliver (Eds.), *Service quality. New directions in theory and practice* (pp. 1–20). London: Sage.

Rust, R. T., Zahorik, A. J., & Keiningham, T. L. (1996). *Service marketing*. New York: HaperCollins.

Ryan, C. (1995). *Researching tourist satisfaction*. London: Routledge.

Sainaghi, R. (2010). Strategic positioning and performance of tourism destinations. In M. Kozak, J. Gnoth, & L. Andreu (Eds.), *Advances in tourism destination marketing: Managing network* (pp. 40–56). Oxon: Routledge.

Sandbach, M. (1997, April 9–10). International competition and structural changes in tourism markets, WTO/CEU-ETC Joint Seminar: Faced With Worldwide Competition and Structural Changes, What Are The Tourism Responsibilities of European Governments, Salzburg, Austria.

Sarkar, M. B., Butler, B., & Steinfield, C. (1995). Intermediaries and cybermediaries: A continuing role for mediating players in the electronic marketplace. *Journal of Computer-Mediated Communication* [On-line], *1*(3). Available http://www.ascusc.org/jcmc/vol1/issue3/sarkar.html

Savitz, A. W. (2006). *The triple bottom line*. San Francisco, CA: Jossey-Bass.

Schertler, W. (1994). Impact of new information technologies on tourism industry and businesses. *The Tourist Review, 2*, 2–8.

Schmalleger, D., & Carson, D. (2008). Blogs in tourism: Changing approaches to information exchange. *Journal of Vacation Marketing, 14*(2), 99–110.

Schmitt, B. H. (1999). *Experiential marketing—How to get customers to sense, feel, think, act, and relate to your company and brands*. New York: The Free Press.

Schuster, A. G. (1998). A Delphi survey on business process re-engineering from the tourism and hospitality industries: The case of Alpha Flight services. In D. Buhalis, A. M. Tjoa, & J. Jafari (Eds.), *Information and communication technologies in tourism* (pp. 224–234). Wien: Springer-Verlag.

Selby, M., & Morgan, N. (1996). Reconstructing place image: A case study of its role in destination market research. *Tourism Management, 17*(4), 287–294.

Selnes, F. (1993). An examination of the effect of product performance on brand reputation, satisfaction and loyalty. *European Journal of Marketing, 27*(9), 19–35.

Shafir, E., Simonson, I., & Tversky, A. (1997). Reason-based choice. In W. M. Goldstein & R. M. Hogarth (Eds.), *Research on judgment and decision making: Currents, connections and controversies* (pp. 69–94). Cambridge, UK: Cambridge University Press.

Sharp, L. (2001). Positive response action: The ultimate goal of website communication. *Journal of Communication Management, 6*(1), 41–52.

Simon, C. J., & Sullivan, M. W. (1993, Winter). The measurement and determinants of brand equity: A financial approach. *Marketing Science, 12*, 28–52.

Sirakaya, E., McLellan, R. W., & Uysal, M. (1996). Modelling vacation destination decisions: A behavioral approach. *Journal of Travel and Tourism Marketing, 15*(12), 57.

Sirgy, M. J., Grewal, D., Mangleburg, T. F., Park, J., Chon, K., Claiborne, C. B., et al. (1997). Assessing the predictive validity of two methods of measuring self-image congruence. *Journal of the Academy of Marketing Science, 25*(3), 229–241.

Sirgy, M. J., & Su, C. (2000). Destination image, self-congruity, and travel behavior: Toward an integrative model. *Journal of Travel Research, 38*, 340–352.

Sivadas, E., & Baker-Prewitt, J. L. (2000). An examination of the relationship between service quality, customer satisfaction, and store loyalty. *International Journal of Retail and Distribution Management, 28*(2), 73–82.

Smeral, E. (1997). The impact of globalization on small and medium enterprises: New challenges for tourism policies in European countries. *Tourism Management, 19*(4), 371–380.

Snepenger, D., Snepenger, M., Dalbey, M., & Wessol, A. (2007). Meanings and consumption characteristics of places at a tourism destination. *Journal of Travel Research*, 45, 310–321.

Song, H., Wong, K. F., & Chon, K. S. (2003). Modelling and forecasting the demand for Hong Kong tourism. *International Journal of Hospitality Management*, 22(4), 435–451.

Sönmez, S. F., & Graefe, A. R. (1998). Influence of terrorism risk on foreign tourism decisions. *Annals Of Tourism Research*, 25(1), 112–144.

Stamboulis, Y., & Skayannis, P. (2003). Innovation strategies and technology for experience-based tourism. *Tourism Management*, 24(1), 35–43.

Steiner, T., & Dufour, A. (1998). Agent-based cybermarketing in the tourism industry. In D. Buhalis, A. M. Tjoa, & J. Jafari (Eds.), *Information and communication technologies in tourism* (pp. 170–179). Wien: Springer-Verlag.

Stephano, R. (2009). *Creation of medical cluster in Chihuahua, México*. Presentation given March 15, 2009.

Stephens, S. (1997, June 13). Eco grading for Scots. *Leisure Week*.

Stern, E., & Krakover, S. (1993). The formation of a composite urban image. *Geographical Analysis*, 25(2), 130–146.

Stipanuk, D. (1993). Tourism and technology. *Tourism Management*, pp. 267–277.

Supphellen, M., & Nygaardsvik, I. (2002). Testing country brand slogans: Conceptual development and empirical illustration of a simple normative model. *Journal of Brand Management*, 9(4/5), 385–395.

Swan, J. E., & Combs, L. J. (1976). Product performance and consumer satisfaction: A new concept. *Journal of Marketing*, 40(1), 25–33.

Syriopoulos, T. C., & Sinclair, M. T. (1993). An econometric study of tourism demand: The AIDS model of US and European tourism in Mediterranean countries. *Applied Economics*, 25(12), 1541–1552.

Tang, K. H., & Zairi, M. (1998). Benchmarking quality implementation in a service context; a comparative analysis of financial services and institutions of higher education: Part II. *Total Quality Management*, 9(7).

Tanrisevchi, A., & Hancer, M. (2008). Examining e-mail response quality in Turkish travel agencies. *Anatolia*, 19(1), 23–40.

Tatko-Peterson, A. (2006, October 5). Medical tourism expanding among Americans. *Contra Costa Times (Walnut Creek, CA)*, Retrieved July 28, 2008, from Newspaper Source database.

Taylor, W. A., & Wright, G. H. (2006). The contribution of measurement and information infrastructure to TQM success. *Omega*, 34(4), 372–384.

Timothy, D. J. (1998). Co-operative tourism planning in a developing destination. *Journal of Sustainable Tourism*, 6(1), 52–68.

Tourism New Zealand. (2007, October). *Tourism News*, pp. 1–24.

Um, S., Chon, K., & Ro, Y. (2006). Antecedents of revisit intention. *Annals of Tourism Research*, 33(4), 1141–1158.

Um, S., & Crompton, J. L. (1990). Attitude determinants in tourism destination choice. *Annals of Tourism Research*, 17, 432–448.

Um, S., & Crompton, J. L. (1991). Development of pleasure travel attitude dimensions. *Annals of Tourism Research*, 18(3), 500–504.

Uysal, M., & Hagan, L. R. (1993). Motivation of pleasure to travel and tourism. In M. A. Khan, M. D. Olsen, & T. Var (Eds.), *VNR'S encyclopedia of hospitality and tourism* (pp. 798–810). New York: Van Nostrand Reinhold.

Vanhove, N. (2006). A comparative analysis of competition models for tourism destinations. In M. Kozak & L. Andreu (Eds.), Progress in tourism marketing (pp. 101–114). London: Elsevier.

Var, T., Beck, R. A. D., & Loftus, P. (1977). Determination of touristic attractiveness of the touristic areas in British Columbia. *Journal of Travel Research*, 15(3), 23–29.

Vaziri, K. (1992, October). Using competitive benchmarking to set goals. *Quality Progress*, pp. 81–85.

Vrtiprah, V. (2001). Managing quality in hotel excelsior. *Journal of Quality Assurance in Hospitality and Tourism*, 2(3/4), 111–126.

Walle, A. H. (1996). Tourism and the internet. *Journal of Travel Research*, 35(1), 72–77.

Wang, Y., & Russo, S. (2007). Conceptualizing and evaluating the functions of destination marketing systems. *Journal of Vacation Marketing*, 13(3), 187–203.

Warnken, J., Bradley, M., & Guilding, C. (2005). Eco-resorts vs. mainstream accommodation providers: An investigation of the viability of benchmarking environmental performance. *Tourism Management*, 26(3), 367–379.

Watson G. H. (1993). *Strategic benchmarking: How to rate your company's performance against the world's best*. Canada: Wiley.

Wijk, J., & Persoon, W. (2006). A long-haul destination: Sustainability reporting among tour operators. *European Management Journal*, 24(6), 381–395.

Williams, C. B. (1997). Benchmarking customer satisfaction with hospital food service within the army's medical command. *Journal of the American Dietetic Association*, 97(9), A106.

Williams, P., & Hobson, J. S. P. (1995). Virtual reality and tourism: Fact or fantasy? *Tourism Management*, 16(6), 423–427.

Williams, R., Rattray, R., & Stork, A. (2004). Web site accessibility of German and UK tourism information sites. European Business Review, 16(6), 577–589.

Wober, K. W. (2002). *Benchmarking in tourism and hospitality industries: The selection of benchmarking partners*. Wallingford: CAB International.

Wood, D. J., & Gray, B. (1991). Towards a comprehensive theory of collaboration. *The Journal of Applied Behavioral Science*, 27, 139–162.

Wood, L. (2000). Brands and brand equity: Definition and management. *Management Decision*, 38(9), 662–669.

Woodman, J. (2008). *Patients beyond borders: Everybody's guide to affordable, world-class medical tourism* (2nd ed.). Chapel Hill, NC: Healthy Travel Media.

Woodside, A. G., & Carr, J. A. (1988). Consumer decision making and competitive marketing strategies: Applications for tourism planning. *Journal of Travel Research*, 26(3), 2–7.

Woodside, A. G., & Lysonski, S. (1989). A general model of traveler destination choice. *Journal of Travel Research*, 27(1), 8–14.

Woodside, A. G., & Sherrell, D. (1977). Traveler evoked, inept, and inert sets of vacation destinations. *Journal of Travel Research*, 16, 14–18.

Xie, P. F., & Lew, A. (2008). Podcasting and tourism: An exploratory study of types, approaches, and content. *Information Technology & Tourism*, 10(2), 173–180.

Yoon, Y. (2002). *Development of a structural model for tourism destination competitiveness from stakeholders' perspectives*. Unpublished doctoral dissertation, The Virginia Polytechnic Institute and State University, Virginia.

Zahra, S. A. (1999). The changing rules of global competitiveness in the 21st century. *Academy of Management Executive*, 13(1), 36–42.

Zairi, M. (1992). The art of benchmarking: Using customer feedback to establish a performance gap. *Total Quality Management*, 3(2), 177–188.

Zairi, M. (1996). *Benchmarking for best practice: Continuous learning through sustainable innovation*. Oxford, UK: Butterworth-Heinemann.

Zeithaml, V., & Bitner, M. J. (1996). *Services marketing*. New York: McGraw-Hill.

Zeithaml V., & Bitner, M. J. (2000). *Services marketing: Integrating customer focus across the fir* (2nd ed.). Boston, MA: Irwin McGraw-Hill.

Internet Sources

Audi, T. (2008, January 6). Your Vegas is showing (We Liked the Old Slogan Better). Retrieved from http://www.filife.com/stories/your-vegas-is-showing-we-liked-the-old-slogan-better

Beirne, M. (2004, October 11). Playing for keeps. *Brandweek*. Retrieved January 5, 2010, from http://www.brandweek.com/bw/esearch/article_display.jsp?vnu_content_id=1000663856

Caribbean Tourism Organization A. Caribbean Travel. Retrieved December 10, 2009, from CTO's Marketing Site, including links to pages for individual destinations Http://www.Caribbeantravel.Com

Caribbean Tourism Organization B. One Caribbean. Retrieved December 10, 2009, from CTO's Business Site Http://Www.Onecaribbean.Org.

Destination Marketing Association International. (n.d.). Development and empirical illustration of a simple normative model. *Journal of Brand Management*, 9(4/5), 385–395. Retrieved September 3, 2009, from www.destinationmarketing.org

Dwyer, L., & Kim, C. (2001). *Destination competitiveness: A model and determinants*. Retrieved August 8, 2003, from www.ttra.com./ pub/uploads/007pdf.

Greenberg, P. (2008, 27 October). CRM at the speed of light. Retrieved February 1, 2010, from http://www.madeforone.com/Articles/index.php/business/crm-at-the-speed-of-light/

Hildreth, J. (2009). *The Saffron European city brand barometer*. Revealing which cities get the brands they deserve. Retrieved December 1, 2009, from http://saffron-consultants.com/wp-content/uploads/Saff_CityBrandBarom.pdf

Kaplanidou, K., & Vogt, C. (2003). *Destination branding: Concept and measurement*. Retrieved July 7, 2009, from Http://Ref.Michigan.Org/Mtr/Pdf/Whitepaper_Branding_Final.Pdf On 07.07.09.

Kim, C. (2000). *A model development for measuring global competitiveness of the tourism industry in the Asia-Pacific region*. Retrieved August 19, 2003, from http://www.kiep.go.kr/project/publish.nsf/243478c1734df97649256d9900210480/546cfe150257031a49256db200487ea8/$FILE/APEC00–03.pdf

Maples, M. F. (2007). *Spirituality, wellness and the "silver tsunami": Implications for counseling*. Retrieved November 20, 2007, from Counseling Outfitters: http://www.counselingoutfitters.com/vistas/vistas07/Maples.htm

Playing for Keeps. (2009). *Brandweek*. Retrieved December 20, 2009, from http://www.brandweek.com/bw/esearch/article_display.jsp?vnu_content_id=1000663856

Wilkening, D. (2007, June 28). *Vegas gambling on new slogan*. Retrieved January 8, 2010, from http://www.travelmole.com/stories/1119671.php#

World Economic Forum. (2009). *The Travel & Tourism Competitiveness Report 2009*. Retrieved December 21, 2009, from http://www.weforum.org/documents/TTCR09/index.html

Yim (Bennett), C. K. (2006). Healthcare destinations in Asia. *Asia Case Research Center, University of Hong Kong*. Retrieved November 15, 2007, from http://www.acrc.org.hk/promotional/promotional_shownote.asp?caseref=863.

Index